W9-BCM-887

# TILL THE END

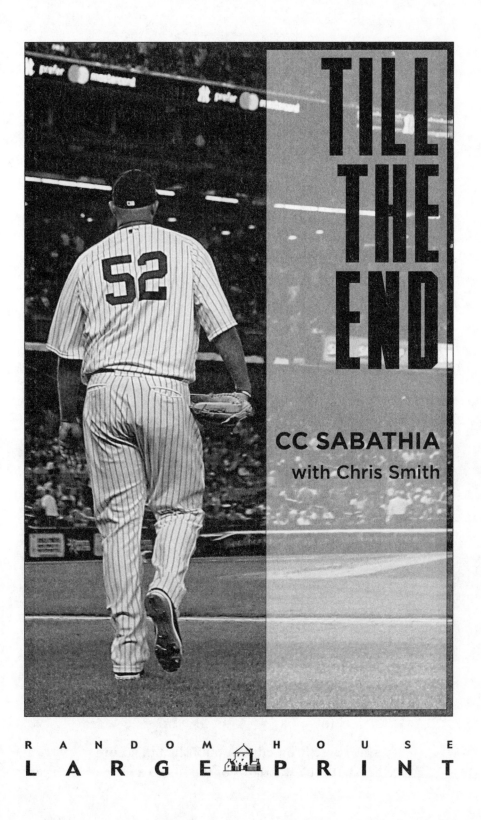

# TILL THE END

## CC SABATHIA
### with Chris Smith

RANDOM HOUSE
LARGE PRINT

**Till the End** is a work of nonfiction. Some names and identifying details have been changed.

Copyright © 2021 by Carsten Charles Sabathia Jr.

All rights reserved.
Published in the United States of America
by Random House Large Print in association
with Roc Lit 101, a joint venture between Roc Nation LLC
and One World, an imprint of Random House,
a division of Penguin Random House LLC, New York.

Photo Credits
Pages v, 2, 196, 212, 246, 264, 316, and 360:
Copyright © NEW YORK YANKEES.
ALL RIGHTS RESERVED.
Pages 12, 48, 72, 114, 152, 238, 258, 302, 340:
Courtesy of the author
Page 130: Focus on Sport/Getty Images
Page 140: Michael Zagaris/Getty Images
Page 180: Jeff Zelevansky/Getty Images

Cover design: Greg Mollica
Cover photograph: NEW YORK YANKEES.
ALL RIGHTS RESERVED.

The Library of Congress has established a
Cataloging-in-Publication record for this title.

ISBN: 978-0-593-50122-1

www.penguinrandomhouse.com/large-print-format-books

FIRST LARGE PRINT EDITION

Printed in the United States of America

10  9  8  7  6  5  4  3  2  1

This Large Print edition published in accord
with the standards of the N.A.V.H.

I dedicate this story to my biggest accomplishment:
Carsten III, Jaden, Cyia, and Carter.
My four children, this is for you.

# TILL THE END

In October 2015, I pitched the game that clinched the Yankees a playoff spot. But I wouldn't be there with the team.

1

'M A WEIRD ALCOHOLIC. I DON'T FIT THE stereotypes. There was no single "trigger" that would set me off on a binge. Not a sad anniversary, not a time of the day, not going to a party. It was all of those things, and none of them. I didn't ever drink more if I pitched bad; I would drink just as much if I pitched good. There was always a reason to drink. I just really liked to drink, and drink, and drink, many times until I blacked out. For a long time it was mostly fun—like when I got my first major league win and five of my Cleveland Indians teammates took me out to a Baltimore bar and stuffed every pocket of my suit with cash. The next morning I woke up wearing $10,000 in crumpled bills, as if I was the world's largest fully clothed stripper. And there was never any trouble finding guys to go drinking with. There's a lot of alcoholics in baseball. A lot. Many of them great players.

But here's the truly weird part: I could turn it on and off. For three days I would get absolutely ripped—starting fights, pissing in the bed, that kind of ripped. And then I wouldn't touch a drop for two days leading up to my next start. Say I pitched on Monday. That night, Tuesday night, Wednesday night, I was hammered. Thursday, Friday—detox, nothing but water and Gatorade. Saturday, when I came out of the game, I needed a Crown and Sprite at my locker. From the last pitch I threw, the cycle started all over again.

I was a disciplined drunk for fifteen years, so good at timing my benders that I'd won a Cy Young Award and a world championship and been paid more than $260 million. My career numbers looked as if they might someday give me a shot at being elected to baseball's Hall of Fame. And maybe what meant the most of all to me was that my teammates—in Cleveland, in Milwaukee, in New York—regularly said that they loved having me on their side and looked to me as a leader in the clubhouse.

It was as if my arm wasn't connected to the rest of my body. No, not just to the rest of my body—to the rest of my life. My mind, my bloodstream, probably my liver, they were addled by alcohol. My left arm, the one that carried me from the streets of Vallejo, California, to the mound at Yankee Stadium, that helped me hoist a World Series trophy, that built a secure life for my wife and our four kids—that arm somehow stayed untainted. Yeah, over the years it required ice and heat and surgeons and rehab, but those were tune-ups. My arm endured. It lifted me from being broke to being rich and famous; it lifted three teams to greatness. My baseball head got wiser, and it made my arm clever and adaptable, but that was my baseball head. As my arm got treated and pampered so it could continue being an asset to billion-dollar corporations and to my family, the rest of me was increasingly a mess. Sure, I was getting old in major league terms, but that wasn't the main thing dragging me down. Mistreating everything that wasn't my left arm was putting my gift at greater risk than any elbow injury. I had to find a way to reconcile my physical talent with the weirdness and weakness and rage and love inside—to lift myself, **all** of myself, this time.

So here I was standing in a damp cinder-block storage room under Camden Yards, the home of the Baltimore Orioles, wearing my Yankees T-shirt and my gray uniform pants, at ten o'clock on a Sunday morning, searching for another bottle of Hennessy. Ever since I got to the ballpark I'd been going back and forth from the clubhouse to the storage room, pouring myself drinks. In half an hour I was scheduled to throw a bullpen, my workout between starts. And I was so blasted I couldn't walk straight. I'd come back from three surgeries and fought through hundreds of hangovers; the one thing I could always do was throw when I was supposed to throw. But now the room was spinning. There was no way I could take the ball and throw it without embarrassing myself. **Man, what am I doing?**

This drinking spree hadn't started for the reasons you might expect. Three days earlier, on Thursday night, I had gotten the start with a whole lot on the line, after a tough regular season. The team had been in first place, or close to it, in the American League East for most of the season; in early August we stretched our lead to six games and had visions of winning another World Series title after a six-year drought. I know that six years between championships doesn't sound like a long time if you're a fan of the Cubs or the Mariners or a whole bunch of other teams. But in the Bronx, six years is an eternity; worse, we hadn't even made the playoffs in two years. In 2015, for the first time in two decades, we were playing without Derek Jeter, the all-time-great shortstop and Yankees icon, who had retired at the end of the previous season. But we still had Carlos Beltrán and Brian McCann and Alex Rodriguez and Masahiro Tanaka, and we felt like we had a real shot. Then, in late August, we started to fade. In September the slide accelerated. Mark Teixeira, our first baseman and one of our best hitters, fouled a ball off his shin and somehow it never healed. Our best starting pitcher, Nathan Eovaldi, went down with a sore elbow. Suddenly we were scratching for just a wild-card playoff spot.

Until that point I hadn't done much to help the Yankees' cause. I was 0–5 before getting my first win in mid-May. My right knee, the one that absorbed my 300 pounds every time I threw a pitch, had been deteriorating for years, and now it was down to bone on bone. In 2014 I'd made only eight starts, the last of them on May 10, before shutting it down completely in early July and getting arthroscopic surgery to try to patch my knee back together, at least temporarily. It was looking like a sure thing that I would need a knee replacement when my playing career ended. I spent nine months rebuilding enough strength in the knee to play, and in 2015, with the addition of a big, bulky brace, I'd managed to survive and pitch until late August. Then the end seemed to be coming up fast again: The knee pain got so severe it felt like someone driving a railroad spike into my leg over and over again. I had to go on the disabled list for two weeks. But cortisone is an amazing drug, and on October 1 I was back on the mound in the Bronx, facing the Boston Red Sox, who were having a terrible year but were still our classic rivals. A win would clinch a playoff slot. The meds dulled the pain long enough for me to come through, allowing one run in five innings. We won, 4–1, and in the locker room the champagne started flying. My knee went back to hurting like shit, but I didn't care.

Guys made sure to pour champagne over my head, just like they did with everybody else in the room. But I didn't drink anything during the celebration. Like I said, I'm a weird alcoholic. I waited until we got on the bus to go to the airport to fly to Baltimore for the final, meaningless series of the regular season. Started downing Henny and kept it flowing on the plane, then on the bus to the Baltimore Four Seasons. The first thing I did when I got to my hotel room that night was open the door to the minibar. Beer, wine, whiskey, tequila, it didn't matter. I'd been mixing liquors since I was a teenager going to Cutty Bang parties in my hometown, Vallejo, California. When the hotel minibar was empty, I called room service. On Friday, the weather helped me keep rolling: It rained all morning, and by midafternoon our game against the Orioles was cancelled, so I sat in the hotel room throwing down drinks and flipping through movies on my laptop. At some point Jomar Connors, my close friend and running buddy since we were five years old, called, worried about me. I was supposed to go over to the house of Adam Jones, an Orioles outfielder and one of my best friends in the game. I hadn't shown up. I told Jomar I would be heading over to Adam's place soon. But I never left the room. I'd fall asleep for a couple of hours, wake up, see it was 2 A.M., down some Red Bull, and have another drink. Or sometimes I'd mix the Red Bull with Grey Goose.

My cousin Darnell Jones was in town for the games and was staying in the hotel, and I ordered him to order me more booze. Later Darnell would tell me he was really scared: He had never seen me this bad and he wasn't sure what to do. He tried to get me to go out and eat, but I refused. Darnell is ten years younger than me. I love him like a little brother, and after everything we have been through together, he is probably my closest family member. But even Darnell didn't feel like he could tell me to stop drinking without sending me into a rage, so he tried slowing me down. When I demanded a bottle of Hennessy, Darnell ordered two doubles instead. I feel terrible now for putting Darnell— and so many other friends and family, for so many years—in that position. But at the time I was having some kind of nervous breakdown, and the only way I knew to kill the anxiety was to keep drinking.

They scheduled a doubleheader for Saturday to make up the rainout, and somehow I found my way to the stadium that morning, staggered into the locker room, and pulled on my Yankees uniform. I'm not even trying to be funny, but I don't remember Saturday at all. Guys must have noticed that I was a mess, but they'd seen me this way plenty of times before, and drinking—at night or, hell, during the game—is such a part of baseball culture that no one paid me much attention. In baseball, if you're getting the job done on the field, your teammates and the organization look the other way when it comes to what you're doing off the field. And I had internalized that logic, that willingness to split a person in two: The leader with his words and his arm could also be a self-destructive human the rest of the time.

They tell me I parked myself on the dugout

bench and tried to stay awake while my teammates were losing two games to Baltimore. Probably what I was thinking about was getting back to the Four Seasons and pounding a few more drinks.

On Sunday morning I was partly drunk and partly hung over when I got into the hotel elevator with Darnell. I was going back and forth, blubbering and then belligerent, my mind racing and my thoughts slurred, my words not making much sense: "Man, you think I need rehab? I've been talking to Amber, I think I need rehab." Couple floors down: "I don't need that shit, man, I don't need to go to no damn rehab." By the time we hit the lobby I was crying: "I'm going to get this shit together, I'm going to get this shit together, I'm going to be all right. I love you, cuz, I'll see you when I get back to Jersey."

When I reached the stadium Jason Zillo, the Yankees' head of communications, found me in the clubhouse and told me to get out before the reporters came in and saw what a mess I was. There wasn't enough time to sober up before throwing my bullpen, so I figured that another drink was what I needed to get through the workout. Every player knows where they keep the alcohol in every stadium. So I headed to the storage room and cracked open another bottle.

And that's when it hit me: **I am about to go do my job drunk.** I had never done that before. I couldn't do that. I needed help. I had fought my way through a lot of things in thirty-five years: Having childhood friends shot to death in my neighborhood. My father disappearing when I was thirteen. Being the youngest player in the entire American League. Frequently being the only Black player on a team. Losing the ability to throw a 95-mile-an-hour fastball. The guilt of becoming rich and famous when many of my buddies back home were still hustling. I had learned and adapted and succeeded at the very highest level of my profession, under enormous pressure, and I loved competing and winning. But all of that survival was wrapped up in protecting and exploiting my ability to pitch, my arm, and deadening the rest of me. Painkillers could numb my knee, but eventually they wear off. This was the mental equivalent. The drinking and the evasions couldn't cover up the hurt and confusion in the rest of my life anymore. This wasn't figuring out how to throw a cutter and fool hitters when I couldn't blow the ball past them. This was about honestly confronting who I was, digging deep into the roots of my emotions and finding out if I could be one person. Standing there in the Camden Yards storage room, more than forty-eight hours into an epic drinking marathon, loaded and crying, I had no idea whether I could win that game.

Eleven years old and representing Foster Lumber,
a powerhouse in the North Vallejo Little League.
Baseball was a big deal in our town.

**2**

FOSTER LUMBER WAS THE NEW YORK YANKEES OF the North Vallejo Little League majors division. They wore red jerseys with yellow lettering, not pinstripes, but they won the championship every year. And baseball was serious in our part of Northern California, and in my family. When my dad was young his favorite player was Oakland's Vida Blue—a ferocious Black lefthander. I grew up rooting for the A's Bash Brothers teams, including the 1989 champs. So when I was eleven years old and pitching for Foster Lumber and my cousin Joey Thurston, playing for Pendergast Auto, stepped into the batter's box, this was an intense showdown. I threw Joey—who would later play seven seasons in the big leagues—my best fastball. He launched it. All these years later I can still see the ball rolling to the outfield fence, the first of two back-to-back doubles.

I fucking lost it. We were still winning, 3–2, but I was crying on the mound, totally inflamed with shame and anger. But I don't resist the feelings, I just let them flow. The next dude to come up was

Poppa, a close friend of mine in sixth grade at Loma Vista Elementary School. He was a right-handed hitter, and he was kind of leaning out over the plate. I couldn't see real well through the tears as I fired the ball just as hard as I possibly could. I did hear, loud and clear, as the ball smashed into Poppa's left forearm, snapping it. I had no desire to hurt him—but, at the same time, I didn't really care. The field was already my outlet for the rage I didn't understand.

On Monday at school the principal called a meeting with Poppa and me, because she thought there were going to be fights. Poppa and I were cool; he knew it wasn't personal, that it was just part of the game. That's how important sports were in Vallejo. We played hard, and during the rugged years when I was growing up, sports were one of the few things that brought people together. But it was also the beginning of my split emotional life, bottling up feelings until they could spill out on the field.

Vallejo is a huge part of who I am. To understand me, why I'm so competitive, why I care so much about sharing my good fortune, and why I have spent so much time wrestling with my demons, you need to know where I grew up.

First, the location. It's North Bay, a blue-collar area just about halfway between two rich and glamorous spots, San Francisco to the southwest and Napa Valley to the north. It's a medium-sized city, about 100,000 people when I was growing up there, but when I was a kid it felt huge. Vallejo is surrounded by rolling green hills and acres of beautiful farmland, and it also has some of the grittiest neighborhoods I've ever seen. Both sides of my family moved out here from the South in the 1940s, part of the Great Migration of African Americans seeking a better life up north or out west. Latino players would see my last name and approach me, especially early in my big-league career, and start speaking Spanish. But my father's side, the Sabathias, is a mix of Black and Native American, and they came from New Orleans, where the name is pronounced "Sah-bah-tee-ay," in the French style. The name seems to trace back to one of the Sabatier families of central France, who were famous for making top-quality knives. "Sabatier" was apparently a fairly common name in Saint-Domingue, the former French colony in what is now Haiti, and slave owners probably attached it to my ancestors. My great-great grandfather spelled it that way until changing it to "Sabathia" at some point.

My paternal grandfather, Al, moved from Louisiana to California and found work painting submarines in the Mare Island Naval Shipyard during World War II. My mother's side, the Rufuses, came to Vallejo from Brookhaven, Mississippi. My maternal grandfather, Sam Rufus, became a welder, building warships to defeat the Nazis. Both sides raised big families—nine Sabathia kids, six Rufus kids—and worked hard to carve out solid, middle-class lives.

Vallejo was pretty integrated in the forties, especially the neighborhoods near the naval base, where people lived in housing projects built during the war years. Many of my relatives were in Henry Floyd Terrace, a project they tell me was the center of local civil rights activism and that was a fine place to live until the early sixties. Then unemployment and crime started going up, and White families headed for the suburbs. The area had become a ghetto over the years, and the city and county shut down Floyd Terrace completely by 1967. My aunt Gloria, who everyone calls Glo, says that probably 90 percent of the Black families were steered by real estate agents to a new development of single-family homes on the very eastern edge of Vallejo. The developers had named the area Country Club Crest. Which might have been good marketing, but it was also kind of a cruel joke: There were two freeways bordering the neighborhood, but there was no country club anywhere for miles and miles. My mom's parents moved to a one-story, three-bedroom house in the Crest on Dieninger Street. At the time it was built, in the mid-1950s, it was the last house on the neighborhood's border, so when my grandparents arrived it must have felt like it was in the country. They re-created a little bit of their southern childhood in the backyard, planting peach and pear and apricot and grapefruit trees and

a vegetable garden, and raising chickens and rab-
bits. My mom talks about how as a kid she would
climb the back fence and roam the hilly pasture on
the other side, hanging out with the grazing cows.

At first my parents seemed to be following the
same dependable path as their parents. My dad,
Carsten Charles Sabathia, was known as "Corky"
since he was a little boy. When he was nine, his
mother died suddenly of kidney failure, leaving
behind nine kids. Hoping to see the world, he
enlisted in the Navy at eighteen, just as the Vietnam
War was ending. So naturally the Navy stationed
him in Alameda. Eventually, though, Dad made it
as far as Seattle and Japan, and it fueled a love of
travel that he passed down to me.

After he was discharged Dad went back to work
in the Mare Island Naval Shipyard warehouse. My
mom, Margie Rufus, worked in the warehouse
office. Mom says she noticed Dad one day and they
started talking. She thought he was good-looking
and asked a girlfriend who he was. It turned out
Corky was four years older and had been in the
same high school class as Mom's sister Denise. After
that Mom started walking past where Dad worked
on purpose, and pretty soon they were going out
dancing to the Commodores, Parliament, and
Barry White. He was twenty-three and she was
nineteen when I was born, on July 21, 1980. Mom
talks about how she was so scared and nervous at
first in the hospital; when they rolled me into her

room and I was crying, she didn't know what to do. A friend who happened to be visiting picked me up and put me in my mother's arms. They say I calmed down right away.

They named me Carsten Charles Sabathia Jr., and my parents called me "Little C." The story goes that my paternal grandmother, Irma, was a regular customer of a butcher in Venetia, California, who had that unusual first name. Apparently my grandmother really liked the sound of Carsten, so she picked it for my dad when he was born. But when I came along, my maternal grandmother, Ethel, could never figure out how to say Carsten correctly. So she started calling me "CC" pretty much right away. The nickname stuck.

My dad was outgoing, always talking, always telling jokes; he was in a singing group with some friends for a while, doing Temptations songs. When he got excited he'd yell, "Damn!" My mom was quieter, but she loved dancing and telling stories. Being young parents is never easy, though, especially when you're making minimum wage and you have a little boy who arrives weighing eight pounds and measuring twenty-one inches long, and who grows fast and likes to eat. Uncle Edwin, my father's older brother, and his wife, Aunt Genia, lived in San Jose, and we'd pack up the van and drive down there for birthday parties and picnics. Aunt Genia tells a story about us visiting her house when I was five years old. Dad warned her that I would wake up very early and liked to have a "warm-up breakfast"—a bowl of cereal. An hour later, when she made breakfast for the other kids, Dad said she should expect me to come back as if I hadn't already eaten.

We lived in a nice, small apartment on Tennessee Street when I was born, near where my parents worked on Mare Island. I guess we watched a lot of TV, because Aunt Glo tells a story about how she had never heard me say a word—until all of a sudden one day I said, "**Soul Train!**" I was a happy kid. I was big into E.T. and Garfield and the animals at Marine World and sports, all sports. There's one particular photo that captures what I remember and what I felt like in those days. I'm about five years old and I'm in the little bedroom I had on Tennessee Street. The walls are covered with sports pennants and a Transformers poster. You can also see some baseball cards and bobbleheads. (I was a big bobblehead collector. Still am.) In the photo I'm standing in the middle of it all, grinning at the camera. That's who I was as a boy.

My parents were trying to figure out life, and though it never felt like I was missing out on anything, I guess money got tight real fast. We moved around a lot. They would be on top of their bills for two or three months, then start falling behind. The end of the month would arrive and they would realize that they couldn't make the rent. The landlord would come knocking on the door, and they'd put him off. My dad would get on his bike, ride over to another part of town, and talk to the land-lord of another apartment building. Dad was a charming guy, a bit of a hustler, loud, the kind of person who always knew how to make people laugh. He would make a deal to move into a new apartment. So that night, after I went to sleep, my mom would pack up everything we owned, which wasn't much—we could fit it all in a few suitcases. In the morning I would go to school and Mom and Dad would move to the new apartment. This hap-pened probably seven or eight times before I turned eight years old. I didn't really understand what was happening at the time; it just seemed like we'd found somewhere better to live. We moved to Admiral Callaghan Lane when I was seven or eight, where we stayed put for a good three years or so, but even then I'd spend many nights at my grand-mother's house. When my mom talks about all the moving now, she's kind of embarrassed. I don't see it that way. I see two kids doing whatever they needed to do to survive tough times and to protect the son they loved. Did the instability have an effect on me? Probably. But that was something I didn't think about until years later.

One thing that has always been clear to me is the fundamental lesson about loyalty I learned growing up. We had lots of family in the Vallejo area, and if one person was struggling, the rest of the family stepped up to help. The Sabathias stuck together, and so did the Rufuses. I was an only child, but I had a big network of cousins and aunts and uncles looking out for me—and as I got older, I wanted to look out for them. For years my mom and her sister Gloria, my aunt Glo, traded off taking care of each other's sons because their work schedules ran back-to-back. My mother's parents, my grandfather Sam Rufus and my grandmother Ethel Johnson, set the example. Grandma always cooked enough food to send some over to her grown sons and daughters—extra meatloaf or ham and big pots of beans. And when I was small, both my parents had jobs, and my grandmother was working as a maid, cleaning big houses in San Rafael and San Francisco. So my grandfather, who was retired, picked me up from school. I loved those afternoons. Sam Rufus was a big, big human—almost six-nine, and full of imagination, like me. We'd take flyswatters and go "fishing" over the side of the bed. My grandfather is the reason I love to fish today—outside!

Our time together changed the summer I was six, when my grandfather suffered a stroke. Walking became difficult; he moved like a very tired bear. I could tell he felt ashamed that he needed help, and that we couldn't play the same way. It was deeply sad to see such a big, strong man diminished, and for the first time in my life, I realized that the things I loved could suddenly be taken away.

Because my grandfather couldn't pick me up from school anymore, in the second grade I started walking about five minutes from Loma Vista Elementary to the Continentals of Omega Boys & Girls Club. The counselors made sure you did your homework every day; they made you read a book and write an essay. But I didn't mind that, because there were also all kinds of other activities, from boxing to cooking classes to "shut-in night," where you slept over with all the other kids. The club had a basketball court, and that was the first time I played for an organized team. But the best part was the founder and director. His full name was Philmore Graham, but to us kids he was always "Mr. Graham." He was a proud, upbeat Black man who was determined to give kids a safe place in the neighborhood, and who always seemed to have time to talk to every one of us. I went to the club every day from second until ninth grade, when sports took over my life.

One particular day at the Boys & Girls Club had a major impact. I was nine, and I remember it like it was yesterday: In through the door walked Dave Stewart. I had been a big A's fan since I was six or seven years old, and I'd even walked on the Coliseum field wearing my uniform during one of those Little League promotional days. And here was the A's star starting pitcher. Major league baseball players did not come to Vallejo; how it happened I still don't know. It was the first time I had been in the same room with a big leaguer, and it was the first time that I realized that my heroes were actual people. Dave had grown up in Oakland, and the local Boys & Girls Club had made a big difference in his life, which made him seem even closer to me. And he was Black, like me. Watching the A's in the eighties felt like watching an all-Black team, and that meant a lot when you were growing up in the Crest. Everybody in the hood wore Washington Redskins jackets because of Doug Williams. We didn't care that he played for a team on the other side of the country. He was a Black man playing quarterback in the Super Bowl. And winning.

I remember shaking Dave Stewart's hand that day. I didn't get an autograph; I have no memory of what he said. But just the fact that he would take the time to visit a bunch of kids made a deep impression, and planted the beginnings of an idea in me—that if I did ever make it big, I'd find a way to reach out and help like Dave Stewart did in Vallejo.

But the person I looked up to the most in those days, the one who was an up-close role model, was my cousin Demetrius Davis. He was the only son of my aunt Glo, who is my mother's oldest sibling. We all spent a lot of time at my grandmother's house. Glo helped raise me and I saw Demetrius nearly every day. He was thirteen years older than me, and everything I wanted to be: a star athlete, a cool guy, outgoing, somebody who was as friendly as a teddy bear and could make anybody laugh but took absolutely no shit. He was six foot five and a rock-solid 225 pounds. His basketball nickname was "Little Nique," after Dominique Wilkins; his football nickname was "Truck." But inside the family we called him "MeMe," thanks again to my grandmother, who doubled one of the syllables in "Demetrius" when he was a little boy. My friends and I would go out to play football in the park with MeMe and he'd be just as rough on us as he would be on guys his own size and age. But if someone from outside the neighborhood said something bad to me? MeMe was there to protect me, every time. He was a star tight end at the University of Nevada–Reno. For three years we drove out to watch every home game. One of my earliest childhood memories is being seven years old and having MeMe lift me up onto his huge shoulders and carry me through the locker room, telling his teammates that his little cousin was going to grow up to be better than all of them. I was thinking, **This is who I want to be.** I never needed to look on TV to find an idol—it was MeMe.

I was incredibly close with my dad, too. He drove a Ford van, silver with red stripes, and on weekend nights he would load up a dozen kids in the back and we'd go to the drive-in movie. He'd open up the back doors and we'd all stretch out on blankets to watch **Home Alone** or **Total Recall** or **Batman Returns**. It's the reason I love movies so much today, especially sci-fi. Dad's favorites were **Willow, Close Encounters,** and that one with the robot who looks like a kid—**D.A.R.Y.L.!** He got me hooked forever on Star Wars. I saw the first one at the great old Empress Theatre in Vallejo, and the second one from the back of Dad's van at the drive-in.

Dad was also a huge sports fan. The Warriors were just down the road in Oakland, but the team mostly sucked when I was a kid. Dad loved the Lakers—he grew up watching Wilt and then Kareem—so I became a passionate Lakers fan, too. It wasn't hard at all: These were the Showtime-era Lakers, with Magic and James Worthy and Michael Cooper. I also loved guys who shot lefty like me, no matter what team they played for, guys like Sam Perkins and Chris Mullin, guys I dreamed of growing up to become. I had a Shaq poster on my bedroom wall. For football, of course it was the Raiders for me and Dad, even though they moved from Oakland to L.A. when I was two. One of my most prized possessions was one of those team souvenir sets you'd get at Toys "R" Us, with the miniature Raiders helmet. Marcus Allen, Bo Jackson, Mike Haynes, Tim Brown, Howie Long—man, those were good teams, full of badasses. Once a season my dad would pile a bunch of cousins and uncles in the family van and we'd make the trip down the 5 for tailgating and a game, the full Raiders experience. I was hooked. We would go visit family for a weekend and I would wear my little Raiders uniform the whole time.

Dad and I also collected baseball cards together, and he bought me a complete Topps 1986 set— I still have it somewhere in storage. Will Clark was one of my favorite players because he was on the Giants, and he was a first baseman and a lefty, just like me. But it was prime time to be an A's fan when I was a kid. I can name the whole lineup for the A's 1989 World Series championship team in my sleep: Mark McGwire, Tony Phillips, Mike Gallego, Walt Weiss, and Carney Lansford in the infield, Rickey Henderson, Dave Henderson, Stan Javier, and Jose Canseco in the outfield, Dave Parker at DH, Terry Steinbach behind the plate. On the mound, Dave Stewart, Rick Honeycutt, Dennis Eckersley. Tony La Russa managing. That was my **squad**.

I was a big-ass kid, so I started playing T-ball when I was four years old. At first I had a lot of trouble picking up the game. One day Mom and Dad and I went to the park to practice. I was swinging and missing, swinging and missing. Couldn't touch the ball. My throws were weak and wild. As a kid I did everything right-handed, and I mostly still do. So naturally I started out swinging a bat and throwing the ball righty. What happened next changed my life, but exactly how it happened is a little fuzzy: I remember my dad suggesting I try hitting lefty, but my mom remembers me asking if I could switch sides and my dad saying, "Hell, yeah!

No son of mine can really be this bad at baseball!" However the change happened, I quickly started connecting, hitting line drives. Pretty soon I was bombing my dad's pitches into the outfield. By the time I was six I could smack the ball way over the orange traffic cones they put out to mark the outfield fence. When I threw lefty, the ball came out fast and easily, and I was pretty good at pitching—when I was twelve, in the first game I played for an all-star team, I threw a no-hitter and struck out seventeen of the eighteen batters. My pal Jomar, who was catching, fielded a bunt for the other out. My dad's best friend was at the game, and when I'd get two strikes on a hitter, he'd yell, "Book 'em, Danno!" like on **Hawaii Five-O**. All night it was "Book 'em, Danno!"

That was fun. But I wanted to be a hitter like the Bash Brothers, Canseco and McGwire, and play first base or in the outfield. Standing alone on the mound, with the ball and the game in your hand—that was fine, but it wasn't as much fun as crushing a homer. Maybe, too, I wanted to be a hitter because I had to work harder to become good at it. My parents were both athletic. Mom played softball and basketball in high school. Dad, when he was nine, broke his left leg so badly that he spent a year in the hospital. He walked with a limp for the rest of his life, but he was six foot three and strong, and in the Navy he became an amateur welterweight fighter. Dad kept boxing for a few years after he left the Navy. He was big and quick, and one of the photos of him I love the most is a black-and-white shot of him in the ring, delivering a jab, looking fierce, lean, and muscular, kind of like Ezzard Charles.

Pretty soon my dad was constantly telling my mom, "He's going to the big leagues." One time he glued a picture of me onto the cover of **Sports Illustrated**. And he'd say, "One day you're going to play for the Yankees." My mom would try to calm him down: "Quit saying that! Let him be, he's just a little boy!" I'm sure there were kids in my neighborhood who wanted to grow up to be teachers or firefighters or lawyers. For me and my friends, though, pro sports wasn't just a dream—it was the only dream. In second grade our teacher asked the students to write about our dream job, excluding sports. "Baseball player," I wrote. Sorry, teach, but I knew what I wanted even then, and there was no talking me out of it, even for a better grade.

My dad did whatever he could to help the dream. Once a month he'd skip work at the shipyard and pull me out of school, and we'd spend the day hitting in a batting cage. He coached my T-ball teams from when I was four till I was six, and my Little League majors teams from when I was ten till I was twelve. In between, the Little League minors, our teams were coached by a friend of his named Junior Little. When I was seven Mr. Little let me play shortstop, second base, all over the field. It's thirty-three years ago now, and that's still one of the best years of my life, maybe the most fun I've ever had on a baseball field. Mr. Little is still playing fast-pitch softball, and I see him all the time when I go back to the Crest.

My dad was always strategizing. He helped coach Kappa, my Little League minors team, but he also was an assistant for Foster Lumber, so that when I turned ten I'd automatically be on the team because he was a coach and they would have a spot to draft Jomar. We were loaded with amazing athletes. Marcel Longmire and Runako Magee, who were twelve; twins Nate and Jay Berhel were eleven; Jomar and me were the youngsters at ten.

One of the many things I'm grateful about to this day is that when I started striking everybody out in travel ball my dad refused to let coaches burn me out. Didn't matter if we had a big tournament game to win—if I didn't have five days' rest, Dad wasn't allowing me to pitch. Things have only gotten worse in youth ball, with year-round schedules and kids throwing a hundred pitches a game at the age of thirteen. But one reason I never really had arm trouble and stayed on the mound till I was thirty-nine is what my dad did to protect me at the beginning.

Besides my dad, the person who taught me the most about baseball in those years was my uncle Rell, Terrell Rufus, one of my mother's brothers. Rell and I played catch and then strikeout against my grandma's garage door for hours every single day from when I was six to when I was twelve. He was tall and lean, a strong guy, and Rell would have been in his mid-twenties back then, but it seemed like he loved nothing more than playing ball with a kid less than half his age. I know I loved it.

My mom deserves just as much credit for me becoming an athlete as my dad and Rell, especially when I got to high school. Her family says my personality is a lot like my mom's: She sees the best in people—she's trusting, until you prove you're not trustworthy. Mom was also a terrific athlete herself, a tomboy as a kid—she would climb any tree in sight and wrestle with her older brothers. The shortest one of her brothers is six foot four; Mom grew to be six feet tall. When Jomar and I played my mom and dad in basketball, they never let us win, even when we were eight years old. Jomar and I were so competitive that we'd fight the whole way home, blaming each other for losing to two grown-ups. When I was a little older and played real basketball against Mom, she would throw some sharp elbows. But she was ferocious about protecting me, too. One summer we were at a nine-and-under tournament in Concord, California. I was only eight years old, but I was already about five foot five and weighed 125. My mom had learned to carry my birth certificate with her to my games, because opposing coaches would argue that I couldn't possibly be in the right age group. That day in Concord I hit my first home run that cleared an actual fence—a grand slam, and it broke some-body's car window! Man, I was excited. I was running around the bases and I heard somebody yell, real loud—and they weren't cheering. Turned out that my mom had gone to the concession stand where this lady, a mother from the other team, started complaining: "He's too big! He's not sup-posed to be playing on this team!" My mother told her, "You're talking about my son." The other woman said, "I don't care!" Mom wound up and punched her. Broke her nose! Mom is actually a pretty quiet person. But you can't talk about her family and expect nothing to happen.

How competitive was I as a kid? Until I was about four years old, I had a friend named Danny. I played Nerf basketball against Danny all day, and I'd trash-talk him: **Come on, Danny. You can't block me, come on.** Danny never won a game. Here's the thing, though: Danny was imaginary. I invented a friend just so I could beat him.

Years later, when I started having some success in the big leagues, sportswriters and fans started speculating about the way I wore my hat, with the brim tilted down toward my right eye. **Maybe he doesn't know he wears his hat crooked. Or is it some kind of NorCal gang thing? Is he trying to start a style trend?** Which made me laugh. Yeah, I did think it looked kind of cool. It added some swagger to my game. Mostly, though, it had just become part of my routine, how I was comfortable wearing my hat. But the way it began wasn't any kind of fashion statement. Not even close. When I was about ten and starting to pitch regularly, I would get really, really upset if I gave up a big hit or a bunch of runs or if I was walking batters. I would start crying on the mound—and I didn't want anyone to see that. So between pitches I'd tug on my hat, trying to pull it down low enough to cover the tears. Jomar, my catcher for most of those teams, knew he was in trouble when the hat started coming down, because I was going to be throwing the ball harder and harder. What eventually became a signature look started with me hiding my emotions.

My mom knew what was going on, of course, and she wasn't having any of it. One time I gave up a home run and started crying on the mound. At the end of the inning, as I walked back to the bench, I could feel her staring at me, hard. "Dude, please," she said to me as I came off the field. "You got to be shitting me." After the game, we got straight into our little two-door Ford Escort. It was a very quiet ride home to my grandparents' house. When we got inside, she steered me into the bathroom, so we could have a little bit of privacy, out of sight of my grandparents, and backed me against a wall. "Who do you think you are? CC Sabathia never gives up a hit?" I could hear my grandmother outside the door, asking if everything was okay, but my mom didn't let up. Same thing if I lost my temper about an umpire's call. When I was fourteen and complained to an umpire, she ordered the coach to take me off the field—in the middle of the game, and even though it was the playoffs. (I'm still sure it was a bad call.)

When I was doing well, she taught me humility. I remember being twelve or thirteen and getting in the car after I'd struck out a bunch of guys and hit a couple of home runs. "Did you see that game?" I said to Mom, all proud of myself.

"Yeah," she said. "But there's some kid in Florida who hit five home runs today. Keep going. Keep working." The message Mom was sending, I figured out later, was that I wasn't above anyone else, that if I made a mistake, I was the one who was accountable—no whining, no crying.

She didn't just care about my progress in sports or my behavior on the field, either. In ninth grade, halfway during basketball season, I got two F's—and that was the end of my basketball season. Next year, tenth grade, I got a D in Spanish—and Mom pulled me from basketball again. Dad could be a really-old school parent, too. I don't remember what set things off, but when I was eight or nine, I started crying about something. Dad got in the car and made me walk home, while he drove slowly alongside.

Most of the time, though, it felt more like she was my older sister and that we were best friends. She always called me "dude," and still does. I trusted her completely, and felt like I could ask her anything, including, one time, "Mom, do you get in trouble for throwing eggs at people's cars?"

"You sure do," she told me with a laugh.

Mom had played fast-pitch softball, and she would strap on an old catcher's helmet, chest protector, and shin guards and take me out to the backyard to throw—until I got to be about twelve, that is, and almost broke her hand with a fastball. "Get someone else," Mom said, pulling the mask off her face, her hand hurting but her voice sounding proud. "You're past me."

That summer of 1992, our Little League all-star team went the farthest any Vallejo team has ever advanced. The team photo is really interesting: It's fourteen Black kids and one White kid. There was another kid who should have been in the photo: Dave Bernstine, my best friend from kindergarten through sixth grade. Bernie was eleven years old but big, and he would hit bombs. One day that summer he ran down the hill outside our friend Jerry's house, stumbled, and broke his ankle. We were a handful of games away from going to the Little League World Series, in Pennsylvania. I still think we would have won it all if Bernie hadn't gotten hurt. I tell him that I'm still mad at him.

Missing out on the chance to go to Williamsport was disappointing, but as far as hurt and trauma, it was nothing compared to the blows that were coming my way soon, one after another. Three or four years earlier, Mom had started spending many nights sleeping in the lower bunk in my bedroom. I didn't think much about it at the time; it just seemed kind of comforting to have her there during the night. Mostly it seemed like my parents were getting along fine. I only ever remember one big argument. We had just moved into another new place in West Vallejo. It was around Christmastime 1992, and they got into a big fight.

One day not long after that, Dad went to work and Mom packed up all our belongings. We were gone. She has never told me all the details—she's still protecting me, even now. "I was good at moving. I had a lot of practice," she'll say with a sort of sly smile. "Your dad and I were just going our separate ways. I still loved Corky. Our marriage just wasn't there anymore." Now, as an adult, I can understand: They were both young, they had a child, and they tried to make it work as long as they could. It sounds like they were done as a couple by the time I was about five years old.

As a kid, I did not see it coming, and it hurt when they split up. But I didn't talk about it with anyone, not even Jomar, whose parents didn't live together, either. There weren't too many kids I knew who had both parents living together. And I was already being raised by a whole bunch of people—my grandparents and my aunts and uncles, in addition to Mom and Dad. My parents seemed to get along better after we moved out. My mother did something that I think was really brave, and important: She didn't talk badly about my dad. Whatever had gone down between them, she wanted me to be on good terms with him. They never officially got divorced.

Mom and I went to stay with one of her sisters, my aunt Denise, who we all called Nieci. My parents' separation didn't faze me too much, but what did make me mad was that Nieci lived completely across town, in South Vallejo. The only people in the area that I knew were a couple of older cousins, Kevin and Javon, so for three years the only time I'd go outside to play was when I went to visit my grandparents in the Crest.

Jomar's dad lived in the Crest, so now we could spend the whole weekend hanging out. We would ride our bikes everywhere together. Our videogame battles lasted for hours—lots of Tecmo Bowl football and a bunch of different baseball games, where I was the A's and Jomar was always the Mets, because he was a catcher and he loved Gary Carter. We'd go in his dad's backyard and spray-paint a little strike zone on the wall and play strikeout. We'd go in my grandmother's front yard and play big-ass games of what we called "Black Man Tackle." You threw the football up in the air, and whoever caught it had to run to one or the other end of the yard to score a touchdown—with a dozen other kids trying to tackle you. Jomar and I would fight, cry, make up, and go right back at it. Later on, as we got older, Jomar would take the blame for stuff I did wrong. Each of us was the brother the other never had.

Because we were so tight, and because we were so obsessed with sports, it helped us tune out the neighborhood's dangers when we were little. Gunfire? Every day. We didn't think anything of it. You heard the fucking police helicopter flying over your house, looking for people, all the time. A sportswriter from Idaho came to the Crest one time to do a story about another athlete from the neighborhood and described it like this: "With the streets abandoned and the windows shuttered, the Crest seems a place where a secret passageway to the middle-class American dream has gone astray."

I'm sure the Crest looked grim to outsiders who lived in richer places. And of course we knew there were gangs and drugs around us. But I never felt unsafe. It was simply part of where we were growing up. When we were little we just wanted to play ball, so we were biking or walking to the park to do it every day, despite whatever craziness was going on around us. No matter how much you tuned it out, though, you also understood, even if you couldn't explain it, that you had very little margin for error. Huge choices were forced on you quick when you were still a little kid. If you were going to have any chance to survive and succeed, you needed to know what direction you wanted your life to go even before you graduated from elementary school.

I had a friend who was a really good baseball player all through Little League, from the time we were nine years old. By the time we were thirteen, he was in juvenile hall. He was far from the only kid I knew who didn't have people to give him hope and who drifted into real trouble real fast. California enacted the three-strikes law in 1994, when I was thirteen. Too many guys from the Crest became part of the prison population.

So my parents not living together was not high on the list of the worst things that could happen. One of those worst things arrived pretty quick, though, and it was the first loss that truly broke my heart. My grandfather Sam Rufus died of lung cancer, in April 1994. He was seventy-two. At his funeral, I just shut down. Learning how to process and channel my emotions has been a lifelong struggle, both on the field and off. For a long time, I tried to just keep all the pain and anxiety inside, to tough it out, to be a man. My only memory of my grandfather's funeral is that I wore one of his suits. I was crushed when he died. That was a big deal to me, to feel myself in his clothes, as if it could keep him with me in some way. I wore that suit to my eighth-grade graduation, that same year, to bring him along, even a little.

That summer my cousin Kevin got out of jail. He was four years older than me, and when I was little, wherever I went with him I felt safe. Kev was incredibly loyal. The downside of this was that Kev would fight anybody, over just about anything. He had a seriously bad temper and he was a polarizing figure in our family. One day that August, my freshman year of high school, during football two-a-days, my cousin Gigi shows up at practice and says, "We need to go home. Now." She wouldn't tell me why, but I took off my jersey and shoulder pads and got in the car wearing my football pants and pads. At home they told me Kevin had been killed—shot trying to rob a gas station. That jolted me. I loved Kev. When I went back to practice, I pounded everyone as hard as I could, in every drill, for the next four years. I was the best practicer of high school football ever, because on the days that we hit, I would just fucking try to kill somebody, because I was mad about something. On the field I would just be lost. Gone, mentally. It's why I loved football, and it's why I got so many penalties as a kid. I could turn into something different on the field—yell, scream—and people were fine with it. I figured that out early.

My parents had split, but after my grandfather's death my dad moved in with my grandmother, his mother-in-law, because she was lonely. Which is an example of how crazy and how close my family is.

Dad moved out of Granny's when I was fifteen,

so Mom and I moved in. That house was my refuge. It's at the top of a small hill, at the corner of Cronin Drive and Dieninger Street. When I stood out front I could see the lights and rides of the Vallejo Marine World amusement park about a mile away, especially at night. Dieninger is one block long, which contributed to the feeling that we had our own cozy little universe. It's a humble one-story house, painted light brown, with a sloped gray shingle roof, set back from the street, with a little hump-backed grass yard out front, and a driveway leading to a one-car garage. Out back is a slightly larger, rectangular yard. My grandparents had fruit trees when I was a kid—one twisty grapefruit tree still survives. But by the time I moved in at fifteen, the cow pasture where my mom used to run around had been filled in with a subdivision.

To enter my grandparents' house, you go up the driveway and across a short, curving walkway to the front door, which opens into the living room. To the right is a fireplace that my grandmother always seemed to have burning; Northern California can get cold, but maybe growing up in the South made the whole year feel cold to her. There were so many nights we'd stay up late watching TV and I'd fall asleep sitting on the floor, the fire good and warm, resting against my grandmother's knee. To the left of the living room is a small dining room, and behind it an even smaller kitchen. How my grandmother fed so many people with her homemade dressings and her banana pudding and her teacakes out of that tiny kitchen I'll never know. A central hallway no wider than an airplane aisle led to three bedrooms. My grandparents had the one all the way in the back. My cousin Gigi had the side room, opposite the kitchen. The front right bedroom, the smallest, was shared by two of my uncles, Seavey and Rell. Most nights I'd sleep on the couch in the living room; I didn't have a bedroom in that house until I was sixteen. Oh, and there was one little bathroom for all of us!

My mom made sure I did my schoolwork. We went to Good Samaritan Baptist Church every Sunday; I was there on Tuesdays, too, for choir practice, and on Thursdays for training as an usher. I would go to take a shower in the morning, and when I came back, my bed would be made and my clothes would be ironed. Was I spoiled? Well, maybe a little. That was my grandmother.

My grandparents' house was always my home base. Even when we were mostly living on the other side of town, a lot of days my mom would drop me off at my grandparents' house. I'd spend the night there and ride my bike to school. Because Vallejo is in the North Bay, my schools were a mix of Filipino kids, Mexican kids, Middle Eastern kids, White kids, Black kids, everything. You knew, especially as you got older, that racism existed in the world, but I never really experienced it directly until I was a grown man and reached the major leagues, which made it even more confusing when people called me the N-word. What I knew was the Bay, where diversity is a common and beautiful thing.

The Crest, though, was the hood. All Black. There were always a lot of kids my age around, and my grandparents' house was where all my cousins gathered to play. I love all of them, but I was closest with Nathan and Jason Berhel. Our grandmothers were sisters who'd come from Louisiana to California together in the 1940s. Nate and Jay's dad, Uncle Aaron, was cousins with my dad, and he helped coach our Little League teams.

Nate and Jay were twins. They were short and stocky and had these raspy, old-man kind of voices even when they were young. Smart, high-energy, tough guys, and really good athletes. They were a year older than me, but we were always on the same teams coming up, in every sport. On every baseball team, Nate was my catch partner. Nate and Jay would both end up being huge influences in my life. They were my cousins, but they were my brothers.

That house on Dieninger is such a fundamental part of who I am that when I signed my first big-league contract, I bought it. A few years ago my mom wanted to sell it, but I never will. There was a lot of love in that little space. And some troubles, too. My uncles would get into huge fights, smashing each other hard. I can remember my grandparents trying to break them up, my grand-mother crying, and me just trying to pretend I was asleep. It's weird, thinking about it now. At the time I felt like, **This is what everybody in the neighbor-hood is dealing with. Everybody's house is like this. This is normal for the Crest.** Sure, you saw crack-heads everywhere in the Crest, and every family went through its drug and drinking problems. We weren't immune. But I told myself I wasn't going to get hurt by any of these people. I had a roof over my head. I had food. It wasn't like I was out on the street and it wasn't safe. So why would I be scared?

No matter how much pain our family went through, we went through it together. There could be a brawl between my uncles in the backyard on Wednesday night, but Sunday morning we were all in church together, and Sunday afternoon we were all having lunch together. There'd be twenty-five people at my grandmother's house, with people eating in the garage and the front yard. All kinds of crazy shit would happen—but our family never broke up. We were still together, all the time.

Growing up in the Crest was probably like grow-ing up in any poor neighborhood—you were always juggling a sense of vulnerability and a feeling of security. You could feel physically safe, even though you knew there was violence everywhere around; you could feel protected by your family at the same time you had the knowledge that things could fall apart at any minute. So you learned to be hard, or at least act hard. The importance of being macho was constantly being taught. A small example: I listened to plenty of Tupac and Dre and Snoop, and E-40—he's another Vallejo guy. But I also loved Prince—we wore out a VHS copy of **Purple Rain**—and I really loved Michael Jackson. But I took a lot of shit for it, because in the Crest, Prince and Michael Jackson were considered soft, and if you liked their music, you must be soft. But I loved Prince and Michael so much I didn't give a fuck what people thought. I had Michael Jackson dolls! I was such a big fan my mom would tease me: We'd be sitting on the couch watching TV, and she'd put her hand over my eyes and say, "Michael Jackson is on! Oh, you missed him!"

When I got to pro ball I'd bring some of my teammates to the Crest, and they'd say it was the roughest place they had ever seen. But what I remember most from growing up there was the awesome, powerful sense of community, of connection. On every street was either somebody I was related to or somebody who knew my parents or my grandparents. As I got a little older, in my teens, the feeling that people were looking out for me made a big difference. About a mile down the hill from my grandmother's house, right across the street from the North Vallejo Park baseball field, in a rectangular strip mall is a place called King's Market. It's the biggest liquor store in the area, with heavy steel bars across the windows, but it also sells the best hot-link sandwiches and it cashes checks. Mac Dre was raised in Vallejo, and when I was around fifteen his music was the only thing we listened to. Mac Dre would be at King's all the time, hanging out, and Dave Bernstine and I would ride over just to see if Mac was up there. King's is around the corner from Gateway Drive, which was pretty much a 24/7 open-air drug market in those days. Scraggly, stoned guys would pound on the windows of cars stopped for red lights, begging for money. One afternoon on my way home from Solano Middle School, I stopped into King's to buy a bag of chips. I was just chilling, talking to people. I had started to get a reputation as an athlete, and this older guy, someone I had never seen before, came up to me. "We know who you are," he said. "We know your mom. You don't need to be down here. Get your bike. Get the fuck out of here. Don't come back, because you're gonna be somebody."

There were two high schools in Vallejo, Hogan and Vallejo. The basketball coach at Hogan, Foster Hicks, was a family friend. I'd known Coach Hicks since I was a baby, and he really, really wanted me on his team—and he thought I was coming to Hogan, because my grandmother's house was in its district. But most of my friends—and, most important, Nate and Jay—went to Vallejo. So I used their address on my school forms, and I went to Vallejo. Oh, the coaches at Hogan were pissed, but they didn't do anything about it. I'm sure they had a few guys at their school who were supposed to be at Vallejo High.

In the nineties, Vallejo had a real sense of pride—kids' sports at Dan Foley Park, community days, block parties, everybody coming out in the middle of the street and hanging together. You barbecued, you listened to music, and you knew your neighbors. Everybody was kind of one big family. You went to the store, you were gonna see somebody you knew.

That's part of what makes Vallejo, for all of its problems, seductive in a weird way. It's familiar. You always find reasons to come back. Or it pulls you back, with a kind of hood gravity. There were so many guys I looked up to as a kid, great athletes who were a few years older than me, who never went as far as their talent could have taken them. Bad decisions, bad breaks—there are a million examples in Vallejo. Runako Magee, he was two years older than me. A phenomenal athlete. Played shortstop and pitched—that motherfucker probably threw 78 miles per hour when he was twelve years old. Plus he had a hammer. Threw no-hitters. He ended up spending a lot of years in prison, until he was released with stage four cancer. Jason Shelley was six years older than me, one of the best Vallejo football and baseball players ever, and the reason I wore number 18 as a kid. He went to the University of Washington and caught three passes for 100 yards in the 1993 Rose Bowl as a freshman. The next year Jason got arrested three times in eight months and was kicked out of school. But he turned his life around, went to an NAIA school, and played in NFL Europe. Some guys were smart or lucky or both. Bobby Brooks, for instance. He lived in the Crest and went to Hogan. Four years older than me. Bobby was the guy from the hood who did everything right. Got the good grades. Stayed out of the streets. He was at the Boys & Girls Club, mentoring us. It took some balls for Bobby to be that way. He went to Fresno State, then played for the Raiders for three years and the Jaguars for one. He's back living in Vallejo coaching high school football and working in law enforcement; his kids and Jomar's kids go to school together.

There have been athletes who did a lot of great stuff in Vallejo. There've been other players from Vallejo selected high in the draft. As good as I was, I was probably fifteenth on the talent list of guys to come out of Vallejo—maybe lower. But stuff happens. Decisions get made. For people who don't grow up in the hood, it's easy to be judgmental: "Well, why didn't he just do the right thing? Make the right choice?" But when you're under pressure from the time you're a little kid, and you don't see people who look like you getting many breaks or living very long, you live for now. A lot of guys I grew up with ran into obstacles they didn't create; I don't blame any of them for not going further in their careers. But I wanted to be the one to have the career. To escape the trap.

Celebrating after a high school basketball playoff win during my junior year. In Vallejo sports, you didn't just try to win the game—you went for blood.

## 3

THIS IS MY LAZY-ASS THINKING: A BIG REASON I played three sports all through high school was so I only had to do conditioning once a year, for football. And then I went right into basketball games and after that right into baseball games. I hate running. One afternoon in the spring of 1994, when I was thirteen, our Babe Ruth baseball team was doing sprints and I was dragging behind. We were on one of the Vallejo High School fields, and the high school baseball players were using the field right next to us. I had a lot of friends on the JV team, so I jogged over to talk with them. A coach saw me and said, "What are you doing? Why are you talking to my players?" I said something smart back to him, but before it escalated, one of the players spoke up: "Coach! That's my cousin! The one we've been telling you about!"

My cousin Nate Berhel was a left-handed center fielder. His brother Jay was a second baseman, and they hit one-two in the batting order. As soon as they made the Vallejo JV team they started talking me up to their coach: "Wait till you see our cousin!" Now here I was, meeting the coach for the first time, holding an industrial-sized Snickers bar in my hand. I was always hungry as a kid, so I always kept a candy bar in my back pocket during practice.

The coach said, "I hear you had a pretty good year with Babe Ruth. Are you excited to come to high school next year?"

I shrugged and said, "Yeah."

He asked me, "What position do you play?"

I looked across the field and saw a group of his JV players running sprints, and I asked, "What position do those guys play?"

"Those are the pitchers," the coach said.

"I play first base," I told him.

That was my introduction to Abe Hobbs. He was just twenty-three years old, an excitable, scrappy little guy who'd grown up in Vallejo and played college ball at Western Oregon. He had a crew cut and looked like a Marine. In many ways we could not have been more different—but the things we had in common were powerful. Hobbs was a baseball guy, he cared deeply about people, and we became tremendously close. Still are. Coach Hobbs became co-head coach of the Vallejo varsity in 1995, with Norm Tanner, then took over completely the next year, all of which was perfect timing for me. We won a lot of games in four years, and had a lot of fun, but he also taught me an enormous amount about life and responsibility.

We were together in the summers, too, when Coach Hobbs ran a Police Athletic League team. We would practice for five or six hours each day—which is normal in Japan, but not in California. Coach Hobbs knew that the more time he had us on the field, the less time there was for us to find trouble off the field, especially if we got home bone-tired. He started doing daily attendance checks, to make sure his baseball players were showing up for all their classes, plus grade checks. He knew that not everyone on the team was going to play professional baseball—most never would even come close—but he kept drumming in the idea that if you worked hard and became a starter in high school, he could find you a junior college, or an NAIA school, or maybe a Division II or Division I school. I can still hear him saying, **Stay eligible, keep playing, and all of a sudden you're walking across a college stage with a diploma, and you have opportunities.** And he's saying it to kids who would be the first in their family to even go to college. He never, ever kissed my ass, not even when I started winning awards and the talk started building about me being a first-round draft pick. Instead Coach Hobbs would say, "Dude, you throw gas and you're phenomenal. Everybody knows that. But what are you doing off the field? What's going on in your life?"

Here is maybe the biggest example of how Coach Hobbs went far beyond just teaching us the game. We didn't have a real home field in high school until my senior year, but when we finally did, that was only because of Coach Hobbs. When he arrived at the school to teach phys ed and health, and to coach, Vallejo High had a football field and some other big open grass fields, but no baseball diamond. Coach Hobbs wrote a bunch of grant proposals, he got a little bit of money from the school district, he borrowed Bobcats and earthmovers, he enlisted students as part of the crew, and in his spare time, over three years, we built a baseball field. And not only a baseball field. Just beyond the right field fence was a big aluminum shed-like building that belonged to the school. Part of the space was an art studio; part of it was an auto shop; part of it was a nursery for high school girls who had babies, so that they could go to class. Coach Hobbs somehow got the school to give him the leftover space to use as a "classroom." Well, he did teach plenty of lessons there, but in the afternoons he pushed aside the chairs and desks and converted the space into our baseball clubhouse. It was big enough that we could take batting practice and throw bullpens in there. It was also where Coach Hobbs started telling me about Jackie Robinson.

I had heard of Jackie Robinson before, of course. Mainstream culture and the school system have a kind of roll call of approved Black pioneers and role models: George Washington Carver, Frederick Douglass, Dr. Martin Luther King Jr., Rosa Parks. Jackie Robinson was in there, of course. And my grandfather, who grew up in Louisiana and lived in California, was a Dodgers fan because of Jackie Robinson. One day, I don't remember why, Robinson's name came up in the baseball clubhouse, and Coach Hobbs could tell that I knew almost nothing about him other than that he'd played major league baseball. "Dude, go to the library," he told me. "Figure it out. It's important for you." The way he said it wasn't condescending, which it easily could have been, coming from a White adult to a young Black kid. It was encouraging and prodding. He would give us books on all kinds of different subjects, and I would come back and ask him questions. But he educated me bigtime on Jackie Robinson in particular. Babe Ruth, Cy Young, Ty Cobb—I'm sure those guys were great players. But there shouldn't be any major league baseball records until 1947, when they let us play.

Years later, Coach Hobbs would tell me that he was trying to build a culture of "moral fiber" with his players, and so he wanted all of us to know who had come before us and what they'd gone through. But he also had a sense I might need to deal with the wider world soon. And he wanted me to be prepared in every way.

One thing he had us do, as a team, was to embrace the inner-city thing. It's not as if we were going to hide the fact that we were an all-Black team. On the other hand, we didn't go out of our way to flaunt it. But we were never going to back down if we were challenged, and the challenges came in different ways. My sophomore year, we won the sixteen-and-under state summer championship, and we took a trip to Indianapolis for a national tournament. We had a game against a team from Miami, Metro Dade, that was made up of elite players from fourteen different high schools. We were a bunch of kids from the neighborhood. Before every game, our team would circle up in center field, which is like a dog marking its territory, and it's kind of provocative when you're not on your home field. The Metro Dade players saw what we were doing—and they came out and circled up around us. We had one or two guys who spoke Spanish, and they told us that the Metro Dade guys were trash-talking us. It was gonna get heated fast. Coaches and staff came running out and separated everyone.

The game started, and we were overmatched; they just had more good players than we did. But I was pitching, and I wasn't giving an inch. We took a lead, and then one of Metro Dade's biggest players hit a home run, one of the first legit home runs I'd ever given up at this level. Our pitching coach saw me tugging down my hat, and he saw my nostrils flaring, and he wanted to come out to the mound and settle me down. Coach Hobbs told him no—he wanted to see how I dealt with adversity in a high-pressure situation.

I drilled the next batter right in the fucking ear.

We ended up losing, but it was a tight contest. Maybe hitting that kid helped scare the Metro Dade batters for the rest of the game. But that wasn't my intention—I wasn't capable of strategic intimidation at that point in my life. No, hitting him was about pure anger. That was me not being able to pull my hat down and cry like I used to when I was ten, eleven, twelve. I had to do something, though, so I took it out on that hitter. Later I'd learn how to put my rage to more tactical use on the field, to knock down guys with a pitch instead of drilling them. Managing those emotions off the field would take a whole lot longer, though.

Being a big, strong kid was a serious advantage on the field, but it was deceptive in other ways. When you are six foot five and weigh 255, people assume you've got your shit together, including your confidence. They forget that you're also fourteen years old. Sure, I was big, but when I got to high school I was nervous. Marcel Longmire was a guy I could walk under, and I don't know what I would have done without him. Marcel is two years older than me, and we'd been knowing each other a long time, since I was ten and we were teammates on Foster Lumber. My mom and his, who I call Miss Jenn, became close friends during those Little League years. Marcel was getting good grades at the same time that he was a star athlete, and he really showed me the ropes in high school. He was always there to calm me down. Sophomore year I played JV football, then got called up to varsity as a backup at the end of the season. Midway through the fourth quarter of our first playoff game our starting quarterback got hurt, and suddenly I'm taking over! My first series, I threw a post corner for a touchdown. But with time running out we were still down by two points. It's fourth and twenty, and I've got one play to keep our season alive. Marcel must have seen the fear in my eyes. We're in the huddle and he grabs me by the face mask and yells, "Just throw me the ball! Don't worry about nothing—just drop back, look for me, and throw me the ball!" So I did, throwing it as far as I possibly could. Marcel jumped up and pulled it in with one hand. We got the first down and extended the drive, but we ended up losing the game. That moment changed me, though. It was an indelible early lesson in how to lead.

By sophomore year I became a starter on the Vallejo basketball and baseball teams. Older guys were the captains, and I looked up to them. But in high school people often expect the biggest and best players to be the leaders. I was getting a lot of attention as an athlete, but being a leader wasn't a role that came naturally to me, or one that I really wanted. Coach Hobbs was constantly in my ear about becoming a leader—what it meant, how I needed to carry myself. I figured he was just trying to get me to run more laps. **Fuck that! I don't want to be the leader!**

My thinking started to change during two trips to the mall, strangely enough. The winter of my junior year the basketball team took a trip, and after practice we were planning to go to the mall. The Vallejo varsity basketball coach, Vic Wallace, pulled me aside and said, "You're the leader of this team."

I was like, "No, man, what you talking about? We got Joe and Scott and Brandon."

Coach said, "You don't even realize. You are one of the leaders of this school."

"Man, I don't know," I said.

Coach—who was a young guy, the same age as my mother—said, "No, you need to own that shit. You need to do the right things because people are going to follow what you do. When we go to the mall today, watch how many people follow what you do. If you say something loud, if you want to get rowdy and act all fucked up, watch how many people just follow that." And so I did. We went to the mall, and I was doing all kinds of crazy shit, and then everybody else was doing all kinds of crazy shit. The lightbulb went on in my head: **Oh, okay. People are looking at me, whether I want them to or not, and they are going to follow my example. So I need to do the right shit. I need to set the right tone.**

I started to carry myself differently, but what it meant to be a leader didn't really sink in until December of junior year. Our basketball team was in a Christmas tournament in Lodi. We had made the finals, and we had some time to kill before the championship game, so Coach Wallace took us to the nearest shopping mall. Back then the nickname for Vallejo High's teams was the Apaches, and we were roaming the mall wearing our red warm-ups. Suddenly all these gangbangers in blue start surrounding us. Crips. The cursing and threats got intense in a hurry, and Coach Wallace was yelling at us to get out of there, but we were teenage boys with our adrenaline racing and we weren't listening. I noticed the panicked look on Coach's face, and something clicked in my head. "We didn't come here for this!" I shouted at my teammates. "We need to get up on out of here if we want to play this game tonight!" It calmed everyone down—at least it calmed all the Vallejo guys down—and we walked away.

That felt good. But I still felt conflicted about that leadership role. From early on, I knew that on the field I was the best out of all of us—and I **wanted** to be the best, the one who made it out. I was so confident. I was so brash, so cocky, I was thinking, **Hell, no. I don't want to be just one of the group.** Off the field, though, I didn't want to stand out. I wanted to stay one of the guys, all in it together, nobody above anybody else. I felt that tension from the time I was a kid, and it has never gone away. And later, once money came into it, things would get really complicated.

At Vallejo High I learned more life skills on the baseball, football, and basketball teams than I did in the classroom. School was interesting at times, but I knew my future was in sports. The high school teachers knew it, too, and some of them went out of their way to try to make an example of me, to somehow prove that I was just a dumb jock. One year, our English final was about **Lord of the Flies**. I didn't pay attention and fucked around during class discussions of the book, because I had seen the movie a thousand times and knew I was going to ace the final. And I did: When the graded tests came back, I'd gotten a 100. But the English teacher gave me an F for the class! He accused me of cheating, said there was no way I could have aced the final, I'd never opened the book, blah, blah, blah.

Okay, that last part was true—but why would I read a book when I knew the movie so well? The athletic director heard about me getting an F and brought me to a meeting with the English teacher. The AD told the English teacher, "If CC gets anything less than a B in your fucking class, you're out of here." Once I saw that, I realized high school was going to be a cakewalk. That English teacher was the only teacher I had trouble with. Don't get me wrong: I knew education was important, I worked hard in school, and I got decent grades. Let's be real, though—there are different rules for athletes. Yes, we get shortcuts other people don't. But don't lecture me that we, especially Black athletes, should be held to the same standards as everyone else until the opportunities and the resources are truly distributed equally. Growing up Black, in a neighborhood that was largely ignored by the people in power, makes the idea of "standards" incredibly biased. Growing up with money gets you access to better schools; growing up white in America typically makes you a beneficiary of everything from more forgiving teachers to standardized testing that's slanted to your culture and experiences. Yes, I needed and wanted a solid education, but sports was going to be my best shot at getting out and rising up, and so that's where I devoted most of my energy and attention. It was clear, from early on, what the system valued in me.

The first time I noticed a baseball scout with a radar gun trained on me was when I was a high school freshman. By sophomore year, there were four or five showing up every time I pitched. In the winter, those same guys were showing up at my basketball games—along with scouts for college basketball programs. In the fall, scouts for Division I football teams. It was cool at first, but I tuned it out pretty quickly and easily. What I cared about was the game I was playing in, and if I kept doing well, the next step would take care of itself.

Sometimes it was hard to ignore, though, and sometimes the attention pumped me up. My senior year, the intensity ramped up. We were playing a team up in Woodland, near Sacramento, that also had a top prospect, a left-handed-hitting outfielder named Tony Torcato. Before the game, I walked out to the bullpen to warm up . . . and thirty scouts followed me. The basketball season had just ended, and I hadn't been throwing regularly, so Coach Hobbs had me on a short leash, limited to forty-five pitches. First inning, I struck out the first two batters, and then Torcato grounded a soft-ass single between first and second. I got out of the inning and cruised through the second and into the third, but then I hit forty-five pitches. When Coach Hobbs came out to the mound, I hid the ball behind my back and told him, "Coach, let me pitch against Tony again. C'mon, just let me throw to Tony." Coach shook his head, but he left me in the game. Four more pitches, and I struck out Torcato and walked straight off the field.

Growing up in Vallejo was what made me hard enough to get out of Vallejo. We all knew coming up that Vallejo, and especially the Crest, was a place where young Black kids did not get second chances, so everything was higher pressure, higher stakes. Even when we were having fun growing up, we knew we weren't far from slipping off an edge. One night we were driving back to the neighborhood, and we had just turned onto Sage Street, maybe six blocks from my house, when the cops pulled us over for no reason. Mom had talked to me for years about being very, very careful around the police, especially when I was in a car. But when you're Black in those situations, you can do everything right and still be a split second from disaster. One cop walked up and told me to roll down my window. The window mechanism was broken, and you had to stick a pen in the handle to crank it open, so I reached down toward the floor. Big mistake. Suddenly there was a gun to my head and my face was pressed to the ground.

The stress of daily life in the hood showed up in the way I played. In basketball, for instance, I wasn't a star—I averaged maybe eight points a game, but double-digit rebounds. My real contribution was talking shit, getting everybody going. I was the Draymond Green of the late-nineties Vallejo Apaches. **Swing on us? What you mean? Nobody going to swing on us. Fuck no—we Vallejo!** One time we were playing Jesuit High School at Arco, the home of the Sacramento Kings in those days, and it was an aggressive game. I went down on the ground and dove for a ball, tied this guy up, and it was a jump ball. I got up before the other dude, and I was talking shit, and I kind of kicked him. Everybody saw it except for the refs. The Jesuit fans were going crazy, booing and yelling, "Fuck that kid! Throw him out!" I just laughed and walked back to the bench. I couldn't have articulated this at the time, but the way I would erupt on the court or on the field wasn't just competitiveness. Between the lines was where I felt the most in control, and where I could release—where I was encouraged to release—the full force of my emotions. In the rest of my life, I would hide what I was feeling, or try to numb it by drinking.

We won against Jesuit, of course. We only lost six basketball games in my last two years of high school. A few times I toned it down. We were playing at Oakland High School and we were beating the shit out of them. I was taking the ball out of bounds and one of the Oakland High dudes guarding me said, "Y'all better stop scoring on us or your bus ain't going to make it out of here tonight." So that night I shut up.

The rivalries and the battles didn't end inside the gym. The Crest, where I lived, had a beef with Hillside, a neighborhood in South Vallejo. Nobody remembered what had started the trouble, but everybody knew that the Crest didn't fool with Hillside. There were multiple gangs in every neighborhood. Older guys in the Crest were in the Romper Room Gang; slightly younger guys were in Sesame Street, or Ses. There were also the Young Players, or YP. The gangs did typical gang stuff—robbing, stealing, selling drugs. Most of it was small-time, but the Romper Room Gang robbed banks, among other things. **Unsolved Mysteries** did a segment about them, saying Romper Room was suspected of holding up at least twenty-nine pizza places. **American Gangster,** a documentary on BET, claimed that Mac Dre was a member of Romper Room. I don't know about that, but all of us went to school together, and I saw where different choices could take you.

My sophomore year, Coach Hobbs hadn't built the Vallejo field yet, so we played our home games at Dan Foley Park, about two miles away from school. One day I was riding to Dan Foley with an older teammate. We left school and were driving up the hill behind it, on Amador Street, when I looked behind us and saw a car pulling up close—real close. My friend saw it, too, but he just turned up the music, ignoring the tailgating car. But the fucking car kept pulling up, pulling up. We were in a Cutlass that had bench seats, and when we got to the top of the hill, we stopped and my buddy said, "C, slide over and drive." He reached under the front seat and pulled out the biggest gun I had ever seen in my life. He opened the door, got out, and went back to the dudes in the other car, saying, "What the fuck?" He was standing there in his baseball uniform with this giant pistol, and I was behind the fucking wheel. If he shot those dudes, I'd be going to jail, too. But I wasn't scared. **Whatever happens, happens. Whatever we going to do, we going to do.** That's just the neighborhood. You wear fatalism like an extra layer of skin.

My teammate hopped back in the car like

nothing happened, and we just drove to the game. Cool. I never said a word about that to nobody. But it wasn't the only time my life could have changed in an instant.

High school was a great four years for our teams. In football I played defensive end, tight end, and even a little quarterback. We made it to the regional playoffs two years in a row. Our basketball team was even stronger. My senior year, we reached the NorCal finals, and three of my teammates went on to Division I colleges after graduation. And in baseball I was being talked about as a guaranteed first-round draft pick. The biggest problem, if you could call it that, was I didn't know what I wanted to do. I realized my chances of making the NBA were slim, but I loved playing basketball. I also loved the ferocity of football. But my future looked brightest in baseball. In October of my junior year I was watching the World Series, the Braves against the Yankees, and saw Andruw Jones hit home runs in his first two at-bats, at the age of nineteen. I thought, **Man, that's going to be me! I'm going to be a teenager in the big leagues!** That's when I decided I wanted to play pro baseball. Still, I seriously considered signing a scholarship offer from the University of Hawaii because they would have let me play both football and baseball, instead of specializing at another college or going into the minors and committing myself to pro baseball.

I got opinions and advice from every direction. There was one major voice missing, though—my dad's. After he and my mom split and he lived those few months with my grandmother, Dad moved to San Francisco and lived with his oldest brother, who everybody called Hippie Joe, because he had long hair, a sixties kind of big Afro. Uncle Hippie Joe was a cool guy. In those years, when I was in junior high, Dad would come around the neighborhood or the house pretty often. The Navy started shutting down its Vallejo base in 1993, and closed it for good in 1996. Mare Island was the city's biggest employer, and when it went away, suddenly fathers started disappearing from the stands at their kids' games. My dad became one of the missing when I was about fifteen. Dad got a new job, at the Concord Naval Weapons Station, south of Vallejo, and he just slowly faded out of my life. Nobody seemed to know why, and I tried not to think about it too much. Mom would talk with him on the phone and keep him up to date on how I was doing, but he wouldn't come to see me. I didn't understand that. I would always look for him in the stands at my high school basketball games. If I didn't spot him, I'd ask Mom afterward, "Did my dad come?" and she'd say, "No, not tonight, but he'll be here another time." Mom talks about dropping me off for high school football practice one day and looking around and seeing all the other fathers watching practice. She says she left in tears, thinking about what I was missing.

For most of my high school years Dad would go months without a phone call, and even longer without coming around Vallejo, and then he would suddenly materialize. One time he took me to see Cirque du Soleil in San Francisco, which was amazing. Another appearance was less fun. At the end of every school year there were all these events leading up to the prom, including a class trip to Six Flags. Junior year, Jomar and I were all dressed up and ready to leave my grandmother's house for the amusement park when suddenly Dad showed up at the house, ordering us to cut the lawn. "I'm going to teach you," he said. "A man's got to know how to do this kind of stuff around the house." I couldn't believe it, but we walked outside. My grandmother followed us and told my dad, "CC don't have to do nothing. I don't care what you say. CC is not cutting the front grass. His job is to play baseball." Jomar and I left for Six Flags.

I don't know where Dad was living many of those years, or how he was making a living most of the time. He drove trucks for a while; he sold weed, Mom told me many years later. But Dad never stopped trying hard to help, even if the way he supplied that help could be mysterious. He would call Mom out of the blue and tell her to meet him right away, sometimes at a nearby store, sometimes just on the side of a road where he'd parked his car. He'd tell her not to bring me along. Mom would meet Dad, and he'd hand her some cash, ask how I was doing, and vanish again. She said he made sure to keep any details of his life hidden from her and me. She said he didn't want his son to know anything bad about him. Sure, I missed him, but his absence wasn't something that I spent much time thinking about.

Besides, as a teenager, there were plenty more interesting ways to spend my time. I was a good kid, but I'll admit I could be a little devious now and then. Mom was working the night shift at the switchboard at Travis Air Force Base, and one time, when I was fifteen or sixteen, I called her job as she was driving to work and left a message saying I was just checking that she was okay, and could she call me when she got to her job, so I'd know she made it all right? Mom got to work and called me, and I could hear in her voice how proud she was that I cared so much about her. Her mood was a little different when she somehow found out, five or six years later, that I had called to make sure she was out so we could throw a party at our house. "Man, you're such an ass," Mom said. "That was some cold shit right there." Now we laugh about it, though.

My first drink came when I was fourteen. I was staying at Jomar's house, and one of us somehow got hold of a bottle of gin. We snuck out that night, went to the park, and downed it. I liked the way it made me feel. It relaxed me, lowered my anxieties about what people thought of me, made me more social. So I started drinking more, and hiding it. I can't tell you how much I drank on average, but it was a lot, from early on. There was a stretch where Jomar was pretty much living with us, and he and I got this big jug of Carlo Rossi and stashed it in the back of my bedroom closet, under a huge pile of clothes. You know how my grandmother did everything for me around the house—made my bed, ironed my clothes? One day when I was at school, she decided to thoroughly clean my room, and she found the jug of Carlo Rossi. She gave it to my mother, who put it on the living room table and sat there waiting for us to come home. We walked in and Mom said, "Jomar, I know this is yours, because CC wouldn't do that." I did not correct her.

Someone was always throwing a party, and I'd go, but even though I was becoming well known on the field and on the court, I was pretty shy, and I'd stay off to the side and never dance. One night during my junior year of high school, though, a house party changed my life. It was at my basketball teammate Brian Douglas's house, at the beginning of eleventh grade. Girls kept coming up to me, asking me to dance, and I kept saying no. The girl that did get my attention was the one who didn't approach me, the one who was sitting on the couch, chilling with her friends. She was tall, with long, light brown hair. There was an energy to her eyes and to her smile that cut through all the music and all the other people in the room. We sat and talked pretty much the whole night. She lived on the south side of Vallejo, so we had gone to different elementary and middle schools, and she was a year younger than me. Her brother, Joe, was a senior—and I had just taken Joe's starting spot on the Vallejo high school basketball team! Right away it was clear that Amber Carter was smart, fun, and formidable. This girl didn't just have dreams; she had a plan for her life. She wanted to go to college and she wanted to be a high school principal. For girls in our school at the time, you didn't hear that kind of thing much. I could tell right away we were opposite personalities, and it's still true: Amber can go into a room and talk to anybody, and I'll try to talk to as few people as possible. I wish I could say I knew right then that we were destined to be together, but I was sixteen and I sort of had a girlfriend already. Amber, however, went home that night and asked her brother, "Do you know CC?"

"Yeah, why?" Joe said.

"That's going to be your brother-in-law," Amber told him.

She was right, as it turned out, and I love how sure she was from the beginning. But I also love

Joe's response. "Oh my God!" he said. "Have you seen CC naked? When he takes his shirt off he has all this crazy chest hair!" Luckily for me, that didn't scare Amber away. Maybe if she'd known how I would test her tolerance in far more serious ways down the road . . .

Getting ready for a Vallejo High School playoff game
my senior year—and on the verge of leaving
my hometown for the Cleveland Indians.

# 4

WANTED TO QUIT. IT WAS THE WINTER OF MY SENIOR year of high school, and from the outside it looked like I had everything to look forward to: Everybody said that very soon I was going to be choosing between a college scholarship and going straight to pro baseball and making money. But because of one day in February, none of that mattered to me.

My mom was my mom, but when we hung out we felt almost like siblings, and for years she worked nights. So my grandmother had pretty much raised me from the time I was eight years old. Granny was warm, full of energy, always laughing, always positive, and strong. When I was in fifth grade I had to be hospitalized for two weeks with pneumonia. I was so sick they had to give me a spinal tap. My mom couldn't stand seeing her son in such pain, so Granny was the one who stayed in the room with me during the procedure.

The most powerful thing about Granny was her love. She would take in anyone in the family who needed help and give them everything she had. Her love for me could be funny at times. Granny never missed any of my games—baseball, football, or basketball—and she watched them as if no one else on the field or the court existed. At Vallejo basketball games Granny would sit in the front row of the bleachers, about three seats down from our team, and lock her eyes on me for the whole night. Other fans would say, "Did you see that?" when someone made a great play, and Granny would just shake her head. At one football game, a teammate of mine got hurt badly enough he had to be carried off the field. My mom had gone to the ladies' room, and when she came back to her seat she asked Granny what had happened. Granny shrugged. "I don't know," she said. "It's not CC on the stretcher." Once I tried to get a job at Marine World. Granny said, "No, you don't have time for that. Focus on baseball."

I wanted to be great for myself—to be the one guy from Vallejo who made it out and made it big. But what motivated me even more was getting Granny out of the hood. After everything she had been through, and after everything she had done to keep our family together, Granny deserved to live somewhere beautiful and peaceful, where she didn't ever have to worry again about how to pay the bills or about bullets flying. It was in her backyard that I remember really throwing for the first time: When I was about five, I picked up a grapefruit that had fallen from one of her trees and hurled it at a folding chair about ten feet away. Even at that age I threw hard enough to knock the chair down.

As I finished my junior year of high school, getting named first team all-league in baseball and basketball, the dream of playing my grandmother's way out of the Crest started to seem within reach. One clear sign was the parade of strangers coming to Dieninger Street, in a neighborhood that college coaches avoided visiting at night.

It started off well. **A coach from UCLA is in my house! Arizona State! A Cincinnati Reds scout! A Cleveland Indians scout! The Giants are here! We got Scott Boras coming in!** But I quickly got sick of the attention. From the end of my junior year until I got drafted a year later, it was a college recruiter, an agent, a pro baseball scout—somebody was at my house every damn day or night. By the time Christmas rolled around after football season, I said, "Ma, you pick. I don't care. I don't give a fuck what school I go to. I don't care who drafts me. I don't care who's my agent. I'm done." It was too many boring questions, too many sales pitches from people you could not trust, too much uncertainty.

Hanging over everything was Granny's health. In October, when she turned seventy, she was feeling great. Then, right around Christmas, she was on a trip with her church group and had a stroke. Granny was tough—she was in church four days a week, but she would cuss you out, just go off on you—so she avoided going to the doctor for five days. The stroke really messed her up, partially paralyzing her right side, and she never really got the proper rehab treatment. After Christmas she got so sick she finally agreed to go into the hospital. Every day after basketball practice I would visit her, and stay until eleven or midnight. We watched the Super Bowl together as Denver upset Green Bay, John Elway's first win. We were in a hospital, but those are some of my best memories—just me and Granny, chopping it up for hours.

Soon afterward she developed pneumonia so severe that the hospital sent her home and said there was nothing they could do for her. She was mostly confined to bed, and it broke my heart to see her getting weaker and weaker, yet feel powerless to help her get better.

Granny had a bell, and when she rang it during the night, Aunt Nieci and I would go in and change her diaper. The night of January 31, she was so uncomfortable she rang the bell every hour. In the morning I was in the shower when my aunt started screaming, "Call 911!" Granny wasn't breathing. The ambulance came. Her eyes were closed when they carried her out of the house. They took her to the hospital, but I knew she was gone.

I went to school that day, and that night I had a basketball game. Somehow I played, but I was completely out of it. I got elbowed in the mouth, was bleeding all over the place, and didn't even notice. I don't remember anything about Granny's funeral, other than it was the most painful day I had ever experienced. I wanted to quit everything—basketball, baseball, school—because Granny was the one person I was doing everything for, and my purpose had died with her. A few days later, I told Mom that I was done. We sat in the living room, surrounded by photos of Granny. The house seemed empty with her gone. We had a long conversation. Finally, Mom said, "Why don't you just decide that whatever your career is going to be—whether it's high school, college, whether you get drafted—you'll dedicate it to her? Play as hard as you can, every day. For Granny."

For the rest of the basketball season my legs were heavier than my heart. But with my mom's words in my head, I kept moving forward. Our basketball team went 32–2, with the second loss coming in the state regional finals, ending our season. In the locker room my teammates were in tears. But I was smiling. We'd played our asses off and I knew my grandmother would have been proud. Compared to losing Granny, losing that game meant nothing.

But my grandmother's death changed the course of my life. College looked like it would be a good time. But we had no money. I couldn't afford to go to college, even with a full ride. For the past couple of years we had depended on my grandmother's Social Security checks, and now those had stopped coming in. What if I went to UCLA or Hawaii and got hurt? So I only talked about going to college to try to jack up my leverage when it came to bargaining for a baseball contract. Playing games had been just fun. Now I had to provide. I had to fucking sign to play pro baseball. And if baseball didn't work out, I was going to have to get a job. This was real life. I didn't consider it unfair. My thinking was, **If we've got to depend on somebody, fuck, let me do it. Let it be on me. Ain't nobody else as good as me to be able to step up right now.** It was the perfect amount of pressure. I was a grown man by that time. Or so I thought.

In June, as the major league baseball draft got closer, my friends and family got more and more excited, constantly trying to guess which team would pick me. The speculation was all over the map, because some teams wanted me as a position player and others wanted me as a pitcher. My only preference was the West Coast, because that's what I knew, and I loved the warm weather. The Giants seemed really interested—I had played for the team they sponsored in the Area Code Games—and they had three first-round picks. Playing in San Francisco, an hour from my hometown, sounded cool.

Later I heard that some teams downgraded me because of Vallejo's reputation—they thought guys coming out of there were undisciplined and hard to coach, so they'd be risky as high draft picks. Which seems to me racist as much as anything factual. The other knock was that I couldn't control my emotions. That's an unfair criticism of any seventeen-year-old kid. But that one hurt because the scouts did have a point. By senior year I was pretty fucked up emotionally. The scouts didn't know what I'd been through growing up, and that even when I was screaming at an umpire or a hitter I was being even harder on myself. I would lie in bed at night, staring at the ceiling. **Where am I going to get drafted? Is this going to work out? Am I making the right decision?** Really, though, there wasn't any other decision to be made.

When the day of the draft came I didn't want to sit around at home with all my relatives and friends and wait for a phone call delivering the news. I got out of there first thing in the morning and went to school. It may have been one of the very few times I actually looked forward to going to school. This didn't exactly seal me off from the nervousness, or from people having fun with me. One hot rumor was that Cincinnati was going to take me with the seventh pick. So my friend Dave Bernstine turned to me in history class and whispered, "Hey, dude, seventh pick, the Reds!" My heart started racing, but Dave just laughed; he didn't know anything.

My mom was at home following the draft on the Internet—remember, this was 1998, so it was dial-up. Some guys who turned out to be pretty good big leaguers were picked ahead of me: Pat Burrell, Mark Mulder, J.D. Drew, Carlos Peña, Jeff Weaver, Brad Lidge. But the teams I thought wanted me passed: The Reds took Austin Kearns. The Pirates took a lefty pitcher from Vanderbilt named Clint Johnston. The Giants, picking nineteenth, took . . . Tony Torcato, a dude I'd played against my whole life, the outfielder I had struck out in that game in

Woodland! When I found out later, I was really mad; the Giants' justification was they planned to grab me with their next pick in the first round. Yeah, sure. I'm not going to lie: My hometown team passing, that hurt. **I'm right here in your backyard, I'm the best player in California—what the fuck are you doing? What else do I need to do to prove myself to you?** It felt like a slap in the face.

I was in third period, art class, when the high school made an announcement over the public address system: "Congratulations to CC Sabathia, who was just chosen in the first round of the major league baseball draft by the Cleveland Indians." The other kids in class applauded. It was pretty cool. We had been talking about this day for years, and it had arrived.

My senior year I went 6–0 as a pitcher, with an 0.77 earned run average, and I averaged two strike-outs per inning. Pretty much untouchable. It lasted all the way until the sectional championship game, in Stockton. I had another shutout going through the first four innings. Then I walked the first two batters of the fifth. Things were starting to spiral in my mind: **Maybe I'm not as great as everyone's been saying.** Somehow I pulled it back together to get two outs—then I hit the next batter, loading the bases, and my composure was gone. This was supposed to be the glorious ending, me the star, carrying my team in my final high school game. I threw a wild pitch, all the way to the screen behind home plate. Two runs scored. The runner on first base took a huge lead, started to steal second—and I forgot about the runner at third, who broke for home and scored easily. The batter then rocked a triple to right center, driving in the fifth run. We lost 5–3. On the bench after the game, I cried, hard and long. "It's the end," I told a reporter.

After the senior prom we were supposed to go to Six Flags, like every year, and then to a party in Oakland, and spend the night in a hotel. I was hyped. The day of the prom, Dad suddenly showed up at Granny's house and told me that two Cleveland coaches were in town and that I had to do a workout—the morning after the prom. "Kiss my ass! I ain't coming back from Oakland!" I told him.

We went back and forth for a long time. I was hot. I was over all of the draft stuff. I did not care. I just wanted to be a high school kid for the night.

"You need to come back tonight and meet with these people tomorrow!" Dad insisted.

So I did. It was the Indians' strength coach and a crosschecker. They took me to the park, told me to take off my shirt, and had me do stupid shit, like it was a one-man NFL combine. Then they gave me a multiple-choice test. I didn't even look at the questions—I just checked off a bunch of answers and handed it back as fast as I could. If they weren't already convinced I was ready to be a pro, I didn't know why the fuck they'd even drafted me. Even now the whole thing still pisses me off.

I was tired and beat up, more mentally than anything else. The stretch from Granny's death through the baseball draft and the end of high school had left me wrung out. I knew I had achieved something special—being selected in the first round—but it felt hollow, because Granny wasn't here to share it with me. It was the beginning of what would become a pattern in my life for a long time: It felt as if every triumph was matched or exceeded by a loss.

The weeks after the draft and after graduation went by in a haze. The pain of Granny's death, followed by the high of getting picked in the first round—I couldn't process the contradictory emotions, so I pushed them away. I celebrated with my high school friends, but I was still nervous about my next step. We picked an agent—mostly because the guy had given me a new suit—and started negotiating with the Indians. The agent dragged things out for a month. Sure, I wanted as big a contract as possible, but also I wanted to get on with it.

One morning Mom came home from work and found me standing in the hallway wearing my glove and holding a baseball. "Mom, I'm ready to go," I told her.

We sat on her bed and called Cleveland, getting Indians general manager John Hart on the line. Mom asked for a $1.5 million signing bonus. Hart offered

$1.3 million. Mom covered the receiver with one hand and whispered the number to me. I nodded.

"We'll take it," Mom told Hart.

When she hung up, we hugged and screamed with joy—and with relief.

There was another big piece of unfinished business, however. What position was I going to play in pro ball? Even when I was drafted, if you had asked me if I was a pitcher, I would have said hell no. I just happened to be good at pitching. And I loved hitting. My senior year in high school I batted .586. In a playoff game against Merced, we were down by three runs late in the game when I came up with the bases loaded. A new relief pitcher came into the game—a guy I had warned earlier not to throw me fastballs. My cousin Nathan was standing by the fence, and I went over and got some sunflower seeds from him. I knew the reliever would throw me a curve; I'd set him up. "Watch this," I told Nathan. "I'm about to go deep." First pitch, curveball, grand slam over some trees in center.

If Cincinnati had picked me, I would have been a hitter. Pittsburgh, I would have been a hitter. And man, I loved to hit. In one high school road game I hit a ball off the light tower behind right field; the stupid umpires only gave me a triple instead of a home run because they lost sight of the ball in the fog. San Francisco wanted me as a pitcher. Cleveland, I had no idea. In July, a few days after I signed, I got on the phone with Mark Shapiro, the assistant general manager, and asked: "Am I playing first, or am I pitching?" Mark laughed and told me not to bring any bats with me to the minor leagues. He said I would be flying to join the Indians' rookie league team in the Appalachian League, in Burlington, North Carolina. I didn't know where that was, but I didn't much care. I was seventeen years old and I was about to get paid to play baseball.

My second-ever bullpen as a pro, with the Burlington Indians in 1998. North Carolina was the farthest I'd ever been from home, and I was so raw I didn't know how to stand on the mound.

# 5

I N 1998 THE MINOR LEAGUE SALARY WAS $200 A week. I probably spent $175 of it on phone cards.

I had been away from Vallejo before, for baseball road trips. But those had lasted a week max. Only twice had I been on trips without a parent or an adult I knew. Now I was in the middle of nowhere in North Carolina, in a small southern town almost 3,000 miles from Vallejo. I didn't know a soul, and I was going to be here for months. The morning after my first night in Burlington I called my mom and asked what would happen if I quit right then: Would I have to give back any of the money? If I did, I'd find a way to get through the season.

I didn't quit, but I cried the first four nights I was in Burlington, and whenever I wasn't on the field I was usually on the phone. Every day at three I called my mom from a pay phone. Every night I called Amber and all my friends. It was the summer, and back in Vallejo they were out of school, hanging out and riding around, partying. I wanted them to tell me everything about all the fun I was missing.

Meanwhile, I was living with my teammates in a

dump of a motel, Kirk's Motor Lodge. It was hot as hell during the day, but you couldn't swim, because the motel owners drained the pool after some of the Dominican dudes on our team peed in it. The rooms didn't have stoves, so you couldn't cook— not that I knew how, anyway. I didn't know how to wash my clothes, either, so when they got dirty, I'd just go to Walmart and buy more.

I was so homesick that after a few weeks I imported Jomar, and he became my roommate and constant companion, just like back home. That helped, though we were still bored. We roamed the mall, killing time; I got my ears pierced. On the field, I was quickly discovering that I knew absolutely nothing about pitching. Nothing. My first bullpen in Burlington, I was really excited. I was wearing my Indians uniform for the first time: **I'm a pro!** The other pitchers were lined up and watching me: **Let's see what kind of shit the first-round pick's got.** The pitching coach, Carl Willis, said to me, "Let me see your four-seamer and then your two-seamer."

I looked at Carl with a blank stare: "What?"

"Your pitches. Your four-seam fastball and your two-seam fastball."

I still didn't know what he meant, so I gripped that ball the way I always had. My fingers weren't even on the seams; I was on the middle of the ball, the open leather horseshoe part.

Carl's eyebrows went up. "Nobody's ever taught you how to throw a four-seamer?"

I shook my head. "Nope. What do you mean?"

Carl took the ball and placed his index and middle fingers perpendicularly across the seams, the pads of his fingers edging just across the laces, the thumb underneath the ball, the open side of the horseshoe facing away from his body. **Oh, okay. That's how you grip a four-seam fastball.**

I showed Carl how I just twisted my wrist real hard to throw a curveball, and how I dropped my arm angle a little bit to throw a slider. I didn't know how to stand on the rubber, either. When I was fifteen I'd gone to a baseball camp run by the Salinas Peppers, a minor league team in central California, and one of the pitchers told me to stand a couple of inches in front of the rubber, because the umpires never pay attention. In high school I was able to get away with that, and with being big, left-handed, and whipping the ball across the plate at 93 miles per hour. That wasn't going to fly in pro ball.

Carl had played for nine seasons in the big leagues, and this was his second season as a pitching coach. He was thirty-eight years old and— fortunately for me—incredibly patient. I could see him thinking, **Man, is this kid raw,** but he didn't say anything critical, and he didn't laugh. After showing me how to hold the ball the right way, he corrected my footwork, turning my left foot—my plant foot, the one a pitcher uses to drive his delivery toward home plate—so it rested against the side of the rubber. After two bullpens, I went from

throwing 93 to throwing 99. One day I threw batting practice and the guys standing behind the cage
were saying, "What the fuck?"

The rookie leagues have a short season, because most
of the players have just come off a full high school or
college season. So I only pitched in five games, and I
gave up more hits than I was used to, twenty in eighteen innings. But I also struck out thirty-five hitters.
The other Appalachian League teams were in tiny
towns scattered in four states, so for road games we
would go on four-hour bus rides, twisting and turning through the mountains to Bluefield, Virginia,
and Kingsport, Tennessee, places where nearly every
face in the stands was White. I hated those bus rides.
But I also started to have some fun as I got a little
more comfortable being out on my own. Before my
starts, I would make the bus driver take us to
Wendy's, and I'd down a Big Classic as my pre-game
meal. You get away with a lot of shit when you're a
first-round pick.

Some of my teammates had cars, so on off-nights
we'd ride to the local club. I hadn't turned twenty-
one yet, so I couldn't drink legally. Sometimes an
older guy on the team would let me borrow his ID.
There was another left-handed pitcher who was
from Venezuela and looked nothing like me. But
he was dark-skinned, which was good enough—the
bartenders didn't look too closely at the driver's
license photo. Or on some nights the little dance
club would let me and Jomar inside even though

we were underage. They just wouldn't give us the wristbands that allowed you to drink. No problem: I'd camp out in the bathroom, and my teammates would bring me drinks in there, two or three at a time, and I'd kill the drinks fast inside a stall.

After the rookie league season in Burlington ended in late August, the Indians sent me to Akron, where they have their AA team, to throw a couple of bullpens so that Mark Shapiro and other front-office guys could come down from Cleveland and see if their investment was making progress. Then in September it was off to the instructional league, the instructs, in Florida. Man, those months were a long haul—the most I'd ever played baseball in a year. By the end of it I was worn-out, and my bonus money was burning a hole in my pocket. I could not wait to get back to Vallejo and cut loose.

The first big thing I bought when I got back to California was a Camaro. It was a beautiful ride. There are two things in the world I really know how to do: pitch and drive. The rest I'm still figuring out. The world will keep teaching you lessons, though. Not long after I bought the Camaro, I took it to the dealer to get it serviced. Jomar and I were hanging out, waiting for the work to get done, and we noticed a brand-new Escalade sitting in the middle of the showroom. At the time the Escalade had just come out, and it was the dopest thing on four wheels, so Jomar and I walked over and climbed in. We were sitting in the front seats, checking it out and talking, when this old White dude came up to the car window and said, in a real condescending tone, "If you guys work hard enough you may be able to get this one day." That shit made me mad. "As a matter of fact," I said, "I'm not getting out of this car. I want this one right here." The White guy was a salesman, and his eyes got big. They got even bigger when I told him I wanted the other salesman, the Black dude, to handle the deal. The funnier part was that because I was eighteen, I had to have my mom come down and co-sign the paperwork. But I drove that motherfucking Escalade right out of the dealership.

There were other times when the combination of youth, money, and anger didn't work out so well. One night we were in Oakland for a party, and we were parked outside in the Escalade. Amber was sitting on my lap in the front seat. I'd been drinking for hours. A friend of mine was in the backseat; his girlfriend had gone off somewhere, and now she was walking back toward us. Some dude we didn't know appeared and started talking with my friend's girlfriend. Suddenly I was yelling at my friend in the backseat: "You're just going to let him talk to your girl like that?" My friend was yelling back at me. By then we were all out of the car. I ripped off my shirt and went after the guy we didn't know, screaming and cursing. It turned into this huge fight in the streets, faster than you can read this paragraph. People were holding me back and shoving me into the Escalade.

It did not take much to set me off when I'd been drinking. Later, Amber would say that in those years I was looking for somebody to say something, for someone to poke the bear. Maybe she's right. But I do know that as much as I had wanted to be the one to provide for people, the reality of having money, and having people expect me to share it with them, was a pressure I had not seen coming. I know the stereotype is that when someone hits it big, people come out of the woodwork with their hands out. That wasn't the problem here, and that's what made it even more painful and confusing: It was some of my family and friends who felt entitled to a piece of the pie. **Set up this rap thing for me! Set up that rap thing for me!** It was nothing compared to what would come later, when I signed a huge contract with the Yankees, and people were on me to build churches, schools, all kinds of shit. I wanted to help them, and yet I resented them for expecting the help. It felt like they were never going to do shit for themselves—they wanted me to do it for them, and they would be dependent on me forever, unless I broke off our friendship, which ended up happening with a couple of people. So, at a time when I needed the support of the people closest to me—for them to care about me, not what I was being paid—money was creating distance between us, making some of my deepest relationships feel impersonal. And yet I had a lot of trouble saying no—some people genuinely needed help, and I didn't want anyone to believe I thought I was better than them. It all contributed to a fury that would come spilling out when I was drunk.

My dad had been coming around more frequently as I got near the end of high school, though I never knew when he might show up, how long he would stay, or where he was going when he left. I didn't care a lot about the details of my dad's comings and goings—I was just really happy when he was around. I knew he wasn't looking at me as a meal ticket, showing up only because I was about to make some real money. He was just genuinely proud and excited for me, and I loved talking with him about what life was going to be like in the big leagues, after all the years we had spent fantasizing about it and working toward that goal.

But then the pattern kicked in: Just as something beautiful was happening in my life, something tragic arrived to even it out. One day in January 1999, not long before I had to leave for spring training, Dad asked me to pick him up from a doctor's appointment. He had looked healthy whenever I saw him, and he didn't mention that he was visiting the doctor for any particular reason. As I drove along the interstate back to the Crest, Dad looked out the passenger side window, kind of quiet for most of the ride. When we got off the freeway and were back on the local streets in Vallejo—I think maybe we were at a stop sign—he said, "Dude, I got some bad news to tell you. I'm really sick."

He wasn't specific. It was clearly hard for him to talk about it. When we reached home and sat down with my mom, she was the one who first said it: Dad had HIV.

My throat tightened, but I didn't cry. That came later. I didn't ask how he'd got sick, either; I didn't want to know, and I didn't care. I didn't wonder if he might be gay; I had never seen him high or using drugs around me, so I didn't guess that it might be from needles. I didn't know much about HIV, only enough to know that in the hood in 1999 it was a death sentence. That was what mattered to me, and what scared me: I thought I was going to lose him right away. I found out later that he had been diagnosed two years earlier and had told Mom about it, but they'd decided they didn't want to upset me and so they'd kept it a secret, which must have been tough on them.

As we drove the final few blocks Dad might have said that he was feeling pretty good at the moment. I don't really remember. I don't think I said anything. All that was in my head was a prayer that began that day and ran through my mind for years to come: **Please let us have Dad as long as possible.**

Amber and I were together most of that off-season. She was working the front desk at a health club, so I bought a membership just so I could hang around and see her. We were definitely in love, but it still seemed like we were being pulled in different directions. She was in her senior year of high school and determined to go to San Diego State after that. Truth be told, I was probably more interested in Amber than she was in me—getting married was clearly not her goal. If things worked out with us, fine, but she had other priorities: She wanted to be a high school principal and she wanted to put Vallejo behind her. Amber's father is Black, her mother is white, and growing up things could be kind of crazy in her house. Years later, she would say her family is like the one on the TV show **Shameless,** and she wasn't completely joking. She was also right to be cautious about me: Her dad had come back from Vietnam with drug and alcohol problems, so Amber knew what addiction looked like.

In February, just before I left for spring training, I remember sitting with Amber outside her house and telling her, "You're going to be my girlfriend." I would call her a lot from the road, often with my mom on the line, too, because Amber wasn't close with her own mom and so I wanted them to become friends.

That spring Amber was voted prom queen, and of course she didn't want to go alone. So she told me she'd asked an old boyfriend to take her, a guy she said she had no interest in anymore. I felt bad that I couldn't be there with her on that special day.

Luckily, I got hurt early that year. I had done

nothing to stay in shape over the winter, figuring I had plenty of time to get my arm ready when I got to Florida. Not long after we started practice, I was throwing my first bullpen. Mark Shapiro and John Hart came over and sat down right behind the batting cage. So of course I started throwing as hard as I fucking could, to show them what they'd gotten with their first-round pick. I ended up with a bone bruise in my elbow. Nothing too serious, but the Indians weren't going to take any chances, so they shut down my throwing and at the end of camp they sent me to Cleveland for rehab until June. In May I asked if I could go home to Cali for a few days. I had a plan to surprise Amber and take her to the prom. It was a good plan, too—except that a week before I flew to Vallejo, the three of us were on the phone as usual and my mom said, "Amber, aren't you excited CC's coming back to take you to the prom?"

My second year in the minors, 1999, I saw a lot of small towns in the South and the Midwest for the first time. Things started slowly, because I was coming back from the sore elbow. The Indians put me with a short-season Class A team in Niles, Ohio, for six games. When I felt healthy and got in a groove they promoted me to a Sally League A-ball team in Columbus, Georgia, in the middle of the summer. I convinced Mom and Amber to come visit me for a couple of weeks. Just after they got off the plane the

Indians told me I was moving to a team in Kinston, North Carolina, right away. Mom and Amber had to jump in my car and follow. We ended up having a good time, but Amber was getting a taste of the unpredictability of baseball life. When it came time for her to head back west and start her freshman year of college, she was very much ready to leave and pursue her dreams. I thought I would be seeing Amber again, and that we would pick up where we left off. But I wasn't sure.

We stayed in that limbo for the next year—seeing each other a lot during the off-season when I was back in Vallejo, staying in touch mostly by phone during the six months when I was away in the minors. Our relationship was part of the split personality that I was starting to develop: When I was home I was one of the guys, just as I had always been, and when I was on the road playing ball, I was more independent with a totally new group of friends. I was still only nineteen and didn't know how to square those two things off the field, which was one reason I was drinking more—it made me more relaxed in social situations.

A few months after signing my first contract I bought Mom a new house, a four-bedroom ranch-style place on a quiet block on Irene Drive in Vallejo. I was so proud to get her out of the hood, and to give her a place where she could be safe and secure and never again worry about needing to leave. I would stay with her in the Irene Drive house during the off-season, and we enjoyed showing it off. Most Friday or Saturday nights we'd throw a party, with maybe twenty to forty people—my mom's girlfriends, my Vallejo guy friends. Amber was home on break from college and came to one of our house parties, and she was surprised: "Aren't you uncomfortable drinking in front of your mom?" No, it didn't bother me at all—and because I hadn't turned twenty-one yet, it was Mom who was buying the alcohol, so what was the big deal? Besides, Mom's thinking was that if I was going to drink, she would rather I do it at home, where she could keep an eye on me.

Most nights that didn't make much of a difference, though. These were what we called Cutty Bang parties. "Cutty" is Bay slang for "shady" or "not quite legal." It sounds like but is different from "cuddie," the Crest word for a good friend—Jomar and me are "cuddies" instead of "buddies," for instance, and you might say, "Wazzup, cuddie?" Anyway, the standard Cutty Bang mixes Tanqueray and Seagram gins, Bacardí Limón, and pineapple juice. That shit is no joke—it gets you buzzed fast—but I could put away a lot of it. We'd go to Costco and buy giant bottles of liquor. I didn't know why at the time, but my drinking always had to be extreme, to go from zero to 100. I would routinely drink until I blacked out. Unconsciousness was actually the preferred outcome, because I was not a happy drunk—most nights if I got loaded and didn't just pass out, I'd want to fight someone. Anyone.

Some weekends I would drive down to visit Amber at San Diego State, and we would go across the border to Tijuana. One night we were walking out of a club and I was blasted, as usual. Some other guy was leaving, too, and I went off on him: "What the fuck are you looking at? Why you looking at my girl?" Of course the guy got pissed and came back at me, and soon we were in each other's faces, screaming. Suddenly the Mexican cops were there. Now, I knew that they were always looking for guys fighting on the street, because it gave them a reason to arrest you and then rob you. You do not want to go to jail in Tijuana as a teenage American Black kid. But I was out of my mind with booze and anger.

The cops grabbed me and the other guy. Thinking really fast, Amber yelled, "No, no! They're friends! They're just talking!" The cops held up for a second, and Amber said in my ear: "Just give them everything you have in your pockets, CC, right now!" I pulled out maybe $200 in cash and handed it to one of the cops.

"Okay, you can go," he said.

We were gone fast, in the car and hightailing it back north over the border. In a few hours I was sober and apologetic. You would think close calls like that might have slowed me down the next time. But I always thought I had it under control.

One reason for that belief was my left arm.

Whatever else was happening in the rest of my life, my arm was still unbeatable. On the mound, I was dominating—and I was getting impatient. In 2000, the Indians invited me to major league spring training for the first time. Cleveland's camp was in Winter Haven, a small town in central Florida about halfway between Tampa and Orlando. There was no chance I was going to make the team that year, but just being around the big-league squad was a thrill. I was getting dressed next to Sandy Alomar Jr., Kenny Lofton, David Justice, Bartolo Colón—players I'd watched as a kid. And Manny Ramírez. My first two years with the Indians, Manny would come by the team hotel during spring training and take me out to eat, and the whole time he thought I was Dominican. He finally asked, "Papi, why you never speak Spanish?"

I laughed and told him, "Dude, I'm from California!"

It all made the dream feel so close. I could even touch part of it now, literally: When I walked into the spring training clubhouse for the first time, I spotted a locker with my name above it, and a bright white Cleveland home jersey hanging inside. I hadn't asked for any particular number—that wasn't something minor leaguers, even first-round draft picks, could do back then. And even if we were able to pick what was considered a desirable pitcher's number—something in the twenties through the forties—the tradition was that younger guys would need to give up their jersey number if a veteran, maybe somebody who had been traded to the team, decided he wanted it.

The jersey in my locker said 52. That was a high number for a pitcher, the kind of number that told people you were just filling out the spring roster and were a long shot to ever play in the majors. But at least they hadn't given me a number in the sixties or seventies. I saw 52 and thought, **Fuck, I'm making the team!** But that wasn't the only thing I saw in 52. What I saw was a number no other player would ever ask to take away from me. It would be mine, one thing in the world that I wouldn't have to worry about losing. I loved 52 right away. I thought, **I'm keeping this high-ass number because it will always be mine.**

Something else really important happened that spring, though I didn't grasp the significance at the time. One day on one of the back fields where the minor leaguers practiced, a tall, lean, dignified man in his mid-sixties walked up and introduced himself. Beginning in 1958, Mudcat Grant had pitched for the Indians for the first six and a half years of his fourteen-year career, and now he worked informally for the organization. He said he thought I had a chance to be a really good pitcher, maybe even one of the "Black Aces": Black pitchers who have won at least 20 games in a single season.

Mudcat also told me that when the team traveled to Kansas City I should make sure to visit the Negro Leagues Baseball Museum and reach out to Buck O'Neil, who had been a star with the Kansas City Monarchs and the first Black coach in the major leagues.

My rookie year, on my first trip to Kansas City with the Indians, Buck was standing by the cage during batting practice. He was eighty-nine years old, but had only recently retired from working as a Royals scout. Buck said, "Hey, big fella, I love what you're doing!"

I was like, "You know who I am?"

He was so embracing, so encouraging. Buck was a phenomenal storyteller, and he had made it his mission to keep the memory of the Negro Leagues alive. He'd sit down with me on the bench before games and say, "CC, you remind me of Bullet Joe Rogan." During games Buck sat behind home plate a little to the third-base side, and I would tip my cap to him when I was walking off the mound. Buck made you feel connected to the Negro League players, the men who paved the way for us.

We lost Buck in 2006, but I go to the museum every time I'm in K.C. I feel like I have to see Satchel Paige and Rube Foster and Josh Gibson. These are my guys, and I miss them like I miss Buck.

At nineteen, though, my focus was on getting to the big leagues as quickly as possible, and having as much fun as I could along the way. It was during the spring camp of 2000 that I got to know Milton Bradley. He was slightly more than two years older than me, had already been in the minors for four seasons, and was an outfielder in the Montreal Expos system. But someone introduced us, and we had a lot in common. He was a Black guy from California who'd grown up with just his mom, and it was hard for him to get along with people and be social, all stuff that I could relate to. We clicked right away. Milt is a lot of different things—loyal and thoughtful and emotional—and I would learn more about the reasons behind his demons a few years later, when he was traded to the Indians. But he's always been a great friend. When we were young Milt and me together were pretty wild. We went to a block party in Fort Myers that spring and I got way too drunk—so bad that I ended up in an emergency room, having my stomach pumped. Shit happens. And I was back on the mound at camp the next day, so nobody in the organization said anything about it, if they even knew.

The Indians started me in A ball again, back in Kinston, North Carolina. In ten games, I struck out sixty-nine batters in fifty-six innings, and it forced them to move me up to double-A, in Akron. Now I was going up against lineups where three or four of the hitters were on track to reach the majors—and I was still mowing them down, striking out a batter per inning. My curveball and changeup were getting sharper, but mostly I was still overpowering people.

That success on the mound could pay off in unexpected ways. One night Jomar and I went to an Akron club; Amber was in the car, too, visiting from California. We were driving home, and our car was weaving down the road. Suddenly I saw flashing lights in the rearview mirror, so I pulled over to the shoulder and stopped. Jomar said, "Put pennies in your mouth! If you put pennies in your mouth, they can't smell the alcohol!" I have no idea whether that's true or not, but we started looking all over the car for pennies. I don't remember if we found any, but I do remember it didn't matter. The cop looked at my driver's license: "Oh, you're CC Sabathia," he said. "Let me escort you guys to make sure you get home okay." It wasn't the first time, and it was far from the last, that being an athlete got me off the hook.

The major league Indians finished second in the American League Central Division in 2000, five games behind the Chicago White Sox. The team's biggest weakness was its starting pitching. At the time it was still common in baseball to have a rotation of four starters. Bartolo Colón, at twenty-seven, was the ace. Dave Burba, a thirty-three-year-old righty, was solid. Chuck Finley, a veteran lefty, was a former ace who was now thirty-seven years old and relying on experience. After that, the

Indians' options for starters dropped off considerably. So going into the winter, they were talking about me as the best prospect in the organization, the starting pitcher who could get them over the hump—if I could win a job in the starting rotation in training camp the next spring.

Back in Vallejo that winter, I saw Amber whenever I could. We had talked plenty about my dad, and one of the things I loved about Amber was that I could open up to her completely about him—my worries about his health because of HIV, my disappointments about the relationship I had with him. But somehow Amber and my dad had never met. One weekend when she was home from San Diego State I told her it was important to me that they know each other, and I wanted her to go with me to visit him.

Mom had told me that Dad was in a hospital in San Francisco. When we walked into Dad's room he was wearing an Indians hat, and he was so excited to finally meet Amber. Dad introduced us to his roommate; he walked us around, bragging about me to the other guys in the hospital. We sat and talked, had some snacks, and after about an hour Amber and I left.

When we got in the car she said, "How long has your dad been in rehab?"

I was stumped: "What are you talking about?" I had assumed that Dad was in a hospital because he was sick from HIV.

But Amber said, "Did you not notice that the place was locked, and that your dad couldn't walk us to the car? That's a rehab facility! Are you that naive?"

I guess I was naive, or maybe I just wanted to block out any difficult, scary possibilities. My mom never said anything bad about my dad, and she always tried to shelter me from as much of the messiness of real life as she could. I was just so happy to see my dad that the truth of where he was simply hadn't clicked.

Amber, as always, took it on directly—but with incredible compassion. One reason I was attracted to her was that from the beginning she told me when I was being stupid, and she never lied to me. Amber keeps things real, but out of love, not games or anger. She had a lot of empathy. Her father had struggled with drinking and drugs for years. An uncle dealt with a crack addiction. "Your dad is totally in rehab because he was on drugs," she told me that day. "We've all dealt with it, so it's nothing to be embarrassed about." Part of me couldn't believe I hadn't realized my dad's situation by myself. But I was grateful to have Amber there when my eyes were opened.

I was even more grateful that my dad got clean in that San Francisco rehab, which was a turning point for him, and the beginning of his real return to my life. That September, we did something together we hadn't done since I was thirteen years old and he left home: We took the ferry from Vallejo to San Francisco to see a Giants game. We didn't watch a whole lot of the game, though. I love new ballparks, and this was the first season the Giants were playing in what was then called Pac Bell Park, right downtown, with the Bay just beyond Barry Bonds and the right field bleachers. Beautiful. Dad and I spent most of the game walking around, checking out all the views and talking. It had been seven years since we'd spent that kind of time together, just hanging out. It was pretty cool.

I worked harder that winter to get in shape than I ever have, before or since. In January the Indians brought a few pitchers to Cleveland to throw, and Charlie Manuel, the manager, said, "If you have a good spring training, you're gonna make the team." I was pumped.

That winter visit to Cleveland also turned out to include a basketball highlight. The Indians' head trainer, Paul Spicuzza, was also a high school and AAU referee. "You gotta come see this kid play," Paul kept telling me. Now, I love just about every sport, and I'm probably a bigger basketball fan than I am a baseball fan. But I was not going to Akron to watch some fucking tenth grader. One night the team, St. Vincent–St. Mary, had a game at Gund Arena, which was across the street from Jacobs Field. So I walked over, and what I saw was unbelievable: LeBron James was sixteen, but he was a grown man. I later got a chance to watch him play football a couple of times, too, and he was a great receiver who could have played in the NFL if he'd wanted. Obviously LeBron went the basketball route, and he's the only athlete who was under that much pressure at that young an age and has delivered on the hype. In sports, I'd say he's the number one guy for handling success well. Someone in Cleveland introduced us, and through LeBron I got to know William Wesley—or World Wide Wes—and Mav Carter, and over the years we've all become good friends.

First, though, I had my own career to build and pressures to navigate. The Indians had invited me to spring training the previous year, in 2000, but everyone understood I wasn't being considered for the big-league roster when the regular season began. All my workouts were with the other minor leaguers, and there was no real pressure; you were there to get in shape. This time around, in 2001, I was nervous but confident when I came to camp. There was no way I was going to let the Indians leave me in the minors again.

A bonus to being on the verge of making the majors was that the team put us up in this place called Southern Dunes, which was a serious upgrade from where most of the minor leaguers slept during spring training, a beat-up Holiday Inn. Southern Dunes had a golf course, and you stayed in small individual houses. I shared one with three other pitchers: David Riske, Devin Rogers, and Ryan Drese. We were a bunch of young dudes who were being paid a little bit of money, so we had shit everywhere: PlayStations, every possible video-game, golf clubs, gadgets. Our house was right by the first tee box, so we would take turns lying on the couch in our living room and squeezing an air horn when we saw a golfer in the middle of his backswing.

The spring training routine is that you show up around eight in the morning to do your work, and unless you're playing in a game that day, you're usually done by the middle of the afternoon. So we rode around in golf carts, played golf, threw barbecues and parties, played beer pong, and started becoming really close friends.

Every spring Bob Feller, the great Indians pitcher from the forties and fifties, would come to camp as a special instructor. Feller was no-nonsense about the game, an attitude that I loved. He would say to me, "How many games you going to win this year?"

And I'd say, "Well, twenty, I guess," that being the measure of an elite starter in those days.

"How many starts you going to make this season?" Feller would ask.

"About thirty-five," I'd say.

"What, you gonna lose fifteen? Go out every start to win!"

That mindset is related to why I never paid much

attention to scouting reports. Scouting reports have gotten more sophisticated over the years, but they always say, "This guy's a good hitter against sliders." My attitude was always, **Not mine! He's gonna see my fucking slider today! Tell me who's hot in the batting order, but that's all I want to know.**

Another reason that spring training with the Indians was so special was that my dad was there, with his best friend, Allen Lake. My dad loved Winter Haven, and people loved him—it was like he was the mayor. We'd walk into Outback Steakhouse, and the staff would call out, "Corky!"

On the mound, I scuffled a bit at the beginning of camp. But I settled down pretty quickly and threw really well the rest of the month. As opening day approached, though, things started getting strange. No one from the front office would tell me whether I had made the major league roster. Charlie Manuel and Dick Pole, the pitching coach, told me to just keep working hard. It had gotten down to the last two days of camp before the team would fly to Cleveland to start the regular season, and still no word. It looked like they were deciding between me and Steve Karsay, a twenty-nine-year-old relief pitcher, for the final spot on the roster. Everyone else was packing their boxes and shipping them ahead.

My dad's flight back to California was booked for the same day the Indians were leaving Florida for Ohio. I had to drive Dad and Allen to the airport in Orlando, and the team buses pulled away from the complex without me. I was pissed and crying. "They fucking told me if I pitched good, I'm going to make the team," I said to Dad. "Now it seems like I'm going to triple-A in damn Buffalo! I don't believe it!"

Dad was cool, and I was so grateful he was there. "It's okay," he said. "You're twenty. Your time is going to come. They just want the older guy for now."

We stopped for gas, and my phone rang. It was Charlie Manuel. "CC," he said, "you made the team. Sorry we didn't tell you sooner, but we just made the decision."

I started crying harder, but I was also smiling and laughing and hugging my dad. One of my favorite pictures is him and me and Allen Lake at the airport, standing curbside as I'm dropping them off, just after I got the news. All of us are grinning. Dad looks so happy that he probably could have flown all the way to San Francisco without the plane.

The Indians wanted me to stay in Florida for another week and throw another bullpen, because my turn to start wouldn't come up for seven more days. I found out later that Hart and Shapiro, who would be promoted to GM after the 2001 season, argued against me making the team—they believed a little more time in the minors would give me a better emotional foundation—but that Charlie and Dick said, "Fuck that, CC is ready, and we need him here the whole way." It's one of the reasons I'll love those guys forever. I was still in Winter Haven by myself for a little while longer. But I was a major leaguer now—the youngest one in the entire American League. The dream was coming true, in a hurry.

Mom caught my pitches in the backyard
when I was little. Now she was visiting me
as I rose through the minor leagues.

# 6

I T WAS A BEAUTIFUL SUNDAY AFTERNOON—SUNNY, and hot for early April in Cleveland, upper 70s at game time with more than 40,000 people in the stands. Including Mom and Amber, wearing Indians jerseys with 52 on the back; Jomar was there, too, and a couple of my cousins. A perfect day to pitch, a perfect day for my major league debut.

I had no idea what I was doing.

For reasons I didn't understand then and don't remember now, the Indians had flown me from Winter Haven to Cleveland the night before. I'd gotten to the hotel, to a strange bed, and was so nervous I could not sleep. I went to the stadium on Sunday and walked out to a mound I had never set foot on before, to throw my first pitch in the major leagues, the biggest moment of my life. As I stepped on the rubber for my eight warm-up pitches I was thinking, **Fuck, man, you should've slept! I am so tired right now.** I couldn't feel my legs.

Somehow I pumped a fastball in for a called strike one, at 92 miles an hour. Brady Anderson, the Baltimore Orioles' right fielder, was the batter, but I don't think I even saw him standing there. On the fourth pitch, Anderson hit a routine fly ball into left field, and Wil Cordero caught it for the first out. Okay.

The next thing I knew, it was the middle of the first inning and I somehow had two fucking runners on base, and I had thrown seventeen fucking fastballs in a row. **What is happening?** Mike Bordick, the second hitter, had doubled to deep left center. Then I walked Delino DeShields. **Damn, this strike zone is so small. I've got nowhere to throw the ball!** I threw a wild pitch, allowing the runners to move up to second and third. And then I grooved a 2–2 fastball to Jeff Conine, who smacked it over the left field fence. **Fuck, man. He didn't even really hit that, and that was a homer? This is going to be rough up here.** I had been in the major leagues for seven minutes and I had put my team down 3–0.

The next batter felt like do or die. If Mike Kinkade, the left fielder and a weak hitter, got on base, I might unravel and not even make it out of my first inning. Deep breath. Called strike one. Foul ball, strike two. Then I missed with two straight. Things were teetering again. But I nailed the low inside corner, and the home plate umpire, Brian O'Nora, punched out Kinkade. My first major league strikeout! The world started to slow down a bit. The next hitter grounded out to Robbie Alomar, and I was back in the dugout. I had taken a punch and kept going.

Top of the second, and the leadoff hitter was Cal Ripken Jr., already a legend and a sure Hall of Famer. **It's Cal Ripken!** I got him to ground out to short, and I rolled through the next seven hitters, starting to feel some flow. I allowed only two more base runners, on a double and a walk, and no more runs before Charlie Manuel walked to the mound with two out in the top of the fifth. I'd thrown 103 pitches. I was disappointed and exhausted.

Here's how raw and naive I was, too. I was in the shower after the game and Dave Burba yelled, "Good job, rookie—you spit the hook!" I was thinking, **What the fuck is he talking about?** As a kid I'd been a first baseman and a left fielder and a pitcher. Then I got drafted and all of a sudden I was a pitcher only, but there was so much I didn't know, even after I reached the big leagues—including the rules about what qualifies a starting pitcher for a win or a loss. Ellis Burks had to explain it to me. We were losing 3–2 when I left the game against the Orioles, and if we'd trailed the rest of the way and lost, officially I'd have gone down as the losing pitcher. Because we scored and went ahead, eventually winning 4–3, I "spit the hook": Instead of a win or a loss on my record, it went down as a no-decision.

There were a lot more lessons ahead. My second start was in Detroit. I was a little calmer, but I didn't pitch particularly well: five innings, five hits, four runs. But we had scored six runs in the top of the first, and hung on to beat the Tigers, 9–8. My first big-league win: April 13, 2001. I have the game ball stashed somewhere.

The wilder souvenir was the way we celebrated, beginning the next night, when we flew from Detroit to Baltimore. I was a little tipsy by the time we landed, but we were just getting started. A bunch of guys—Burbs, Chuck Finley, Ellis, Richie Rodriguez, Jim Thome—took me out to dinner, and then to a bar. I remember waking up the next morning with money, handfuls of wadded-up cash, stuffed in every pocket of my suit. It turned out this was the Indians' ritual when a pitcher won his first major league game: His teammates congratulated him by getting him drunk and giving him a bunch of money. In my case, something like $8,000 to $10,000!

The guys on that team who were good to me were really good to me. And on the field the 2001 Indians were a terrific team. Einar Díaz was the starting catcher, taking over from Sandy Alomar, who had left as a free agent, and I relied big-time on Einar's knowledge of the hitters I was facing, almost all of them for the first time. Thome was the first baseman—a power hitter and really outgoing and funny, a big personality in the clubhouse.

Robbie Alomar was the second baseman, a fantastic fielder and hitter and probably the smartest baseball guy I have ever played with. At shortstop was Omar Vizquel, one of the greatest to ever play the position. The starting outfield was solid: Marty Cordova, Kenny Lofton, and Juan González, who had signed as a free agent over the winter. Ellis Burks was the primary designated hitter. This was a team going through a transition. The Indians had just missed the playoffs the previous season coming up one game short of Seattle for the wild-card slot. Manny Ramírez then left to sign with the Red Sox as a free agent. Charlie Manuel's job was in jeopardy. It was a veteran team where just about all the regulars were at least ten years older than me, and the pressure was on to win now.

That Indians group was unusual in that everybody mixed pretty well, whether they were older or Latino or everyday players or relievers. But a lot of times I still felt alone. Russell Branyan was the next-youngest starter, and he was twenty-five. So it was huge for me when the Indians brought David Riske and Ryan Drese up from the minors for parts of the season. Riske I'd met in the summer of 1998, when we played instructional ball together in Winter Haven. He's about four years older than me, grew up in a suburb of Seattle and spent a year in community college before being drafted—in the fifty-sixth round. But Riske had a live arm and incredible determination. We hit it off right away.

Drese is also a little older, but he's a Bay Area guy like me—grew up in Oakland and went to Berkeley. The three of us were tight all the way through the minors.

The older teammate who really looked out for me was Ellis Burks. One of the first days of spring training in Florida he came up and introduced himself, and said, "Meet me at this place tonight. Let's go eat. Let's hang out." Ellis was thirty-six years old, this was his fifteenth big-league season, and he'd seen a whole lot in his career: He'd come up with Red Sox when he was young, he'd been an All-Star, he'd been to the playoffs with four different teams, he'd been hurt, he'd been traded. He was just a good dude. He had a lot of baseball wisdom to share. If he wasn't playing, or if we were on the plane, Ellis would talk to me about how hitters think, and about how to attack them. He taught me about becoming a team leader by the way I carried myself on the mound: If I was starting the first game of a series, it was my job to dominate, to set the tone.

It was off the field, though, where he had the biggest impact. I was hugely worried about people judging me—where I was from, what I wore, how I talked—and I badly wanted to fit in. Ellis showed me how the vets did things, and it made the adjustment to this new life somewhat easier, especially since most of the 2001 Indians were married with kids, and their interests weren't mine. I wore jeans pretty much everywhere—on road trips, to clubs at

night. Ellis put a stop to that. "You've got to represent yourself as a young man," he said, and then he
took me to his tailor to pick out custom-made suits:
"This is how you need to start dressing." Ellis was
always making sure I had money in my pocket, or
taking me out to dinner after a game on road trips,
in cities like Seattle or Chicago or Arlington, Texas,
places I'd never been before.

My introduction to the big leagues was a whole lot
less entertaining in other ways. When we were on
the road, one veteran liked to have lunch in strip
clubs, and he'd take me along sometimes. The food
wasn't great, but the scenery was definitely more
interesting than eating in the hotel restaurant.
Mostly, though, the veterans, they would beat you
down. Hazing rookies was still common at the
time—lame stuff like older guys making the new
guys carry their bags or wear goofy outfits on road
trips. Most first-rounders with big bonuses got roy-
ally shit on by veterans. I avoided most of the abuse
because I was quiet and wouldn't talk back. I made
sure to carry the ball bucket for vets. You came up,
put your head down, and just tried to fit in. Which
sucked. You weren't free to be yourself until you
had an All-Star Game under your belt. I was twenty,
and I didn't say a word in the clubhouse until I was
twenty-three. Basically I was trying to hide.

But it didn't always work. Though most of the

hazing I dealt with was pretty random and childish, it still sucked. I would be sitting in the food room after a game and a vet would walk by and stick his fingers in my sandwich. Or I'd be sitting on the couch in the clubhouse, watching TV, and a guy would yell, "What the fuck are you doing on the couch, rookie?" and take the remote out of my hand. Shit to just make you uncomfortable and remind you of your place. The worst, though, was a guy who was always making stupid racial comments. On the bus from the airport to the team hotel this guy would get drunk and take off all his clothes. He'd be buck naked, except for his shoes and socks, and he'd make a point of sitting next to me. As soon as Riske or Drese came up from the minors I made sure one of them always sat next to me so the naked drunk vet couldn't.

John Rocker was a part of the Indians bullpen that season. We traded for him in June, sending Steve Karsay to Atlanta. At first I was really cautious around Rocker: He had a terrible reputation because a couple of years earlier, in a **Sports Illustrated** interview, he had said a bunch of bigoted stuff about gay people and immigrants. I couldn't avoid Rocker, though: The Indians put his locker right next to mine, and because I was a rookie, I couldn't go sit on the couch in the middle of the clubhouse— that belonged to the vets. Surprisingly enough, Rocker turned out to be a regular guy and a great teammate. We chopped it up a lot, and there was no sign of Rocker being prejudiced, at least with me, anyway. He worked his ass off, cared only about winning, and he pitched pretty well.

One of the moments from that blur of a rookie season that will always be vivid in my mind happened in July. We traveled to Cincinnati. Ken Griffey Jr. had been one of my heroes growing up: a power-hitting lefty, a tremendous outfielder, and a Black guy who played with such joy. My mom was a big Griffey fan, too, so anytime he came to Oakland, in his early years playing for Seattle, she'd take me to the game. Now that I was in pro ball, I couldn't let Griffey hit a homer and have my boys back home get on me. I needed to strike him out, so I decided to throw as hard as I possibly could—and with my two-two pitch, I hit Junior right in the back. He was pissed. I wanted to cry. **You don't know how bad I want your autograph!** I was thinking as he headed to first base, glaring at me.

Overall, though, I pitched really well in 2001, good enough to win seventeen regular-season games. The Indians trusted me so much by the end of the year that I started game three of the first round of the playoffs, our first game at home against Seattle in the AL Division Series. The Mariners won 116 regular season games that year, the most in baseball and 25 more than us. But this series was best-of-five, and we came so close to knocking them off. We had won the first game and the Mariners took the second, so game three shaped up as a huge turning point. What I remember most about that game, though, was that in the first inning me and Einar Díaz were having a lot of trouble getting on the same page. I kept shaking off the pitches Einar was calling. The second or third time he came out to the mound to talk, Robbie Alomar came in from second base. "Okay, I'm calling the pitches," Robbie said. He came up with a gesture for a fastball and a gesture for a curve; he'd flash them to Einar, and Einar would relay them to me. "Do not shake them off," Robbie said. I trusted the shit out of him. Smartest dude I have ever seen play. So Robbie called the pitches from second base for the rest of the game, and it worked. It took all the tension out of my head, and I pitched great: six innings, two runs, and five strikeouts; I struck out Bret Boone three times, and he was pissed. We won 17–2. But Seattle stunned us by taking the next two and advancing to face the Yankees in the AL Championship Series. A few weeks later, one of the Mariners beat me out in the Rookie of the Year voting, too—Ichiro Suzuki.

But inside my head that whole first season felt like my first big-league game: unsettled. I never felt comfortable on the mound or in the clubhouse. I worried constantly that I was going to be sent down to the minors. Every day, coming to the field, I was sure somebody was going to be coming off the disabled list and I was going to be the one shipped to Buffalo to make room. Nobody in the organization ever said anything to create that fear; in fact, after I had a bad start, I would read in the paper that John Hart, the GM, or Shapiro or Manuel had said, **No, we're not sending CC down.** But I still wouldn't trust it. It took me probably five or six years before I felt any security. Because in my head, I wasn't anywhere close to where I needed to be. I wasn't Pedro Martínez or Bartolo Colón or Roger Clemens, and that's where I knew I wanted to be and knew I could be, and I knew that was what people were counting on me to be. And it felt as if the only alternative to being an elite pitcher was being a failure.

It was great to be back in Vallejo that winter and decompress. As much as I enjoyed hanging out at home, though, I was also beginning to see the opportunities that come with being a big leaguer. It's a strange thing: When you're broke, nobody offers you anything. When you have money, people are eager to give you stuff. In November, I was offered a free trip to Las Vegas to see the Lennox Lewis–Hasim Rahman heavyweight championship fight. Rahman had scored a huge upset in April, knocking out Lewis, and this was the big rematch, so of course I went. Free plane tickets, free hotel room, free seats at the fight—this was all new and amazing. It just kept getting better: One night I was in a VIP room at the casino, and my financial advisor at the time introduced me to Serena Williams, who's smart, beautiful, and obviously a helluva athlete. We talked. In February, both Serena and I went to the Super Bowl in New Orleans, and we saw each other at an ESPN party.

A few days later, I got a heads-up: There was going to be a poll on ESPN asking who would be a better choice for Serena to date, Redskins linebacker LaVar Arrington—who was rumored to be her boyfriend at the time—or CC Sabathia. **Oh, shit.**

I called Amber: "Babe, what's up?" We laugh about it now, but even back then Amber had figured out that when I called her "babe," it was a tip-off that something was wrong. "I just found out this is going to hit ESPN. I don't know why they're saying this. I know her, but we're not dating. It's not true." Amber didn't yell. She got quiet. I knew she wasn't buying it. So we broke up. It hurt, but I was twenty-one, Amber was determined to stay in college, and I was just starting to live the pro athlete life. We would stay friends. But we decided, **You do you and I'll do me.** Maybe we would get back together someday. Maybe we wouldn't.

I didn't like the way things had ended with Amber, but the future was still looking pretty bright—including, when I arrived at spring training in February, signing a four-year contract for $9.5 million, with an option for a fifth year. The deal boosted my confidence some, but even before it was final I had decided that this season I wasn't going to take any more shit.

Back in the day, if you were a Nike-sponsored athlete, they sent you a catalogue, and you wrote down all the stuff you wanted: shoes, shorts, shirts, hats, pants, whatever, for you and your family. So there I was with what seemed, at the age of twenty-one for a kid from the Crest, like a mega-contract—and Nike was giving me stuff for free. **This is dope!** I ordered my gear and had it shipped to the stadium in Winter Haven. One random day I came in from doing my running, and there was a stack of Nike boxes at my locker, like jock Christmas morning. But one of the boxes was open. I walked around the corner, heading to the shower, and there was a fucking guy—the naked guy from the team bus rides—wearing one of the Nike shirts I had ordered for Amber! Like, a half shirt, with his fat belly sticking out. I lost it. I almost killed that motherfucker. They had to pull me off him.

That was it. He was never a problem after that. Not one person ever said anything negative to me again. It was weird. It was almost like the veteran guys who had hassled me before were waiting for me to do something like that in order for them to accept me: **Sure, you can pitch good and help us win and all that shit, but we'll see about accepting you.** They weren't going to stick up for me until I took care of shit on my own. But once that happened, it was like I was one of them. And for the rest of my career, I made sure no rookie joining my team had to go through any of that kind of crap.

We started off really strong in 2002, winning eleven of our first twelve games, and I won my first two decisions. Coming off winning 17 games in my rookie year, I was starting to think, **This is going to be easy! I'm going to win 25 every year!** Then both me and the team cooled off fast: By May 1 the ball club was under .500, and I got hit hard, losing three out of my next four starts. It was a night we didn't play, though, that caused me the most trouble that year. More than trouble: That night could have easily ended my career and my life.

Cleveland was my baseball home for almost eight seasons—and a place I thought I would never leave.

# 7

T HURSDAY, MAY 16, WAS AN OFF-DAY, IN BETWEEN a series with Baltimore and one with Kansas City, so it was a chance to meet some fans and make some extra money. I did a card signing at a Cleveland mall that afternoon, and it paid in cash, so I walked away with probably $3,000 in my pocket. Jomar and I went out for a nice dinner, then hit one of our regular clubs, WISH. It was tucked away in the Warehouse District, a neighborhood that had become a nightlife hub in Cleveland; you had to enter the club through a dark alley, which made it feel even cooler.

A few weeks earlier Mom had visited me in Cleveland, saw our nightly routine, and tried to warn me. "Dude, I'm not feeling good," she said. "You're going out too much. You need to slow your roll."

I smiled and shrugged. "Nah," I told her. "It's cool."

We knew the hosts at SpyBar, WISH, all the spots. That night they showed us to our normal roped-off VIP area. Jomar and I were just drinking and chilling. There was a birthday party for a model we knew. The hosts brought a couple of other guys to our section; we assumed they were okay, because they were in the VIP area, too, and as we talked it turned out they had been big college basketball stars at Cleveland State. After a few hours it was getting late and the club was getting ready to close, but everybody was having fun, and someone said there was going to be a party at a suite in the Marriott downtown. Great. The major league baseball schedule is mostly night games, and you're back and forth between different time zones every few days, so players become part vampire: I didn't usually get into bed until four or five in the morning.

Jomar and I headed over, and there were maybe fifteen people in the hotel suite. Good music, good-looking women, lots more booze. After a while the crowd thinned out and we were ready to head home. When we reached the hotel lobby I realized that my watch was missing. It was a $60,000 Rolex, and at one point I'd taken it off my wrist in the bathroom to wash my hands. I think. Maybe. By this point I was loaded, so not much was clear. And my head was woozy in a different kind of way than when I'd been drinking for hours. Everything was kind of slurry and dense.

Jomar said he would go back upstairs to look for my watch. As I was waiting in the lobby, two dudes from the party appeared and said they'd go back up with me and help us look. Not that they were giving me any choice: One of them flashed a gun as he steered me toward the elevator. They shoved me into the suite. Jomar saw this and looked stunned. So was I: **This can't really be happening.** Jomar could be kind of a hothead, and he started yelling, "Fuck you guys!" Somehow, though, as messed up as I was, I knew we didn't want to get shot. Maybe having a 9-millimeter pistol in my face sobered me up just enough, but I calmed Jomar down. The two guys forced us to lie facedown on the floor. Then they started reaching into our pockets. There went the cash from the afternoon's autographs. They took my diamond earrings, which were worth $15,000. They took my $26,000 gold and platinum necklace. Then they backed out the door and left us there, shaking, at around 4 A.M.

They'd stolen our cellphones, too, but somehow we called the cops. When the police showed up, they seemed to have no real interest in what had happened. They were just going through the motions of asking questions: **Yeah . . . yeah . . . uh-huh . . . right.** Their attitude seemed to be: **A couple more fucked-up Black guys who say they got robbed by a couple other Black guys.** Then one cop nudged the other and leaned in to say something. I couldn't hear what he said, but from the reaction of his partner I knew what the message had been: **That guy plays for the Indians.** Their whole demeanor changed. Now they wanted to know all the details.

When we got to the precinct, I asked the cops for a favor. I borrowed a phone and dialed Amber. Now, it was probably around 5 A.M. in Cleveland, so it was 2 A.M. in San Diego. When Amber answered I'm sure she assumed it was just me drunk-dialing again. "Babe," I said, "I'm going to put the police on the phone. I'm okay, but you've got to talk to the police." Which probably woke her up quick.

The cop said, "Hi, Amber. I have CC here. He's safe. He's fine. He didn't do anything wrong." And then he explained what had happened that night with the robbery.

When I got back on the line Amber sounded relieved, but also irritated—which was totally understandable. I had already put her through so many scenes and so many close calls. We had broken up a month before, and here I was waking her up in the middle of the night after yet another episode. "CC, what do you want me to do?" she said. "I'm in San Diego! I have school in a couple of hours!" But even as tired and scared and half drunk as I was at that point, I knew this wasn't just another crazy night. Me and Jomar had gotten out of control with the partying, and we could have died on that hotel room floor.

"If you were here, none of this would have happened!" I blurted out. I wasn't blaming her; I was pleading with her. "You need to be here. I need you here! Let's just get married!"

Not exactly the most romantic proposal, I know.

And Amber didn't know it at the time, but two weeks earlier I had called her dad and asked for his permission to ask his daughter to marry me. I had been drinking pretty good that night, too, but I meant every word. I was trying to figure out who I was and who I wanted to be, and I couldn't do it alone.

The day after the robbery, Amber told her dad what had happened to me and that she didn't know what to do. "I think this guy is serious," he told her. "And if he's asking you to be there and he needs you, you've got to go." Amber finished her spring exams, packed up her apartment, and flew to Cleveland. It wouldn't be the last time she would rescue me.

All that craziness had started late Thursday night at the club. To make it even more insane, on Friday I was scheduled to move out of a rental loft and into a house on the other side of town. Jomar and I went from the police precinct to packing boxes, still partly hung over and still shaken by being robbed at gunpoint. Sometime later that day the cops called and asked us to come back down. They had the surveillance tape from the hotel lobby. They had recognized right away who robbed us, and once I watched the black-and-white video I saw it clearly, too: the two Cleveland State basketball players! They were arrested almost six days later. One of the guys was wearing my diamond earrings.

I managed to get a few hours of sleep in our new

place Friday night, and on Saturday afternoon I made my start in the first game of a doubleheader against the Royals and threw six strong innings, giving up only two earned runs. I was separating whatever was happening off the field from my pitching, just as I'd always done.

With Amber moving in, Jomar went back to Vallejo. That calmed things down some off the field. But for the Indians, it was pretty much a lost season. Over the previous winter the ownership wanted to cut the payroll, so Robbie Alomar had been traded to the Mets and Juan González hadn't been re-signed. After our hot start in the first twelve games we went sideways for the next five months. In June they traded our ace, Bartolo Colón, to Montreal, and the teardown went into full swing. We were 39–47 in early July, 9½ games out of first place and going nowhere, when they fired Charlie Manuel— a couple of hours before I started a game against the Yankees. I knew we were playing badly and that's when managers get cut loose, but it felt personal: It had been only a little more than a year earlier that Charlie had fought for me to make the roster out of spring training, and I felt like I'd let him down. I would have a couple of pretty good games, and then a couple where I walked five or got hit hard and gave up four earned runs. Most nights it felt like I was just out there throwing as hard as I could as long as I could, with no real plan. This was the first real losing team I'd ever played on, and I hated it.

Something special did come out of that 2002 season, though, and it flowed from the night when Jomar and I got robbed and could have been killed. Dad moved in with me and Amber right after the robbery, putting him back in my day-to-day life full force, clean and sober, for the first time in nine years. I needed him again, to put some structure in my life, and he loved being needed and doing the dad thing again. Dad was the only person in my life who could yell at me and I would listen.

He supervised the building of a basketball court with a hoop above the garage door. We played one-on-one any chance we had, with me finally beating him. Sometimes he seemed to think that me and Amber were still teenagers: He'd come down to the poolroom in our basement at 10 P.M. and announce, "Okay! Time for bed," then shut out the lights. Though in some respects I did feel like a kid again. When I was little, we had the kind of relationship where I could talk to my dad about anything. I had missed that more than I was willing to acknowledge, and now I got that relationship back. It was an unexpected gift, so I just enjoyed having him around again. I didn't ask him about what had gone wrong.

Dad became my driver, taking me to the ballpark in Cleveland every afternoon, then coming back for all the games whether I was pitching or not. He looked healthy, but he was secretive about being HIV positive. "Don't tell anybody," he'd say all the time. "I don't want anybody to be nervous about coming over to the house." He kept his own set of silverware for meals, even though he knew, and we kept telling him, that the disease couldn't be spread that way. Dad said he wanted us to be more comfortable around him, though maybe the real reason was he was scared and that ritual made him more comfortable being around us.

Amber and I used to joke that Dad was a classic mean old Black man. He would get annoyed really easily. He could be really social, but he didn't like most people. Dad would say, "If you're going to have a party, let me know—I don't want to be here." He was incredibly protective of me, and suspicious of everyone around me: **I don't trust that financial advisor—he's out to get CC's money. Why do CC's friends want to drive his cars?**

Amber had taken a class about HIV and AIDS at San Diego State even before she knew about my dad being sick, and her knowledge was really useful now that Dad was living with us. He looked and felt better when he wasn't taking his medication, so I'd say, "Just let him keep doing what he's doing." Amber knew better. The drugs might have some nasty short-term side effects, but they would help keep him alive. The meds were in the refrigerator, and she'd check to make sure Dad stuck to the schedule; she also stayed on him to make sure he was eating right. The three of us sharing that house in the summer of 2002 were some of the best days of my life to that point. And even though the team ended up in third place, 20½ games behind the Twins, I finished the season strong, throwing strikes with some consistency, winning five of my final six decisions to put together a 13–11 record. I had made the most starts of any pitcher on the staff, and I liked that Mark Shapiro kept telling the sportswriters I was one of the pieces the Indians were planning to build around.

My dad was back in my life. Amber and I were together. The Indians roster was getting a lot younger: We had traded for my friend Milton Bradley halfway through the 2001 season, sending Bartolo Colón to the Expos, and the deal brought us other guys with real potential—Grady Sizemore, Brandon Phillips, and a skinny lefty pitcher from Arkansas named Cliff Lee. Over the winter we had hired a new manager, Eric Wedge, who was only thirty-four and seemed to be a good guy, and Carl Willis, my minor league tutor, would be promoted, becoming the major league team's new pitching coach. I couldn't wait for the new season to start. It looked like 2003 was going to be a great year.

In 2007, I pitched in the All-Star Game
in San Francisco—something my dad had
envisioned but didn't get to see.

# 8

AMBER WAS LATE. IT WAS THE MIDDLE OF JANUARY and we were in Arizona. We had been there for about a month, because during the 2002 season I had cracked 300 pounds for the first time—up from the 255 I weighed when I was drafted in 1998—and the Indians wanted me to do an intense off-season workout program at one of those training academies. We rented an apartment, and Amber would drive me back and forth to the facility. Every day she would pick me up at 4 P.M. Except this one day, she didn't show. I called her cellphone, left a message; called again, left a message. I must have called fifteen times, and I was getting seriously worried.

After about an hour Amber arrived. She said that she had fallen sound asleep and didn't know why. She had been tired lately, for no real reason, and wanted to sleep all the time. "What's wrong with me?" she said. Then she realized she was late in another way: She should have had her period a week earlier.

I shouted, "Yes! You're not going back to San

Diego now!" We had been arguing for months about Amber returning to college or coming back to Cleveland with me. I hadn't exactly helped my case by not following up on my proposal from the police precinct the night me and Jomar had been robbed. I kept meaning to make the engagement official, but something was holding me back—an anxiety about whether I could really handle being married, do what it takes to be a good husband. I'd always looked up to my father's younger brother, Uncle Edwin, and his wife, Aunt Genia, who had been through ups and downs but had stuck with each other and become a rock in our family. Uncle Edwin and Aunt Genia were the role models when it came to marriage, and I didn't know if I could live up to their example. So I kept putting off buying a ring. Amber's friends had been telling her they were sure I would do it on her birthday, in September, so she got her hopes up. Nope. We celebrated her birthday, but not with an engagement ring. Then Amber figured that it would happen at Thanksgiving, when we were back in Vallejo and the whole family would be around to share in the big news. Nope. "You're not ready," she told me. "The whole reason I took the fall semester off was you told me we were going to get married. I'm going back to San Diego and finishing college. I'm so close to getting a degree. I've got to finish. Then we can figure out what we're doing together." I needed Amber, badly, and over the years it came at a high cost to her—an unfair cost, as much as she loved me. I was reluctant, but I agreed she should go back to school. At some level I understood—and admired—that this was a Black woman trying to break cycles in her family history and make her own way. And I had a new plan for solidifying our engagement: Christmas morning would be perfect.

I bought a beautiful ring. I rehearsed what I was going to say. I planned the scene with my dad: On Christmas morning, I would wait until Amber was in front of the tree, and I would get down on one knee. Dad would capture the whole thing on videotape. And then the anticipation started eating at me. I didn't sleep for a week. What if I messed it up? What if Amber said no? My head started vibrating with anxiety. I was sweating. The nerves kept building.

On Christmas Eve, we were getting dressed to go over to Amber's mother's house. I had the engagement ring in my pocket. Amber's back was to me. I couldn't wait. When Amber turned around, I was kneeling, holding the ring box out toward her. Somehow I managed to get out the words: "Will you marry me?" When we went downstairs my mom and dad were pissed that I'd panicked instead of following the plan, so no one has any photos of the big moment. We joke about it now, that it was the worst proposal ever—except for the fact that Amber said yes.

Amber still went back to San Diego State for the spring semester. My mom insisted that the mother of her future grandchild could not live with three other college girls, so I rented Amber an apartment and bought her a little dog for company. In June she moved back to Cleveland, and at some point we went to a doctor's appointment. We were sitting in the waiting room when the nurse came out and called for her: "Amber Carter." That bothered me a lot. Maybe it was my old-fashioned side; maybe it was my macho side; maybe it was somehow knowing that I wanted us to be all in, together, in every way; maybe it was insecurity that I could lose Amber, the most important person in my life. Probably all of that, and when we got in the car afterward, it busted out of me: "That's embarrassing to me, that I'm sitting here and they call you and it's 'Carter,' not 'Ms. Sabathia.' I can't take that your last name is Carter and we're having a child together. We've got to get married. Now. Let's go to the courthouse." Amber hadn't pictured her wedding that way: She wanted a big ceremony, with family and friends enjoying the day. She did not want to get married while pregnant. Her way was much more romantic, and understandable. I countered with a practical argument: Amber hated the hospital that went with her insurance plan, but if we were married, she could be on my (much better) Indians insurance. And I promised we would have the big wedding back home, in Vallejo, when we had time to plan it. So I suggested that we go down to the courthouse right then, and just not tell anyone.

We compromised a little: We told my mom and my dad and Aunt Glo, and they came from California to join us, sworn to secrecy. Amber and Margie have always had a strong mother-daughter relationship, and at the time Amber was kind of distant from her own mom. We found an off-day on the schedule, June 9. Amber wore a gorgeous but simple green dress. The judge was grinning as he pronounced us husband and wife. I was relieved and thrilled, and no one seemed to have recognized me, which meant we could keep things quiet until we were ready for the "real" wedding in Vallejo.

That night we were sitting at home, watching TV, some local Cleveland station—and all of a sudden there's that line of type that delivers breaking news, a crawl, running across the bottom of the screen: INDIANS BACHELOR PITCHER CC SABATHIA MARRIED HIS HIGH SCHOOL SWEETHEART TODAY. Amber picked up the phone and called her mom.

A month after we got married came another amazing, joyous moment, this one a baseball highlight. We had dug ourselves a big hole in April, going

7–20, but then we picked it up some, putting together a winning record in May. With two years of experience behind me and Carl Willis in my ear, I was beginning to feel more confident on the mound, and I had better control, spotting the fastball to the corners of the strike zone instead of just always trying to blow it past hitters. By early July I was 8–3 and among the American League leaders in strikeouts and earned run average. But I can still remember the shock and joy when Eric Wedge called me into his office before a game one afternoon and told me I had been chosen for the All-Star Game. Some of the other starters on the American League team were Roger Clemens, Roy Halladay, and Mark Mulder—great, great pitchers who had been stars for years. And twenty-three-year-old me, from Vallejo. I was tripping.

A few minutes later my phone rings. It's my mom, and she says, "I have some news."

"Oh, you heard already! I'm going to the All-Star Game!"

"No. Your dad has been having stomach pains, and he went to see the doctor. They say it's terminal stomach cancer. They're giving him six weeks to live."

Everything went blank with sadness and disbelief. After all those absent years, my dad had come back, and we had grown close again—and now he was going to be gone, this time forever? I had already seen too many people die early, but this was more than unfair. It was cruel. Instead of going to Chicago I caught the next plane to San Francisco and then went to the hospital in Vallejo. When I walked into his room, Dad got pissed. "What are you doing here?" he yelled. He might have been sick, but he was fired up. "I'm going to be fine! I'm going to see Lil' C born! Get out of here and go to the All-Star Game!" So I did, the next morning. Sure, I was worried about Dad. But once he said it was fine for me to go, my mind was good.

I did not pitch in that All-Star Game, and I don't think I said three words to a soul the whole time I was there, I was so young and so nervous. I do remember meeting Barry Bonds, who had come to the Giants when I was twelve, and that was a thrill. Oh, and somebody said "Nice of you to show up" when I arrived on Monday right before the home run derby. He didn't know what I had been dealing with, and I didn't explain.

Amber was due in September and Dad vowed to be there, even as he got weaker over the summer. When the date got close he pulled together enough strength to fly to Cleveland with Mom. He was exhausted, skinny, and shaky when he arrived; his skin looked three shades darker from the medication. He was completely bald. Even his eyebrows were gone. But he was there on September 15, just past midnight, when I walked out of the maternity recovery room carrying an 8-pound, 14-ounce baby boy: Carsten Charles Sabathia III. I handed my son to my father. To his grandfather.

The Indians' season was just about done by then. We went backward in some ways, losing more games than in 2002, and our ballpark, Jacobs Field—the Jake—was less than half filled many nights. But a few pieces of the puzzle were fitting into place. Jhonny Peralta, an incredible fielder, showed signs he could eventually take over at shortstop from Omar Vizquel, who was a year away from free agency. Casey Blake and Travis Hafner flashed some power. Milt had a great year in center field, hitting .321. Cliff Lee was sharp when they brought him up from the minors near the end of the year.

Me, I finished the season as the only Indians starter with a winning record. One reason was that I kept working on the mental side of the game, and on channeling my emotions. It didn't come quickly or easily. Sometimes my mind would be racing even before the game started. I remember one time in 2004 my uncle was coming to Cleveland, so I went on the team website to buy some extra tickets for the game, and I see "CC versus Pedro Martínez!" **Oh, shit! Now I gotta be great! Now this is the seventh game of the World Series!** Pedro struck out eight and gave up only two runs. Me, I gave up eight hits (including a homer by Manny) and four runs, struck out nobody, and we lost. My arm was strong, but my mind could be my worst enemy.

Early in my career I would live and die with

every pitch, no matter who we were playing or who was in the stands. If an umpire didn't give me a strike on a checked swing, I would get so pissed that I would completely lose focus. Suddenly three pitches had gone by, I'd given up a home run, and I had no idea what had just happened. It was my emotions and my demeanor that were holding me back, not a lack of physical talent.

The Indians were ahead of the curve in baseball in emphasizing the psychological side of the game, and they'd hired Charlie Maher as the organization's mental skills coach in 1995. He would hold meetings and talk to us about simplifying our thinking, letting go of the results after you let go of the ball and just concentrating on next pitch, next pitch.

A lot of the older players back then thought this was all some New Age bullshit, and that somehow talking about your emotions was a sign of weakness. Me, I was really interested, and I gradually tried to put it to use. In baseball everyone needs someone they can talk to off the field, but that's especially true for pitchers. You're out there for three hours by yourself, you and your thoughts, so you better be thinking about the right shit. I also learned a lot from watching Kevin Millwood, a veteran pitcher who had signed with us as a free agent. Millie was one of the best I had ever seen at slowing the game down when he started to get in trouble. He'd give up a couple of hits or walks, the fans would be screaming, and he'd take a stroll off the mound to regroup; usually he'd get out of the jam. We were teammates for only that one season, but for me, still struggling to channel my emotions, Millie was an important example.

And the whole time I was in Cleveland, Mark Shapiro would sit me down in his office regularly and talk about taking the umpires completely out of my thinking, and concentrating on throwing one pitch at a time, 120 times each start. Mark was always the boss, but he became a cross between a father figure and an older brother for me; Lil' C was born right in between Mark having his first child, a son, and his second, a daughter. So I listened to Mark, I understood what he was saying, and it helped, but it took years to really buy into that mindset. And no matter how long I was in the big leagues, I was never able to completely ignore the umpires! I still screamed at them, got tossed from games—but I picked my spots better, managing my on-field emotional life way better than I did when I was out of uniform.

The changes kept coming fast and hard even after the season. Dad went back to Vallejo shortly after Lil' C was born, and his condition kept going downhill. By October he was so sick he couldn't eat solid food very much; mostly he would drink Ensure. Mom went over to Dad's apartment three times a day, talking with him, trying to keep his spirits up, making sure he took his pills, changing his bedding. Some friends couldn't understand how Mom gave so much of herself to him after the ways he'd hurt her and me. "This is my son's father," she would tell them. "I will love him regardless." Amber was just as loyal. She would visit Dad every day, bringing him money, bringing the baby for him to see. When I got home in the off-season I would visit Dad all the time. He loved Popeye's red beans and its gumbo, so I would bring those and he'd eat as much as he could.

In December Dad needed surgery. He tried to be optimistic, telling everyone it was going to help, and as they rolled him into the operating room, he gave a thumbs-up. I remember me and Glo sitting in the hospital waiting room, and me telling her I hoped this wasn't the last time I would see Dad. When he came back out, he was on life support.

A few weeks later, I was scheduled to fly to New York to tape ESPN's **Top 20 Under 30** and go to the big party they throw for it. Amber tried to talk me out of it, but I told her no, Dad would be fine, Dad would want me to go.

I was on my way to the airport when Mom called Amber: "Corky passed away this morning." He was forty-seven years old.

Amber called me and told me to turn around. "Why?" I said. "What is me turning around now going to do?" I felt a familiar emotional daze start to overtake me. I spent the weekend in New York drinking my goodbyes.

With Amber, the love of my life, at our first wedding, in November 2004. Our bond would be severely tested.

**9**

**D**AD'S DEATH LEFT ME MORE NUMB THAN SAD. I tried to tell myself that at least we had had the gift of becoming friends again, and that I was lucky Dad had lived long enough to hold his first grandson. But it turned out that losing him was just the beginning of the shocks. And with the next two, I couldn't find any way to rationalize the hurt.

In March I was in Winter Haven, finishing up spring training. We had a bunch of new players in the lineup—the young guy taking over at catcher, Victor Martinez, a switch-hitting power hitter, looked like he could be a star—and optimism was starting to build. A few days before we headed north to start the season Mom called, and I could tell it was bad news just from the way she said hello. My uncle Aaron Berhel—the father of my close friends Jason and Nate, and my dad's closest cousin—was gone. A heart attack. No warning. He was fifty-three. First my dad, and three months later Uncle Aaron.

At the beginning of April came a baseball loss. Milton Bradley had had a bunch of run-ins with Eric Wedge in 2003, and near the end of spring training in 2004 things boiled over. Omar Vizquel hit a pop-up and didn't run hard out of the batter's box. Wedgie didn't say anything. Then Milt hit a pop-up and barely made it to first base. Wedgie said something. Milt lost it. So instead of heading north with us as the Indians starting center fielder he was shipped to the Dodgers for Franklin Gutierrez, one day before the regular season opener.

Yeah, Milt did a lot of stupid shit—we did it together! But I was pissed at him—pissed at both of us—because we couldn't figure out a way to play together for a long time. Milt should've been there with us when the Indians started winning again—he would've been a big part of those teams. But Milt needed treatment for his emotional issues, and nobody helped him get it. Just the opposite— people, including the media, egged him on, to see him act out. I didn't understand it at the time, being young, too, and having my own issues.

The next punch hurt much worse. Our season had started off slowly, but by early June we were playing better, and on a Wednesday night in New York we beat the Mets 9–1 to get back within a game of .500. I went eight strong innings for the win, giving up only one run, and because we were the visiting team in an interleague game, I also got to hit, which was even better, and I went one for four. Back at the hotel that night I was feeling really good. This time Amber delivered the jolt.

It was Nate Berhel, my cousin. He'd been my teammate from the time I was six until I was seventeen. If we weren't on the same baseball team, Nate was the one supplying me with sunflower seeds between innings. He made me laugh everywhere we went, on the field and off, and when I made the big leagues Nate would come to Cleveland and hang every chance he got. One night in June he went to a party in Benicia, like we'd all done a hundred other nights. There were dozens of other people there, and nobody would ever say what happened. But Nate ended up on the ground, bleeding from a severed artery in his arm. They took him to the hospital, where he died. Nate was twenty-five, one year older than me.

I flew home from New York the next day. I can still see Nate lying there in the coffin in the funeral home, can still hear his mother crying. My next start was scheduled to be in Chicago on the same day as Nate's funeral. At the time it seemed like the best tribute to my friend was to go out and pitch, so that's what I did, with Nate's initials written on the side of my Indians hat. I threw 123 pitches that day, every one of them with Nate on my mind. Losing him still feels fresh, even all these years later. That's why, if you looked closely, you could see that I had "RIP NB" stitched into the side of all my gloves ever since. I carry Nate, and all of Vallejo's other lost souls, with me every step that I take.

Some people look to God for explanations when tragedies hit, and in some ways I envy them. I grew up going to church regularly, and I still believe, but I have never been able to chalk up misfortune to a divine plan—or, alternatively, to shrug it off as random bad luck, or to pin all the blame on the bad choices of an individual. Being Black and poor in America is clearly part of why these things happen. The extra stress of everyday life raises blood pressure. With guns and drugs and anger so common, mistakes are more dangerous. We are all responsible for our own actions. But the deaths of Uncle Aaron and Nate came in a context that too many of my friends and relatives, and too many other Black Americans, are forced to deal with every day.

I didn't understand that when I was twenty-four. Not that it would have reduced the pain even if I had. I certainly didn't know how to process my rage and sorrow. So I tried to bury them. I tried to drown them. Anxiety has always been just below the surface for me. Sometimes it comes out in ways most people probably don't even notice: When I am talking to someone and the conversation goes in a direction that makes me uncomfortable, my knees start bouncing. Or when I worry so much about wearing the right thing—I want to look good but not stand out—and I'm sure I will pick the wrong stuff. So for years Amber has picked out my clothes each day. She packs for me on every road trip. Once we had a fight and she refused to pack my clothes; it was the worst I have ever pitched on a road trip. A few years ago Dellin Betances and his wife invited us to a baby shower. We thought it was a casual kind of party, so Amber went wearing jeans and I went wearing sweats—nice sweats, but sweats. When we walked in, though, the shower looked more like a wedding. The women were in dresses and heels, the guys in suits and ties. Probably nobody cared what we were wearing, but it didn't matter. My anxiety kicked in hard right away: "We need to leave, now. I'm done." Back in those days, alcohol seemed like the best way to dull the anxiety. No matter how much I drank, though, the feelings still found their way out.

I had promised Amber a real wedding, and we planned one for November 2004, back in Vallejo. The weekend before the big event about two dozen of us went to Las Vegas for a bachelor and bachelorette weekend. Friday and Saturday nights the women did their thing and the guys did ours. On Sunday night, we all got together to celebrate. At the end of the night a waitress came over with the bill, and Amber began to sign it. I was drunk, and that set me off: "I can sign the damn bill!" From there it turned into a huge fight. Nasty, mean things got said, as if the booze was some kind of truth serum, releasing all the anger and insecurity in me. Suddenly I was yelling, "I'm not marrying you!" and Amber was yelling back, "We've been married for a year! You can't go back now!" I escalated it, of course: "You're just with me for my money!"

Amber had the good sense to eventually walk away. But not before I had driven all her friends to tears. They couldn't believe what I'd said; they thought the wedding was off. Amber just laughed; she knew that before the night was done I would be equally over the top with apologies. She was wounded, I know, and I hated that. But she understood, better than I did, what was tearing me up inside.

The wedding itself was beautiful—what I remember of it. We were sort of celebrities in Vallejo now, which generated expectations, so we couldn't turn down anyone who wanted to be there. We ended up with about three hundred guests. I could pitch in front of thousands of strangers, but being the center of this show made me nervous. At the same time, I felt like I needed to be the life of the party. The combination meant I started drinking bright and early, in the groom's room at the hotel. All my guys had to get haircuts, so we had a barber in there, and we spent hours drinking and telling stories. I was good and drunk by the time we got in the limo to go to the church. Standing at the altar, I was equal parts wasted and anxious. I couldn't look Amber in the eye. We got through the ceremony. By the end of the reception, though, I was in a chair in the corner of the room, curled up and crying: "My dad should've been here. I just want my dad back." Our honeymoon night didn't last long. After reaching our suite I passed out immediately, still in my tuxedo, and peed in the bed.

The next morning my head was pounding and I had almost no memory of the mess I'd made of our big wedding. Amber was not happy. But she was still there.

My baseball education was bumpy, too, but it was moving in the right direction. The veteran Indians pitchers, guys like Chuck Finley, taught me something important when I was really young: that you're only gonna feel really good maybe five times each season. The rest of pitching is figuring out how to win when you don't feel good. As the Indians rebuilt, though, the roster got significantly younger. This was great because there were more guys in the clubhouse I could relate to. Every team has groups that develop according to race or position—the Latin guys hang out together, the everyday players, the pitchers—but the most common bond is generational, because you like the same music, the same clothes, and you're at a similar place in your careers.

On the other hand, even though I was still really young, my success on the mound meant that more teammates were looking for me to be a leader. Fortunately, I had some great teachers in how to fill that role. But lessons could arrive unexpectedly.

One Saturday night in July we were in Seattle. This was 2004; the Mariners were heading for last place, and we weren't going anywhere, either. Out of nowhere, though, things seemed to take on real urgency. Eric Wedge was really young for a major league manager in those days, and so the Indians had brought in Buddy Bell as our bench coach for Wedge to consult with. Buddy had experience as a manager in Detroit and Colorado. He was also a baseball lifer—his father had been an All-Star with the Reds; he'd played eighteen years in the majors, seven of them in Cleveland; and two of his sons would play in the big leagues. Buddy was fifty-two and tough. That day in Seattle, as I was getting ready to go out and pitch the bottom of the first inning, Buddy came over to me in the dugout and quietly said that I needed to hit Justin Leone with a pitch. The night before, we'd crushed Seattle 18–6, hitting eight home runs; the Mariners had responded by hitting three of our guys, Matt Lawton, Travis Hafner, and Lou Merloni. Why Leone was picked to feel our reply was never clear. And it didn't matter: Buddy Bell told me to drill him.

Leone came up for the first time in the bottom of the second. I had just given up a walk, a two-run homer, and a single; we were down 2–0, so this was no time to put Leone on base. I got him to hit a weak grounder to shortstop. He batted again in the bottom of the fourth. We were still losing 2–0 and I'd just walked Jolbert Cabrera, who then stole second, so again there was no room to mess around; I got Leone to fly out to center. Bottom of the sixth, he came up again. We were still down, but at least Leone was leading off the inning, so the damage would probably be limited, and the way the game was going I wasn't likely to be pitching much longer. First pitch, I got a called strike. **Okay,** I thought, **now it won't look so obvious.** I aimed a fastball at Leone's front knee—and missed. Three more times I went after him, and three more times I missed both Leone and the strike zone. He walked.

When I got to the dugout Buddy was pissed. I mean, seriously losing it. Right there in front of all my teammates, letting me have it. He was calling me all kinds of pussy, screaming "You're supposed to be the leader of this team!" and just going off. He kept it up after the game. He kept it up for the next two days! I loved it.

I don't think Buddy had anything personal against Justin Leone. The intensity was the point. The old-school competitiveness. The idea that we were in charge, that other teams should fear us. That we were fighting to get better, and that this is what I needed to be, **dominating.** Buddy and I had been kind of close even before that night in Seattle, but after that, we were as tight as any player and coach separated by nearly thirty years could be.

Now, I'd been ruthless on the field since I was a little kid. When I was eleven, we beat a baseball team from Calistoga 51–3, and we were chanting, talking shit, the whole way, like the game was close. In high school our basketball team was really good, and the starters would play the whole game, trying to score one hundred points when we had no business being on the floor in the fourth quarter. That's just how it was in Vallejo. You got somebody down and you did not risk them coming back. You're just going for blood all the time.

But as a young player with the Indians I was unsure of myself. There seemed to be all these rules I didn't understand. How much passion was too much? Would the veterans smack me down for not acting like a big leaguer? People like Buddy Bell and Dick Pole, the pitching coach my first season with the Indians, encouraged me to treat every start like a war, a mentality that I carried for the rest of my career.

Alex Cora was big, too. He wasn't with us long in Cleveland—the Indians signed him as a free agent before the 2005 season, and traded him to the Red Sox in July that same year for Ramón Vázquez, an even weaker-hitting utility infielder. But Alex made a huge impression during the six months we were teammates. He was twenty-nine and in the middle of what ended up being a fourteen-year playing career. He had to battle the whole way to make it last that long—he was an undersized, light-hitting middle infielder who kept finding ways to help his team. One of those ways was by staying on the field, no matter how beat-up he might be physically. I came to understand what that meant one night. I don't remember the exact game, but I thought I'd pulled my hamstring, and I walked off the mound at the end of the inning, down into the dugout, and without stopping headed straight to the training room to tell them my hammy was messed up. Alex met me halfway down the tunnel. He asked me what was going on. "Are you hurt right now, or are you fucking injured?" he said. "Are you really injured, or do you think you can pitch? Because you need to know this: Whatever you're about to tell the doc, they're probably going to put you on the DL for four to six weeks. If you're really fucked up, if you're really injured, go in there and tell them. If you're hurt, go sit at your fucking locker and you'll be fine tomorrow."

I went to my locker and didn't say shit to anyone. I just kept pitching. That was the beginning of what I did for the rest of my career. If you really, really can't go, if something is broken, fine. Otherwise, you find a way. You man up. You play. You compete. You put your body and everything you've got in your heart out there, for your team and for yourself. Till the end.

One part of my pitching education was less traditional. Mom spent much of the baseball season living with us in Cleveland, and after my home starts, I would come back from the ballpark and we'd sit in the garage, drinking and talking, with Mom smoking a few Capris. She's a serious student of the game, and we would go through what I'd done that night inning by inning, good game or bad game. Inside the house, Amber would be putting the kids to sleep; inside the garage, I'd be saying to Mom, "Man, I shouldn't have thrown that pitch." And she'd ask what had been going through my mind leading up to it, why I'd decided to do what I did, what had been good or bad about the execution. It was fun to talk it through with her, and it helped me get the game out of my system. We had a little ritual to end it: "Love you, Mom," I'd say. "Love you, dude," she'd say. We'd leave the garage and we'd leave the game behind.

If my growth as a player was uneven, so was the progress of those Indians teams. In 2004 we made what seemed like a big step forward, finishing third behind the Twins but winning twelve more games than the year before. The next season, 2005, we made an even bigger leap, going on a late-summer tear to pull ourselves into the pennant race with the White Sox. The atmosphere was intense, and I loved it. In Chicago, in the visiting bullpen, there used to be just a chain-link fence behind the mound, and White Sox fans would be talking shit. I was warming up for one game and a guy was getting on me, so I turned around and kicked dirt off the mound right in the dude's face, right in everybody's drinks. After that they put up a screen, because of me! I'm kinda proud of that.

On the last Thursday night in September I threw eight shutout innings to beat Tampa and keep us three games behind the White Sox with three games to play—in Cleveland, against the White Sox. We lost the first game of that series by one run, a heartbreaker in thirteen innings, and we were done. Still, we finished 93–69, our first winning record in four years. The Jake was packed and loud again every night.

Things were pretty exciting at home that fall, too. In late September we were on a road trip to Chicago, to play the White Sox. Amber was pregnant, and the due date was getting close. She called me one afternoon right after we had gotten to the field and said, "I'm about to have this baby today, but I'm going to finish my shopping. Your mom's with me, but I'm not going to tell her." She's always cool and in control, but I couldn't believe it: **Amber is in labor, and she goes to Costco, A Pea in the Pod, and Red Robin.** I left the ballpark, went back to the hotel, packed up all my shit, and got a plane back to Cleveland. By the time I got to the hospital our first daughter and second child, Jaden Arie, was already wrapped up like a burrito. It was the only birth I've missed. All the others I've been in the delivery room the whole time, taking pictures. We'd been talking about having a big family ever since high school, even picking out most of the names for our kids, so being there for the delivery was special every time. And I like watching surgery.

The next spring, 2006, we came into camp with huge expectations—and flopped when we went north. Injuries, down years for a bunch of guys— we fell under .500 in mid-May and never recovered. Even though I had pitched pretty well, by the middle of June the frustration was eating at me.

That's when the Cubs came to Cleveland for a three-game interleague series. Even if our season was going downhill fast, I had something to prove in my start. The Cubs' starter for that first game was Carlos Zambrano, who was one of the hottest pitchers in the National League in those years. More important to me, though, was that Dick Pole, who had meant so much to me in my rookie year with the Indians, was now the bench coach with the Cubs. Dick had been tough on me. The attitude he taught was "Never apologize for shit. Go hard. Be a bull." Now I was going to show Dick how far I had come as a pitcher. I wanted to show him what he'd made. That I had arrived. I wanted him to be proud of me.

The first inning, I was so hyped I was not sharp, giving up a walk, a single, a double, and one run. The second inning was better—a single, but no damage. The third inning started with a soft single to left that I thought should have been caught, then a line drive to right for another single. Then came two ground balls that should have been double plays; the second one would have ended the inning. But we didn't turn either of them, so there's still no outs. By then I was mad. Dick Pole was watching, I was making good pitches, and I wasn't getting any help behind me. Instead of pushing through it, my mind went, **Fuck it. Whatever.** I just started throwing the ball right down the middle. Fastball, fastball, fastball. **Here you go—hit it.** Which the Cubs did. I lasted only 2⅓ innings and gave up nine fucking runs.

I went to my locker and started drinking. Drinking after you came out of a game but while it was still going on wasn't uncommon. I had a big red tumbler and a special stash of booze waiting for me. This night I was able to put away even more because there was a rain delay, and everyone waited around for more than an hour before they finally called it after seven innings. By the time the beat writers came in for interviews I was pretty drunk—and too blunt. "What was inexcusable tonight was for me to give up," I told the reporters. "I'd like to apologize to my teammates, the fans, my family, and whoever else was in the stands. That's the first time in my career that's happened to me. I just lost focus."

The next day people on the Cleveland sports talk radio station tore me up. Called me a quitter, said I was a bad example. It didn't bother me, because I knew I had fucked up. We were a young team and a close team, and we held one another accountable. And even though 2006 was turning into a disappointment, we were on the way to being really good. I felt like I had the respect of my guys, but that night I'd let my guys down. That has always been the worst feeling for me, ever since I was a kid. No matter what, you go out there and battle. No matter what happens with errors, no matter what happens with the umpires, no matter what's going on with your wife or kids or girlfriend or with your contract, that was always my thing: I was going to go and fucking leave my heart out there on the mound. And I didn't that night. Then I made the mistake of being a little bit too honest in the postgame comments.

Here's the strangest—and best—part of that episode, though. I came into the clubhouse the next day and apologized to Hafner, Casey Blake, Grady, all the core guys who cared. "Man, last night I fucking gave up. That was bitch shit. That's on me, and it will never happen again." They shrugged. Hafner said, "What are you talking about? Didn't look like that to me." Maybe Travis really hadn't noticed, or maybe he was letting me off the hook, but it made me love those guys even more, and it was a huge relief to know I still had their respect. I pitched my ass off for the rest of 2006. Didn't even let the fact that I needed knee surgery slow me down. Back in December 2005 me and Amber, plus her brother, Joe, and Joe's girlfriend at the time, drove out to Tahoe. My first time on a snowboard, I hit a mogul and twisted my right knee, slightly tearing the meniscus. It didn't hurt that much, though, and I didn't really want to tell the Indians what had happened. So I waited until the 2006 season ended to get the knee cleaned up.

We had become a really, really close team, and it showed in 2007. Ryan Garko, who had become the starting first baseman, hit 21 home runs. Josh Barfield arrived from San Diego in a trade and was solid at second. But mostly it was our core group of young guys—Sizemore, Hafner, Martinez, Peralta—peaking at the same time. And we finally had a solid pitching staff. Fausto Carmona (later known as Roberto Hernández) moved from the bullpen to the rotation and won 19 games. Paul Byrd, with his old-timey arm-waving windup and his off-speed stuff, added another 15. Jake Westbrook and Cliff Lee didn't win a lot of games but pitched well in big games. Joe Borowski, a free agent pickup and our new closer, a guy who had kicked around with six other teams, had the best season of his career, racking up 45 saves. We beat the White Sox, who had edged us out on the final weekend of the previous season, the first two games of the year, and after that we never stopped rolling.

I didn't, either. By early July my record was 12–3, and I was selected for the American League All-Star team. The 2007 game was in San Francisco, which meant I had to round up a ton of tickets for my Vallejo friends and family. Jim Leyland, who was with the Tigers at the time, was the AL manager, and he brought me in to pitch the bottom of the fifth inning. As I climbed the mound something stirred inside me. When I was little my dad told me, "You're going to be in an All-Star Game. You're going to pitch in San Francisco, your hometown." Mom's face had an expression that said, **Corky, you've really lost your mind.** But now I walked behind the mound and took a moment. I looked up and said, "I'm here, Dad." I took a deep breath, got back up on the hill, and threw a scoreless inning.

That was the year I felt everything come together as a pitcher. It was my seventh season and I knew the hitters. More important, I knew myself. I had my 95-mile-an-hour fastball, but I could also spot my slider, and I had finally found a consistent feel for my changeup. I won my first five decisions, lost a game, then won the next four. I was averaging six strikeouts a game and holding the walks down to just one. Every time I went out there I knew we were going to win. I finished 19–7 and cracked 200 strikeouts for the first time. The Tigers stayed within a game or two of us until late August, when we won eight straight to take control of the Central Division race. We ended up with 96 wins, tying us with the Red Sox for the most in the big leagues. Heading into the playoffs, we didn't just know we were good enough to win the World Series. We **believed** we were going to win the World Series.

There were a lot of guys who piled up great stats for the Indians that season, including me. The guy who made the biggest difference, though, got over-looked by the fans and the media. Trot Nixon had been the starting right fielder for the Red Sox for most of eight years, but they'd dumped him for J.D. Drew, and the Indians signed Trot as a free agent, not even sure if he would make the team out of spring training. Trot only played 99 games for us in 2007, only hit .251, didn't have much power, wasn't fast. He was thirty-three years old, a year away from being out of the game for good. But bringing in Trot was the most important change the Indians made. He brought the energy every day, screaming and hollering in the dugout, in the clubhouse. When we were playing the Twins or the Tigers, the teams we had to beat in the division that year, Trot was talking shit to them. We knew we had a chance to be good, but our confidence took off with him on our side. Trot showed us how to win. He was the reason we won the division that year.

A shot at a championship is always special. For us in 2007, the urgency was even greater because we knew it was going to be the only shot for this group. Older guys like Trot and Kenny Lofton probably wouldn't be brought back. I was one year away from free agency and Vic Martinez wasn't far behind. Cleveland is a smaller-market team; if we won the World Series, they would probably make enough money to re-sign us, but if we didn't win, they would shop me and eventually Vic for trades and start rebuilding again. So we needed to get it done now.

Things started off a little scary. We opened at home, against the Yankees, and as the ace, I got the start. I was amped, maybe too much. When that happened I overthrew the ball, like I wanted to run it to the plate. And when I overthrew, I walked too many people, and my pitches flattened out. So on my fifth pitch I threw a straight fastball to Johnny Damon and he clubbed a line drive into the right field seats. **Okay, breathe, first inning, lot of game left. Make the next pitch.** That settled me some. But Derek Jeter was the next hitter. An all-time-great player, obviously, and he was one of my toughest outs: In the five years I ended up facing Jeet he hit .500 off me. So I felt like this was already a turning point: If Jeter got on base, the Yankees would really start rolling and I would really get nervous. But if I got Jeter out, I'd get it under control. Jeter knew that, too, of course. We went back and forth: A ball outside. A fastball for a called strike that I really needed. A foul ball, and then I was ahead and ready to put him away. I missed high, so it was 2–2. Jeter fouled off a slider. And then I beat him with a fastball—he popped up to Asdrúbal Cabrera at second base. One out.

That at-bat looked even bigger after I walked the next two guys, Bobby Abreu and Alex Rodriguez. Then I got Jorge Posada to swing over a 2–2 slider for a strikeout, and Hideki Matsui grounded out to Cabrera. It wasn't pretty—thirty-three pitches that inning, that Damon homer—but I escaped. The boys bailed me out in the bottom of the inning, scoring three runs, and from there I kept battling. Robinson Canó got me for a solo homer in the fourth and Abreu doubled in a run in the fifth to cut our lead to one run, but then we broke it open and won 12–3. I only went five innings, throwing way too many pitches and walking six, and I was mad about that. But we had taken the first game in a short series, which is huge, and then we won a thriller in the second game, walking it off when Hafner singled with the bases loaded and two out in the bottom of the eleventh. Man, that was fun.

The next games were in New York, at the old, original Yankee Stadium, a place I never liked playing in. I understood and appreciated the history. It's just that I hated the cramped, smelly dugout. They kept the visitors' locker room in good shape, but the rest of the place seemed to be falling apart. We blew an early three-run lead and lost game three, then jumped in front 6–1 in game four, hanging on to win 6–4.

Next stop, Boston. We had won the same number of regular-season games, but the media had built the Red Sox up as the best team in the league that year, which only motivated us more. This was the Red Sox of David Ortiz and Kevin Youkilis and Curt Schilling and Daisuke Matsuzaka. And Manny Ramírez, who had become a star playing for the Indians. We felt like this was going to be the real 2007 World Series—whoever won would handle the National League champs easily, whether that turned out to be Colorado or Arizona.

Fenway Park is worse than the old Yankee Stadium. The visitors' clubhouse is so small you couldn't turn around when we were all in there getting dressed. You'd see mice in the hallways. The dugout roof is so low I couldn't stand up straight. And the fans are really bad. It's not just that they're on top of you everywhere because the seats are so close to the field. It's that they're nasty. I never understood that: They paid to come watch me play! I get rooting hard for your team; I go nuts at Raiders and Lakers and Man U games. But I'm not cursing out the other team. In Boston, you'd be warming up in the bullpen and fans would be hanging over the walls calling you the N-word.

After seven seasons, I knew what to expect, and I could tune out the yelling. My heart was still racing, though, because this was a big moment. I hadn't pitched well against the Yankees, and now I was going to make up for it. Instead I went out there and stunk it up. Manny, who always killed me, drove in a run in the first to tie the game. In the third, with the bases loaded, I walked him; Mike Lowell doubled in two more, and Jason Varitek drove in a fourth run on a groundout. I was done after 4⅓ innings, pulled from the game with us down 7–1. It wasn't even that I got hit that hard—it was that I threw as many balls as strikes and was constantly behind in counts, constantly on the defensive, walking five guys and being forced to throw fat pitches.

The next day I was sitting on the couch in the clubhouse, deflated and stewing, and Joe Morgan came up to me. He was broadcasting the games for ESPN. "Attack these motherfuckers!" he said. "You're out there nibbling, trying to throw around the strike zone. If you're going to lose, lose giving up hits, not fucking walking people! Go at these motherfuckers!" Joe was exactly right, and I needed to hear it.

The team picked me up: We won the next three games, which put us at home in Cleveland with a chance to close it out—and me on the mound for game five. Perfect. Redemption time. Fuck yeah. It didn't matter that I'd pitched shitty in game one. That was gone. One win and we'd be in—we'd be going to the World Series. **We're about to win the World Series—and I'm about to be the hero.** All day that was running through my head. **I'm about to go out and fucking dominate this game.**

Here's how confident we were as a team: None of us brought any suitcases to the ballpark that day. If we lost game five, we would have to travel to Boston for game six and maybe game seven. But we weren't going to fucking lose, so we didn't pack.

Maybe that was a bad move, messing with the baseball gods. Second batter of the game, Youkilis, hit a home run. Manny doubled. Lowell singled. Fortunately, Manny got thrown out at home on a great play by Franklin Gutierrez, or the hole would have gotten even deeper. But in the third Manny got me again, driving in Big Papi. I kept it close; we were down 2–1 heading into the seventh. Then Dustin Pedroia doubled leading off, Youkilis tripled, and Wedge took me out of the game. We ended up losing 7–1.

I had taken Joe Morgan's advice and attacked— but this was all on me. I was too amped up, too determined to throw a complete game and win it all by myself. Afterward, I was too down to process it, but that playoff game ended up teaching me a huge lesson: I didn't have to do too much. I was in the ALCS, I was playing for a team that was really good, so I had good players around me. I just had to go out and do my job, and the guys would pick me up.

That loss changed so much for the Indians. We went back to Boston and got blown out 12–2 in game six. **Okay, no problem, we still just need to win one. We'll take game seven.** Then crazy shit started happening. That night, maybe three or four in the morning, the hotel fire alarm went off. All the Indians players and our families were out in the street in the middle of the night. We figured the hotel did it to mess with us. Then the **San Francisco Chronicle** broke a story that one of our pitchers, Paul Byrd, had years ago received shipments of HGH—human growth hormone, a performance-enhancing drug. We got to Fenway for game seven and all the reporters were asking about was PEDs. Probably it was a coincidence that George Mitchell, the former senator leading an investigation into steroid and PED use in baseball, was also on the Red Sox board of directors. Mitchell has always denied having anything to do with the story. But that day, it sure seemed like a strategic leak, and it was a huge distraction.

No excuses, though. We were down one run going into the bottom of the seventh, and the Red Sox pounded our bullpen for eight runs. Dustin Pedroia drove in five runs; Youkilis hit a two-run homer to seal it. The final was 11–2.

The feeling leaving Boston was fucking devastation. We were the better team—the Red Sox just had more experience. I was going to put that team on my back and carry it to the World Series, but the weight just got too big. I hadn't been able to figure out how to pitch to Big Papi because I was so worried about dominating and becoming an iconic playoff pitcher. I had let down the Indians fans, who hadn't won a championship since 1948. I'd wanted to be the reason we won it all, but I was the reason we lost.

The hurt went deeper than that, though. Equal to when my grandmother and my father died. Me, Cliff, Vic, Grady, Jhonny, we'd grown up together. We'd had barbecues and spent holidays together. Our kids were the same ages. It was the tightest group I would ever be part of in pro ball. But we all knew that the only way the Indians could afford to pay us was if we won the World Series that year. Otherwise, if we lost and got off to a slow start the next spring, people were getting traded. So I felt that my responsibility wasn't just to win a ring—it was to keep the family together. And I blew it.

I don't have many regrets in my career, but that's the biggest one: not winning a championship with the Indians, not having the mental ability to fucking power myself down and be able to pitch great in the playoffs. On the bus to the airport, we were all crying. A lot of the wives were on the plane with us back to Cleveland. It was so quiet the only thing you could hear was people sobbing.

I cried when Cleveland traded me—but I loved every minute of pitching the Milwaukee Brewers into the playoffs, and having so many Black teammates.

# 10

APPRECIATE IT SOMEWHAT MORE NOW. REALLY, I do. But a month after losing to the Red Sox, I shrugged at the news that I had won the Cy Young Award as the American League's top pitcher. It felt like being handed a weak consolation prize. The Cy Young is chosen by a vote of sportswriters, so anybody can win that shit once. Winning the Warren Spahn Award, as the best left-handed pitcher of the year—I'm cool with that, because it's based on statistics. But fuck individual awards. I've never been into that. And there weren't any awards that could have made up for the disappointment of how our 2007 season ended. I would have switched it up with Josh Beckett, of the Red Sox, in a heartbeat. He could have the Cy Young; I'd take the World Series ring. One really good and important thing did come out of winning the Cy Young, though. Amber went with me to the awards ceremony in New York, in January, and that's where our third child was conceived. When she was born, in October 2008, we named her Cyia.

. . .

A whole lot of things changed during those nine months. We all know the game is a business, and that without a fast start in 2008 the Indians were going to start trading off the most valuable parts of the team, because we were about to get too expensive. To his credit, Mark Shapiro sat me down in his office that winter and was honest about his plans. Cleveland would talk to my agent and make what it thought was a fair offer, but if I wanted to become a free agent at the end of the year and be almost certain of making a whole lot more money, he'd understand. If it looked like negotiations were heading toward a dead end, Mark said, he would try to trade me by the July deadline and get back some prospects for the Indians.

I understood all of that, of course. But there was a big part of me that didn't quite believe it. I never really thought they were going to trade me, as stupid as that sounds. I loved Cleveland. I was an Indian! They'd drafted me. This was my home. These people were my family, top to bottom—from the front office to the lady at the stadium gate to the vendors selling T-shirts. It was all I knew. During eight seasons I'd seen a bunch of guys going back and forth between teams, but I just never thought that I would be in that situation in Cleveland. **They ain't going to fucking trade** me.

Sure enough, the team got off to a bad start in 2008. We were five games under .500 after the first two months and sinking in the standings. I was worse. My ERA was almost 8 after the first month; my only good start was against the Yankees, and we lost that game 1–0. Physically, I was fine. But all I could think about the whole first half of the season was free agency. Any player who says they are not thinking about free agency is fucking lying. That's all you think about, especially if you've got a family. And we had a young family at the time. I didn't know where we were going to live. We wanted to live year-round wherever I was playing, so we could raise our family in one place. We wanted to make a home. But what if I got hurt and my value cratered? What if I got a bunch of offers and made the wrong choice? That whole year was sleepless nights, worrying about what might happen, what might get messed up, where we were going to end up. I could deal with uncertainty on the field. Being uncertain about where we were going to land was something else. It had taken me seven years to get comfortable in Cleveland. I didn't like the idea of being forced to make such a big change. I didn't know if I could change.

Wine was my drink of choice in those years, from about 2005 until around 2009. Not that I turned down anything else, but now I could afford what I wanted—red wine, white wine, didn't matter. Silver

Oak, a nice NorCal cabernet, was a favorite. We also had cases of Far Niente, a Napa chardonnay, at our house. Twomey—I went through a lot of bottles of its pinot noir. I always felt like I played out of my era: I should have been a seventies or eighties guy, when going out at night after games and living as hard as you played were standard. Players of my generation don't hang out like those guys did.

There were nights where I would stir up trouble, and a lot of mornings where I woke up with a bad headache. So I would cut down on the drinking for a while. But I never thought I had a problem, and we never talked about me getting any help. Why would I? In 2007 I had won my first Cy Young Award and made my third All-Star team, and now I was on the verge of becoming the hottest free agent pitcher available. My routine was working.

The wine took the edge off the trade talk a little bit at night, but the next day, every day, the reporters were all asking what I thought about the latest rumor. In June, the talk was that I was definitely headed to Los Angeles, with Casey Blake, in exchange for a couple of top prospects, maybe Carlos Santana and Andy LaRoche. I liked the idea of going to the Dodgers—back to the West Coast! Besides, the Dodgers were the team I wanted to sign with as a free agent, so that would be a head start. Then the Los Angeles rumor went away, without explanation.

A different one kept percolating: Milwaukee.

The Brewers were on the fringe of the pennant race, but they hadn't made the playoffs since losing the World Series to the Cardinals in 1982, they had an aggressive, fairly new owner, Mark Attanasio, and maybe they were willing to gamble. I hated the up-and-down and I tried to block it out. But I couldn't ignore a call from my buddy David Riske. We had been close friends since we were teammates in the Cleveland minor league system, but the Indians traded him to the Red Sox before the 2006 season. We kept in touch as he bounced to the White Sox and the Royals before signing with the Brewers for 2008. During the Fourth of July weekend, Riske called me and said, "They're making your jersey up here!"

Still, when it happened, I was shocked. We got off the plane after a series in Minnesota and I saw a text on my phone from one of my friends, before anyone from the team had told me anything officially. Then I saw our traveling secretary, Mike Seghi, crying. I was trying to hold it together, so I just hugged Mike, left my bags at the airport, and got in my car and got away as fast as I could. When I got home and saw Amber, that's when I cried. For a couple of hours. Until I said, "Fuck this! Fuck them! I'm gone. Get me a plane to Milwaukee!"

I was hurt, and I turned it into anger. I was glad, in a way, that I had been traded instead of leaving on my own as a free agent, so there was no ill will between me and the Cleveland fans. But I went from heartbroken to **Fuck that. They don't want me here? I'll show them.**

Doug Melvin, the Milwaukee general manager, sent word that I could take my time joining the team: "I know your wife is pregnant, I know you've got two little kids." So it would be fine if I started a game in a week, the final game before the All-Star break. Which I appreciated. But I was not waiting around. The trade went down on a Sunday and was announced on Monday; I told Doug I would be in Milwaukee later that day and start Tuesday's game. Best decision I ever made.

I got there so fast they had to paint my red Indians spikes blue so they would go with the Brewers uniform. When I walked out to the mound that night to face Colorado, the 42,533 Brewers fans—a sellout crowd—rose for a standing ovation. It pumped me up even more, maybe a little too much, since I was kind of wild, walking two batters in the first inning, before settling down, going six, and getting the win. Making it even more fun was that the reliever who took over in the seventh inning was Riske.

I'm sure that Dave being the one to follow me was purely a strategic choice by Ned Yost, the Brewers' manager. But it fit perfectly with the instant feeling of welcome. When I walked into the Milwaukee clubhouse for the first time, I looked around and couldn't believe what I saw: five Black faces. That may not sound like a big number, but on a major league baseball roster, it was huge. I had played on Cleveland teams where I was the only Black player. It was something I thought about but didn't dwell on, and I had plenty of White and Latino friends on the Indians, and some guys, like Riske, were practically Black in their attitudes and outlook. But it wasn't until I got to Milwaukee that I fully realized how lonely I had been, and how much more fun it could be to play alongside a group of guys who looked like me. To be Black in America is to constantly be on guard. With the Brewers, for the first time in my baseball life, I could be more at ease.

Mike Cameron was the leader of that Brewers team, and he immediately felt like an older brother to me. Cam was thirty-five, this was his fourteenth season in the league, and he was just a wise old soul and a baseball warrior. Rickie Weeks was super, super quiet, kind of shy, so the rare times when he'd throw out some jabs, it killed. Prince Fielder was the jokester of the bunch—loud, talking shit all the time. Billy Hall was from Mississippi, a real down-home dude. B and me are kind of the same personality—whatever is going on, we're with it. If you want to chill in the hotel room, we'll do that. If you want to go out and tear it up, we can do that, too. Tony Gwynn Jr. was a real pro, just like his dad. And the Brewers traded for Ray Durham a few weeks after I arrived.

We knew this group was something special, and

we appreciated every minute of it. I quickly became friends with J.J. Hardy and Jason Kendall and Ben Sheets, all great dudes. But the Black guys spent all our time together—on the bus, on the plane, going out after games. No disrespect to my friends in Cleveland, but I got to Milwaukee and felt like I had been there ten years already. Amber was pregnant, so she mostly stayed in Cleveland, which meant I had even more time to hang with my new crew. The only bump was that the Brewers put me up in the Pfister, this big old hotel in downtown Milwaukee. It was nice, but it was spooky at night. The rooms were huge and the lights were dim. You felt like you're in **The Shining**. I couldn't sleep for a week. I was running on fumes. I called up Amber and said, "You gotta find me a house, now!"

The personalities in the locker room combined with being airlifted into a pennant race made for an electric three months. When I arrived the Brewers were four games behind the Cubs for the Central Division lead. By late July, we'd caught them. Then the roller coaster turned down again. We slumped through August, though we still had a winning record. Our shot at the division championship disappeared, but we were still in good position for a wild-card slot—until mid-September, when we dropped seven out of eight games and fell into a tie with the Phillies. With twelve games left in the season, the front office made a big gamble to turn things around, firing Yost and promoting Dale

Sveum, our third-base coach, to be the manager. I started the next day, the first game with Dale as manager, going up against the Cubs at Wrigley, wanting badly to help move us in a better direction. It didn't go according to plan: I gave up nine hits and four runs in seven innings, and we lost, 5–4. But that would be my last bad start in 2008. I had been brought to Milwaukee to lift the Brewers to the playoffs, and my left arm was going to deliver them, no matter what it took.

Before I arrived, Ben Sheets had been the Brewers' ace. But he had dealt with injuries pretty much all of his career. In early September 2008, the doctors told Ben his sore elbow was in danger of blowing out if he kept pitching. Not only that, Ben was about to become a free agent, so a bad injury now could cost him a big payday at the end of the season. The same day the doctors gave Ben the warning, he went out and threw a complete-game shutout. He was one of the toughest guys I've ever known, and he kept trying to gut his way through the pain, but eleven days later he had to leave a game after two innings. Which left us short a starting pitcher heading into the last ten games of the season, with our chance to reach the playoffs slipping away.

**Give me the ball.** That's what I was thinking, and that's what I told Dale. Starters usually pitch on four or five days' rest, but with Ben down I volunteered to go on three days' rest, in a season where I had already thrown nearly 232 innings, the most in the majors. **Give me the ball.** My agent at the time, Brian Peters, who I loved and trusted, argued against it, hard. I was set up to become the most desirable pitcher on the free agent market that winter; I was a couple of months and one contract away from taking care of my family for life. The opportunity could disappear fast, though—Ben Sheets did the right thing for the team, the unselfish thing, the competitive thing, and it might have cost him $100 million.

**Give me the ball!**

After going seven innings in that loss to the Cubs, and after three days of rest, I started against the Reds and threw 105 pitches. Another one-run loss. After three more days off, I was scheduled to start against the Pirates. Now Brian was pissed. We were arguing, a lot. He thought I was going to burn myself out. "I'm good," I'd tell him. Brian and a lot of other people were thinking about the negative: What if he pitches bad? What if he gets hurt? I was thinking, **I'm gonna pitch good. I'm ready. I'm having fun.** There was the competition part driving me, and the city was going nuts—Milwaukee is a pretty small city, and everywhere you went, you could feel the excitement, how much they were behind you. But the even bigger thing was that this Brewers team had such good chemistry. We were having a blast on and off the field, I had never played with that many Black dudes, and I didn't want that shit to end. When you get into a pennant race or into the playoffs, you're chasing the feeling. Whatever I had to do to keep the feeling alive in Milwaukee, I was going to do. Brian stopped talking to me.

Now we were one game behind the Mets for the wild-card spot, with five games left. Our margin for error was slim. This time I came through: seven innings, one run, eleven strikeouts. The last of my 108 pitches was a fastball; Jack Wilson swung and missed, and I punched the sky and roared, "Let's fucking go!" We beat the Pirates, 4–2, with Salomón Torres closing it out. In New York the Cubs finally did something good for us, beating the Mets in ten innings. So we were tied with four games to go. The Mets won two of their next three; we won two of our next three. That brought us both to the final day of the season, tied. Me on the mound with three days' rest, at home in Milwaukee, against the Cubs. **Give me the ball.**

I don't remember whether it was a quirk of the schedule or Major League Baseball manipulating things to dial up the tension even more, but that Sunday our game, in the Central time zone, started at nearly the same moment as the Mets-Marlins game back in New York. The Cubs had clinched the division title weeks before, so they weren't going to burn a starting pitcher before the playoffs. They threw seven relievers at us, all of them going two innings or less. Which should have given us the advantage, but after six innings we were down 1–0, and you could feel the nerves of the 45,299 Brewer fans in the stands getting raw. The Cubs had scored a cheap run in the second—a single, an error, an RBI groundout—but otherwise I was mowing them down. We finally tied it in the seventh, when Craig Counsell drew a walk with the bases loaded; in the eighth, Cam singled and Ryan Braun hit a two-run homer to give us the lead. In New York, the Mets and Marlins were tied in the seventh inning, while we were up 3–1 with one inning to go. I'd thrown twenty-seven and two-thirds innings in the past twelve days. I was at 107 pitches in this game, and Torres, our closer, was warming up in the bullpen. There was no fucking way I was coming out of this game.

I got Alfonso Soriano to fly out to Braun in short left field. Ryan Theriot singled to center, though, which brought up Derrek Lee as the tying run. He was having a good year—20 homers, 90 RBI. A big, strong right-handed hitter. Lee had done pretty well against me over the years, hitting .333, but I had handled him three times already that day. None of that history meant shit in a moment like this, though. I knew he'd be aggressive, and I got him to swing at a fastball just off the plate, fouling it off for strike one. Then he took a ball and a called strike. I came inside, on his hands, with a fastball, and jammed him. The grounder went straight to Durham at second, who flipped to Hardy at short, who whipped a throw to Fielder at first. Double play, game over, and I'm screaming, "Fuck, yeah!" and pumping my arms Hulk style. Amber calls it "the beast coming out," which is exactly right. I hugged Jason Kendall so hard I'm surprised I didn't break one of his ribs.

We danced around on the field, waving to the fans, who were losing their minds. I was ecstatic and absolutely wiped out at the same time. Just as we got into the clubhouse, we heard that Wes Helms had hit a homer to give the Marlins a lead on the Mets. Florida held on, we were in the play-offs, and the champagne started to spray. We were all good and soaked and my eyes were stinging, but I could see well enough to spot my agent, Brian Peters. He was shaking his head and laughing. After the celebration, we ended up back at my place. Our first-round playoff series would start in Philadelphia, in three days. I looked at Brian: "You know I'm starting game one, right?"

This time he didn't laugh. "You're tripping!" Brian yelled, and our fight kicked in again.

This time, unfortunately, Dale Sveum was on the same page as Brian. I didn't go until game two, on three days' rest. I still believe we were a better team than the Phillies that year. Maybe we were dragging a little from the push we had to make in the final week of the regular season. But Cole Hamels shut us down in the first game, and I was on fumes in game two, giving up five runs in only 3⅔ innings, and we dropped that one 5–2. We rallied to win game three back home in Milwaukee, and then the Phillies put us away pretty quickly in game four. About the only upside was that I was back home in Cleveland when Cyia was born five days later.

After the intensity and the high of how we made the playoffs, the end of our season came so fast it felt like an afterthought. Those three months in Milwaukee remain unbelievably special to me. I didn't realize it at the time, but the gigantic disappointment of losing to the Red Sox in 2007 and the trauma of being shipped to Milwaukee—and succeeding in a new place—were necessary, perfect preparations. But all I could see in October 2008 was that, **bam,** I was again leaving people and a place I loved—and the scary thing was, I didn't know where I was going next. The one thing I was sure about? I sure as hell did not want to play for the Yankees.

I was sure I was going to the Dodgers when
I became a free agent. The Yankees
had other ideas.

**11**

OH, I WAS PLAYING FOR THE DODGERS. NO question. That was where I was going next. Because I was from Cali. Because L.A. was just far enough away from home. I wanted to play for one of the historic teams and have a chance to win all the time. In 2008 the Dodgers had won the National League West before losing in the League Championship Series to the Phillies (them again). The Dodgers had a great manager, Joe Torre, who owned four World Series rings. They had Russell Martin, Matt Kemp, and Andre Ethier in the everyday lineup. What the Dodgers needed was an ace to go with Chad Billingsley, Hiroki Kuroda, and this twenty-one-year-old kid named Clayton Kershaw. Perfect setup for me. I was going to spend a couple of months over the off-season visiting all these other teams, go to the Winter Meetings in Las Vegas acting like I was shopping around and try to have the other teams drive up the price, then sign with the Dodgers. Hell, I would sign with the Dodgers even if the price didn't go up very much, though I sure wasn't telling them that.

When I got back to our house in Cleveland after

the season, Cyia was still a newborn, so I was happy to focus my attention on her. We were packing up the house and getting ready to sell it, so there was a lot of chaos and uncertainty, but I'm thinking, **Man, this is about to be so much fun. I'm about to be flying around to all these different cities and be offered all these contracts.** Brian had put together a book with my statistics, comparing me to everyone else on the market and to comparable free agents in the past, with how much money they had signed for and why I was projected to be even better than them. We thought a contract for six or so years was a good target. But we really didn't have a set number for that, or for the dollars I would accept.

Amber didn't care where we signed, with one exception: She did not want to live in Vallejo, which at the time I still thought could work if I signed with the Giants. There was a small part of Amber that kind of wanted to return to Milwaukee, because those three months with the Brewers had been so much fun and the city would have been a safe, known choice. Otherwise, for Amber, it didn't matter. We could have moved to fucking China as long as she and me and the kids were all together in the same place year-round. We were tired of moving around. Lil' C would be starting kindergarten in the fall of 2009. So wherever we signed was where we were going to live.

I did have some other standards, if somehow I was forced to consider signing anywhere other than with the Dodgers. At the top of the list of my requirements:

I was not going to play in an old stadium. I am too much of a germophobe. Wrigley? Fenway? Those places were awful. Old and gross. The walls sweat, everything is tiny, and they stink—you can't get away from the smell anywhere. Ernie Banks, Ted Williams, romantic attachment? Make it a museum. I love to see pictures of baseball history. But I don't want to play a game in it. I have no sentiment for that old shit. That's a part of the larger problem in baseball: People don't want it to change. The world changes all the time, and baseball, too, needs to change.

The other thing that was big for me was the clubhouse. Not the physical qualities, but the atmosphere. I wanted to go somewhere where all the focus was on winning. And after the Milwaukee experience, it had to be somewhere I would be comfortable with the group of guys I would be joining. I was always used to baseball being fun and the feeling being light after the game, with the guys going out to dinner and hanging out together and shit. So I would go to New York and check it out because the Yankees had a new stadium opening in 2009, but everything I knew about the clubhouse told me I did not want to be there. I had heard all the stories. I talked to guys I trusted who had played for the Yankees and they told me it was a nightmare. What I heard, from every player I talked to, was that the media was brutal, the tension between Derek Jeter and Alex Rodriguez was weird, and the grind was relentless. "There are always big expectations with the Yankees, and if you're not winning, you can't go in the clubhouse and have fun. It's miserable," guys said. That's what stuck with me, because while every team is going to have bad years, in most cities, even if you're struggling and the media's beating you down and the fans are beating you down, at least you got your boys, and you're in it together. What I heard, consistently, about the Yankees was, "No one will have your back. Everyone is on his own." That's hard. That can become some mental health shit real quick. And wherever I signed, I wanted to be there six or seven years. New York? No fun. No thanks. I did not want to play for the Yankees. I **really** did not want to play for the Yankees.

It made sense that New York would be interested in me, though. The Yankees had missed the playoffs by six games in 2008, and their starting pitching was a mess: Mike Mussina was retiring, and their fourth and fifth starters had been Darrell Rasner and Sidney Ponson, borderline guys nearing the tail ends of their big-league pitching careers. But we underestimated just how interested the Yankees would be. I filed to officially become a free agent as of midnight, October 31. Ten minutes later the Yankees' general manager, Brian Cashman, was on the phone to my agent with an offer: $140 million for six years. When Brian Peters called me later that day we were both pretty shocked. That was not what I'd been expecting. It was a great offer. But I was still not interested. I'd wait for the Dodgers, and all the other teams, to make their bids.

Thanksgiving came and went. Silence. The only other team that called to show interest was Anaheim. Maybe everyone was expecting me to take the Yankees deal, but I knew where I wanted to go, and I wasn't worried. Back in June, when I was still with the Indians, we had played an interleague series at Dodger Stadium. I thought I'd given them a pretty good audition in the second game, throwing seven innings, giving up one earned run, striking out ten. Before one of the other games I ran into Joe Torre, and he said, "Man, I would love to have you here." So it was only a matter of time until I was wearing Dodger blue.

Mark Shapiro, from the Indians, seemed more concerned about the lack of action than I was, and he tried to help stimulate the market, calling around to other teams and talking me up, telling them how much they'd be getting if they signed me, which was a really generous and unusual thing for a general manager to do for a player he'd already traded. Mark called Jim Hendry, the general manager of the Cubs, and Brian Sabean, with the Giants. Nothing happened. But I didn't really expect the bidding to pick up until early December, when the annual baseball Winter Meetings happen. The Winter Meetings are a kind of job fair and swap meet for all levels of the game, from kids just out of college looking to break into an entry-level job in the minors to free agent players shopping for a new franchise. All thirty general managers are in one hotel, and fans roam the lobby asking for autographs. In December 2008, the meetings were in Las Vegas. I figured I would go and make the rounds talking to the GMs, and finally the contract offers would start flowing.

It seemed like a really good sign when my phone rang as I was boarding the flight to Vegas with Dee—my friend Dureyea Johnson, who is also from the Bay Area. It was the Angels, offering five years and $100 million. But they said I had to answer right away.

I hung up. **You can't tell me to make a major life decision on the spot! I got a wife. I got kids. You're not going to strong-arm me. Why would I want to go to Anaheim under those conditions? Get the fuck out of here!**

So I arrived in Vegas pissed off, with one less team as an option. But it still didn't matter, because all I cared about was signing with the Dodgers. In the hotel lobby I bumped into Ned Colletti, the Los Angeles GM, and I told him I wanted to be a Dodger. He said he didn't know if they could offer me enough years. We shook hands, said we'd talk again.

Later that night I was watching ESPN and the crawl read, SABATHIA WANTS TO SIGN WITH DODGERS. Brian texted me: "Bro, stop talking to people." My up-front desire might not have been the best negotiating tactic, but I'm always going to be honest. However to my amazement and disappointment, no meeting with the Dodgers ever happened. We only sat down with the Yankees, the Mets, and the Red

Sox. Frank McCourt, the Dodgers' owner, called me once or twice, but the conversation seemed like he was going through the motions; the Dodgers never made an offer. Their lack of interest hurt, bad, and the whole free agency process, the uncertainty, was ripping me up.

That night, about 3 A.M., I couldn't sleep, so I went over to Dee's room. Woke him up. We were sitting in the dark, talking, and I was crying. "I need your help. I don't know what to do," I told Dee. "I have no idea. I feel like I'm being pulled apart. I want to sign with the Dodgers, but they don't want me. The Yankees want me, but I don't want to go there. I don't know if I should stay in Milwaukee for less money." I counted on Dee to see things straight, and to tell it to me straight.

"All the negative feedback about New York, about how the organization is—don't listen to none of that," he said. "What do you think is going to be the best for you and your family? Make a selfish decision—do what you want to do, not what other people want you to do, and you'll make it work for everybody."

Dee was right, but I couldn't absorb it completely right then. The next day I carried my disappointment about the Dodgers into our next meeting with the Yankees. I was also nursing a hangover, from going to a fight and a club the night before. But so what? This meeting was just a courtesy. The Yankees were going all out, though. Brian Cashman came to my hotel and brought Joe Girardi, the manager at the time, plus Reggie Jackson. My dad had been a huge Reggie fan, and so was I—so him coming to the meeting was both cool and distracting: I didn't hear anything Cash said about the contract because I was focused on Reggie. He talked about what it was like going from the West Coast to New York, and how playing for the Yankees had taken his stardom to another level. The Yankees also brought a DVD showing off all the features of the new Yankee Stadium, which would be opening the next spring. I don't think the Yankees knew about me being a germophobe, but playing in a brand-new stadium was kind of intriguing. The video included construction workers saying, "Come to New York, CC!" It was dope. But the DVD and Reggie were not enough to change my mind. It was still the Yankees. The clubhouse was still toxic.

Dee was watching and listening to as much TV and radio as possible from the cities where I was thinking about signing, and he was keeping me posted. New York sports talk radio was killing me: "He's taking too long to sign." "He wouldn't be able to handle the pressure in New York." "He's too fat." **Fuck that. I'm not signing there.** I left the Yankees meeting with a shrug: **Whatever.**

I talked with Cash some more the next morning, then flew back to California. When I landed, Brian, my agent, called: "Hey, Cashman wants to come to your house in Vallejo and meet Amber." **Shit.** In the first meeting with the Yankees I'd repeatedly played it off on Amber: "Yeah, well, I got to go talk to my wife, see what she's thinking, talk about where we want to live, it's a family decision . . ." Blah, blah, blah. I thought I had stalled Cashman and put off needing to figure out what I was going to do. Now, though, Cashman was calling my bluff. His determination was starting to make an impression, but that wasn't even close to enough to overcome what I was sure I didn't like about the Yankees.

I had only ever said, "What's up?" to Jeet; I had never talked with Mariano Rivera or Jorge Posada or Andy Pettitte. The only guy on the Yankees roster at that time that I knew, even a little bit, was Alex Rodriguez. During spring training in 2008 I'd pitched against the Yankees in Tampa. After my innings I went to one of the back fields to do my running, and Al happened to be there working out. "Man, we would love to get you here in free agency next year," he'd said.

Now, the Major League Baseball rules say that recruiting players while they are under contract to another team is a violation, that it's tampering. But fuck that. The players have to stick together and look out for one another, because this is a business, and the owners and the front offices will cut you loose as soon as you're not performing or you get too expensive. So what Al said to me in Florida that day is the kind of conversation that goes on all the time. If you're a competitor, you're always going to try to beat whoever you are up against that day, no matter what's happening with your contract or what someone says to try to get you interested in their club. Besides, at that point I had zero interest in the Yankees. So even as I was telling Al, "Oh, yeah, that'd be great," in my head I was saying, **Fuck out of here, no chance.**

Nine months later, there was a $140 million offer from the Yankees on the table and Cashman was sitting on our couch in Vallejo. He started talking about quiet neighborhoods in New Jersey, where the best schools were, connecting us with real estate agents. He said he'd be going all out to sign other free agents, so if I signed with the Yankees I wouldn't be carrying the pitching staff by myself. Amber mentioned that she loved the Macy's Thanksgiving Day Parade. Cash said he could get us front-row tickets—and if I was playing for the Yankees, we could even be in the parade if we wanted.

That was all good. But this time, unlike when we talked in Vegas, I had to be real with him. "What I'm worried about the most is the dynamic in your clubhouse," I told Cash. "All the guys I talk to, guys I trust, tell me it's a mess."

He didn't argue. In fact, he nodded and agreed. "We've got a broken clubhouse. That's why I want you," Cash said. "I've been watching, I've been talking with people, too. You can make a huge difference in that dynamic. You can make it fun. You can make it work."

I couldn't tell whether he was bullshitting me, but in any case I didn't really believe him. And if he was telling the truth about the clubhouse being "broken," that was almost scarier. "You've got fucking Jeter and Posada, and they can't make a difference?" I said. "You want **me** to make a difference? Those guys are great players and they're stars. What am I going to do that these guys can't do?"

Cash smiled. "We've got great players, you're right, and they are leaders in their own way," he said. "But the combination of how competitive you are and how much fun you have competing, that can lighten things up and bring guys together in a different way. We really need that."

In Vegas he had made a sales pitch. In Vallejo we were having a real conversation about whether this could work. I appreciated how highly he seemed to think of me, and the extra effort he was making. But I still wasn't buying it.

"Look," Cash said, "I'm so sure that you're going to love playing for the Yankees, I'll give you a six-year contract with an opt-out after three. If you're not happy after three years, you're a free agent again."

Damn. He was convinced, and he was starting to convince me.

But when Cash left, it was Amber who understood what was in my mind, the combination of insecurity and anxiety that was holding me back. "Babe, he's telling you you could make a difference in the clubhouse—that's what you do!" she said. "Don't sell yourself short!"

I hadn't seen myself in that light in Cleveland—

after the rough first few years, I was just one of the guys having fun. But Amber was right. I had been a big part of why the Cleveland clubhouse was fun, and why we won, even if I didn't want to take credit. I was ready for the free agency uncertainty to be over. Right then I decided to sign with the Yankees.

I called Brian Peters to tell him my decision, and a few minutes later he called me back. "Oh, by the way," Brian said, "it's seven years and $161 million." We started out talking about a contract for six years and $140 million. Somewhere between Cash leaving the couch and reaching the airport he had upped the value and left in the three-year opt-out. The boost made it the biggest guaranteed contract in baseball history for a pitcher up to that point. That wasn't something I'd set out to achieve, but if there was any doubt left in my head about how much the Yankees wanted me, it was gone now.

Six weeks earlier I'd been sure I was going to Los Angeles. Instead I was heading to the Bronx, the last place on my list, with a challenge beyond pitching that I had never seen coming.

I got a text from Jeter and a call from Pettitte right after I signed. Those were great. They calmed me down, and started me thinking that this might work out. On the flip side, the news that I had signed a huge contract instantly dialed up the expectations from friends and family even higher. Motherfuckers were lining up at my door like the $161 million was gonna hit my bank account at midnight.

The Yankees were planning to hold a press conference in New York to introduce me to the city. I wasn't looking forward to being up there alone in front of all the reporters. Fortunately, two days after I agreed to sign, the Yankees made a deal with another free agent pitcher, A.J. Burnett. This was great. Not only was A.J. an excellent right-hander—he was coming off his best season, winning 18 games with Toronto—but he had a reputation as a really fun guy and a winner. He had lots of tattoos, a nasty curveball, and a nasty attitude—on the mound, anyway. I didn't know A.J. well—we'd only pitched against each other once, when he was with the Jays and I was with the Indians—but I knew I wanted him at the press conference, too, instead of holding separate ones. Sharing the spotlight would help me be less nervous. But doing the press conference with A.J. would also send a message about all of us being in this together. I wasn't thinking, **Here's how I start becoming a leader on the Yankees**—guys see through that kind of calculation right away. It's just who I am. I always want to bring people together. I always want to be a part of something bigger. Everything is more fun that way. So I called up A.J., and to my relief he agreed to do it together.

Even with A.J. there, I was still plenty nervous. When Joe Girardi handed me a pin-striped jersey with 52 on the back, I didn't even unbutton it— I pulled it straight over my head. The night before,

I'd gone out to dinner with Jason Zillo, the Yankees' head of communications, to go over questions I might be asked and practice some answers. Jay said he knew I was used to being totally honest, and he appreciated that—but in New York I might need to hold back a little bit. Which was good advice. When it was my turn at the press conference, I got in some great jokes—and nobody fucking laughed. George King, the Yankees beat writer for the **New York Post,** sat there straight-facing me. I was pissed. But mostly I just spoke from the heart about what I was feeling. "Me and my wife were out house-hunting yesterday, looking for a place and we were in Alpine. We were walking through a house and the guy says, 'So, what team do you play for?' And I said, 'The Yankees.' And it kind of gave me a chill."

Which was totally true. But it was nothing compared to the goose bumps I felt saying those words out loud in front of a crowd of people at the press conference. Not for the reason that fans or sportswriters might expect: I knew about the Yankees tradition before I came to New York, but I didn't care about it, not until the first spring training made it real, meeting Yogi and Gator and Goose, having a relationship with them and understanding what it meant to be a Yankee, and wanting to be a part of it. No, the tradition was one of the reasons I **didn't** want to come as a free agent, because you're always compared to these old ghosts. The goose bumps at the press conference weren't about the Yankees history. They went back to my dad. Because for the longest time, he told me the Yankees were where I was gonna end up. He knew that I needed to come here to be great. This is where he wanted me to pitch, the best baseball franchise on the planet. And I didn't want to be here! Now I had to live up to my dad's vision. The goose bumps were made up of both thrill and fear.

The press conference took place in the original Yankee Stadium, and then we walked over to the new one, which was still being built, and posed for more photos. On the mound where I would be standing in four months stood a Christmas tree. Christmas was one week away, and I already had a pretty damn good present. We needed to celebrate.

We headed downtown to the 40/40 Club, Jay-Z's place. We talked about what it meant to be a Yankee, the legacy I was stepping into. One of Hova's business partners, Juan Perez, better known as OG, told me, "Man, you need to win the World Series the first year."

"Nah," I told him. "Our team is dope. We going to be fine. We got time. I've got a seven-year contract!"

OG smiled and shook his head. "Win the first year and take the pressure off. This is the Yankees. This is New York."

I didn't really get it. But I soon found out how right he was.

I came to New York to win a World Series—
and in 2009, my first season with the Yankees,
we delivered.

# 12

I T WAS A HECTIC WINTER. MOST OF OUR TIME WAS spent figuring out our move east. I sought out Gary Sheffield for advice, because he'd played for the Yankees and he was one of the wisest Black big leaguers. Sheff had become a good friend. He recommended we check out Alpine, New Jersey, where he had lived when he played for the Yankees and then the Mets, and it turned out to be a great suggestion. Big houses, big yards, quiet neighborhoods, plenty of kids. It was an easy half-hour drive to Yankee Stadium, at least when the traffic cooperated. Alpine also seemed to be a welcoming place for successful, high-profile Black folks who wanted a safe, low-key spot to decompress. Andre Harrell, Lil' Kim, Chris Rock, and Diddy all had houses in Alpine. We settled on a six-bedroom place that was under construction on a hilly, tree-lined street, and redrew the plans to get exactly what we wanted, because this was going to be the home where we raised our kids and put down roots. We decided on an office for Amber, a big open kitchen where everyone could hang out, and a downstairs TV and recreation area, including a full-sized basketball court. A pool and a guesthouse out back, so friends and family could come and visit for weeks. My vision, since I was a little kid, was to someday have a big-ass aquarium, floor to ceiling, with sharks, that would be the first thing you saw when you walked into my house. Turns out that would have been crazy expensive to maintain, and Amber wasn't into having live sharks in the house. We had a big fight about it, and I settled for a tank that runs along one wall of the family room. While our permanent house was being finished, we rented a second one around the corner.

Alpine was a different universe from the Crest, and sometimes I felt pulled between the two, or that I didn't completely belong in either one. Signing the big Yankees contract while so many of my friends and family were still going through hard times in Vallejo also increased the expectation that I would share the wealth. It was rare for relatives to outright ask me to send them money, but they found ways to make it clear they could use some help, often by talking to my mom or to one of my aunts. I genuinely wanted to help as much as I possibly could, and not just blood family. When I heard that Coach Hobbs's son, who has autism, needed a sensory stimulation device known as a hug machine, we sent him one right away.

Amber says I have survivor's guilt. I'm not sure that's exactly right. I have always felt I've earned and deserved whatever teams paid me—not just because I have delivered on the field, but because the owners wouldn't be paying me and my teammates millions if they weren't making plenty of money themselves. What Amber describes is close to the truth, though: Being the one who made it out and made it big created a sense of obligation I wasn't prepared to handle. I didn't know how to say no, and before long I was buying cars for several cousins, paying their school tuition and rent and child support. And slowly starting to resent it.

The baseball season seemed to kick in even faster that year. I couldn't wait to get to Tampa and to spring training with the Yankees. I function best when I have a routine. Every spring I would pick six songs that I'd listen to in the shower every morning I was starting a game that season. For ten years with the Yankees I would eat the same lunch— a chicken sandwich with lettuce and tomato on a burger bun, plus barbecue chips—every day I pitched. But in February 2009, after nine years in Winter Haven with the Indians, I needed to learn my way around a new camp and a new system, everything from the best route to drive to the airport to finding a new barber, and I was on edge for the first few weeks.

At Steinbrenner Field, the Yankees' spring training home, I was given the locker that had belonged to Moose—Mike Mussina. My only request to the Yankees was that I be next to Joba Chamberlain. He was a big, fun-loving twenty-three-year-old guy with tons of potential, the Yankees' hottest pitching prospect. I knew what it was like to be young and dealing with large expectations, so I thought I might be able to help Joba, who was being moved from the bullpen into the starting rotation.

Toward the far end of the row of lockers was Andy Pettitte. He intimidated me. Not just because he had already won four rings and was one of the best left-handers in the game, but because when you watched Andy pitch from the other side of the field he looked cold as ice, covering his face with his glove and glaring as he stared in for the catcher's signs.

And on the surface we couldn't have been more different as people. Andy grew up in suburban Texas, near Houston. He's White, eight years older than me, and soft-spoken; he doesn't drink, and he's a devout Christian. He wasn't a big prospect in high school; he went to junior college and worked really hard on his game. Totally opposite from my experience. I knew I wanted to try to learn everything I could from Andy about pitching. But I didn't know what to expect in the way of a relationship.

At the end of one of the first days of camp I was starting to wander off the field without doing any poles—poles being the traditional way that pitchers finished practice, by running dozens of times from one foul pole to the other and back again. I'd had surgery on my right knee once already, and I probably should have had it cleaned up again that winter, especially after having pitched so many innings on three days' rest with the Brewers. But no way was I going to start my big new contract with the Yankees on rehab. When I got to Florida the knee still hurt and I didn't want to make it worse, so I figured I just wouldn't run at all in spring training. And for the first week or so I was doing a good job of avoiding it.

But as I was heading off that day I looked up and saw that Andy was running poles. **This guy is thirty-six years old and he's got four fucking World Series rings. What the fuck are you talking about, you're not running? You better get out there and fucking run!** That's how I developed a relationship with Andy, running poles and talking, which is the weirdest thing, because I still hated running. Turned out we have a whole lot in common. We both have huge families. Andy and his wife, Laura, met in high school and have four kids, just like me and Amber. Our friendship developed from not knowing anything about each other and wanting to find out. Andy wanted to understand where I came from; I've always been that way when I meet new people, too. It went from talking while running to talking while sitting on the bench during games, sometimes about baseball but more often about our upbringings. During the regular season teams will send the pitcher who is starting the first game of a road trip to the next city a day early, so he can get better rest. When that pitcher was Andy—who we called "Teetay," after the pair of double T's in his last name—he didn't like to travel alone, so he'd recruit me and, eventually, Hiroki Kuroda, because we followed him in the rotation, to fly ahead with him. That was great because it gave us even more time together. Andy had one restaurant in every city where we would always eat—a steak house in Toronto, an Italian place in Minneapolis—and he would order the same meal every time. Some people might call that superstition. Pitchers call it having a routine. You could talk to Andy about anything, and he would listen, think about it carefully, and offer wise opinions but not judgments. This would become incredibly important to me over the next few years.

Mike Harkey, the Yankees' bullpen coach, quickly became my new big brother, someone who made a huge difference in my adjustment to New York on and off the field, especially in a season when there were only two other Black players on the roster, Jeet and, as of July, Jerry Hairston. Early one morning during spring training I was sitting on the couch in the food room watching television. Mike walked in, looked at the screen, saw that I was watching BET, and burst out, "Yeah! Finally! Black chapel! We don't have to watch MTV anymore! It's not **SportsCenter** every day!"

. . .

I got a very different kind of introduction to the Yankees world during the first week of spring training. SI.com, the **Sports Illustrated** website, had published a story saying A-Rod had tested positive for anabolic steroids in 2003, when he was playing shortstop for the Texas Rangers. At first Al didn't comment. Then, after more evidence came out, he criticized the reporter, Selena Roberts, before saying he'd used "something." So this was a huge controversy, and the Yankees decided to try to deal with it by holding one big press conference at the start of spring training. It was mobbed. There must have been two hundred reporters, plus TV camera operators and photographers elbowing one another for space. I hadn't seen this many media people during eight seasons in Cleveland added together.

I stood off to one side of the stage with most of the other Yankees players. We were there to support Al; whatever drugs he had used in the past, and whatever lies he'd told about not using them, we needed him to play well if we were going to win a championship in 2009. My attitude toward guys who used PEDs is kind of contradictory. It's definitely bad that players who followed the rules probably lost jobs to players who cheated. And I hate giving up home runs to guys who I know are juiced and shouldn't be able to hit the ball 400 feet. On the other hand, I played with a bunch of fucking guys who were on steroids and who were still trash. You've got to be really good to do what Barry Bonds and Roger Clemens did. Those guys deserve to be in the Hall of Fame, whether or not they were using. A-Rod was a fantastic player, obviously. His baseball IQ is off the charts. And he didn't need the chemical help, physically. I just think he started using the drugs when he was so young that his mind got mixed up—he didn't know if he could be great without them.

All the media attention focused on Al that spring training allowed me to skate in more easily and quietly, instead of having to deal with stories every day about whether I was going to be worth $161 million. There's a lot of hours to kill during camp, so some nights I'd organize a trip to a restaurant for six or seven of us. Other times I would buy tickets to Orlando Magic games and invite a bunch of guys. I wasn't trying to follow some plan to loosen up the clubhouse and bring people closer together. Jeet had been the captain since 2003, he deserved to be, and everyone looked to him as the leader of the team. I just wanted to get to know the guys I was going into battle with, and I felt like everybody should be included. In Cleveland, that meant a group of us going to Cavs games or coming over to my house for a cookout. During spring training I didn't want guys just sitting around bored in the hotel room at night if I could help it. Naturally, I invited the pitchers first—A.J., Joba, Phil Hughes,

Brian Bruney. Chien-Ming Wang, a great guy, is from Taiwan and had been in the United States for ten years, but he'd never been to an NBA game. Wanger got a bonus the first time we went to see the Magic: The team invited us onto the floor and let us shoot around before the game. It was cool. Joba hit a few in a row. Wanger airballed his first couple of shots, but then he hit one off the back-board. Yeah, I might have drained a few myself. It was just a fun night, but this kind of stuff seemed to be unusual around the Yankees.

They had plenty of guys who cared about win-ning, but the approach had been all business, treating the game like it was a job—show up at your office, take BP, compete for three hours, go home. Jeet became a close friend; people on the outside don't realize that he's really funny. As the Yankees clubhouse loosened up, Jeet was right in the middle of it, yelling and joking. We always had some kind of bet going. He's a huge University of Michigan fan, so I'd find anything happening— a Michigan water polo game—and bet on them to lose, against Jeet. But his style as a leader was mostly to set an example by playing hard and conducting himself as a professional. For the seven months of the season he was absolutely locked in, down to eating a peanut butter and jelly sandwich every day before a game, one hour before the first pitch. On the field, things need to be buttoned up, and that perception helped us: **The Yankees aren't fooling**

**around. We're gonna come in and kick your ass.** If someone on the team was really out of line, Jeet would say something. Otherwise he was going to leave people alone and expect them to take care of themselves the right way. Jeet was happy to hang with guys after a game, as long as it was on his clock—if you got dressed fast enough, great, you'd go out to dinner with him, but Jeet wasn't waiting around. The other biggest star on the team, A-Rod, was a great guy in many ways, but more often than not he was off on his own after games. So Al wasn't going to be the one to create unity.

One other important new relationship for me was with Dave Eiland, the Yankees' pitching coach. First I had to buy my jersey number from him—he was wearing 52, which had been his digits as a player with the Yankees in 1988. I can't remember exactly what it cost me, but probably around ten grand. I freaked out Dave the first time I warmed up for a game. When I was young I would just go straight from the locker room to the bullpen mound and start throwing. No real stretching, no time in the weight room, no riding the stationary bike, none of the standard stuff most pitchers do. I wouldn't even play catch in the outfield. I would just walk out to the bullpen, young, loose, and ready to go, and start throwing. And throw and throw. I would do an almost sixty-pitch bullpen before starting a game. Before my first spring training start with the Yankees I threw seventy-three pitches in the bullpen. Dave saw this and said, "What the fuck are you doing? Wait. Wait. Wait."

I shrugged and laughed. I had won a Cy Young Award, I had been in the big leagues for eight years, but in a lot of ways I was still raw: just doing what was working right then, without much of a plan for tomorrow.

"You can't do that," Dave said. "We're going to be asking a lot from you this year. How long have you been doing it this way?"

"I don't know. This is how I warm up."

He looked like he might explode. We scrapped what I had been doing and came up with a whole new routine, beginning an hour before the first pitch with a hot tub. Over the years, as my body broke down, the pre-game part would get longer and longer. But the bullpen work stayed the same for the next ten years. Instead of sixty pitches, we dialed it down to thirty-six: three fastballs inside to a righty hitter, three fastballs away, three fastballs in again, three fastballs away, three changeups, three sliders. Then I'd repeat the whole mix out of the stretch. Never more pitches, never fewer. I loved the precision. It quickly felt more like a ritual than a warm-up, something I needed to follow down to the last detail or I wouldn't be ready.

The Yankees made a couple of other important additions to the roster over the winter. We signed Mark Teixeira, a power hitter and a switch-hitter, to be the new starting first baseman. And we traded for Nick Swisher, who could play all over the field. More important, Swish was a crazy person—in a good way. He was pure upbeat energy, with no off switch. With Swish and A.J. and me, we now had a trio that could keep things light. It also cut down on the talk about me coming in and saving the organization. Sure, I was the biggest deal that winter, but the team was making it clear that there was more than one thing that needed to be fixed, which took some of the weight off me. On the downside, we lost A-Rod to a torn labrum in his right hip just before the season started, and it wasn't clear when he would be back. As spring training ended, most of the so-called experts were picking us to finish behind the Red Sox in the AL East.

I have always hated opening day, and in 2009 I pitched two of them. We started the regular season on the road, in Baltimore, and I was bad: eight hits, five walks, no strikeouts, and six earned runs. Part of it was nerves. Throughout my career nervousness was always very much part of how I pitched. The day of my start, my stomach always hurt. I always had to take a massive dump before the game, but that didn't make the anxiety go away, even though I tried to believe it would. Catchers learned to expect the nervousness from me. One time Austin Romine came out to the mound and I said, "Fuck, man, why is my stomach hurting?" Rome kind of laughed: "Your stomach hurts every time you pitch." He was right. But the first game of a season, I always felt worse. In Baltimore in 2009 there was also the extra pressure of trying to prove myself to my new team right away. I was gone after just 4⅓ innings and we lost 10–5. Five days later, in Kansas City, things went much better, and I got my first win as a Yankee.

Then we finally headed to New York—and another opening day. The reason I hate opening day is that it gets way too much hype. I understand that fans are excited to have baseball back. But it's one game. It counts the same as the other 161. And there is all this sentimental stuff about being named the opening day starter for your team, how it's a big honor. It's cool, I guess, but I always would have preferred that someone else do it. Nobody remembers who the fuck pitched opening day. It's meaningless. I wanted to pitch the first game of the playoffs. That's when shit matters.

And in 2009, it felt like all I did was firsts. Not only was I starting the home opener for my new team after signing a huge contract, I was starting the first game in the new Yankee Stadium. As if all that wasn't enough tension, we were playing the Indians! The batting order was filled with my friends. The opposing starting pitcher was Cliff Lee, one of my best friends. I hated it. It was not fun. Somehow I pitched okay—5⅔ innings, only one run, but five walks and 126 pitches—but Cliff was better, and we ended up losing 10–2. The thing I remember most about that day is being glad it was over.

Our record hovered around .500 for the first six weeks of the season, and I was alternating good starts with bad ones. The question started coming often: "Are you feeling the pressure to live up to your new contract?" Honestly, I never did. The way I saw it, I wasn't being paid for what I was doing now or in the future—I was being paid back after being underpaid during my years in Cleveland. It just happened to be the Yankees who were writing the checks.

The New York fans and media were getting restless, though. The chatter about Joe Girardi being fired was growing. It took until May 8 for A-Rod to get back into the lineup after his hip surgery. His first game, his first at-bat, the first pitch he saw, Al crushed it to deep left center, 374 feet, for a three-run homer. It was crazy. That was exactly what we had been missing. Up until then we hadn't hit a big homer, we hadn't taken on our personality as the Yankees. With that one swing, the feeling became, **Holy shit, this is us, let's go, it's time to roll!** There was a long road in front of us, of course, but as the fans were screaming and we were pounding Al on the back, I was thinking, **We are winning the World Series for sure.**

I was on the mound that day against the Orioles and threw a complete-game shutout with eight strikeouts. I didn't feel pressure because of the big contract. But what I did feel was that the Yankees had brought me to New York to deliver a championship—so I had to win every game I pitched! In the middle of May, when I was driving to the park, the usual beat was pounding in my head: **I've got to win this game. I've got to win this game.** Then, and I don't know why, a little light went on: **Damn—I've got A-Rod. I've got Jeet. I've got Tex. I've got Robbie—if he goes off and gets a couple of hits, man, this might be kinda easy! Mo has the ninth inning locked down. If I just go and do my little part, and not try to throw a fucking no-hitter, just pitch like I can, we might get on a roll.** My next start I went eight innings and beat Toronto, one night after Andy had shut down the Jays, and we ignited, winning nine in a row. A sense of calm started to settle into my head. At the end of the month A.J., Andy, and I pitched three straight solid games to push us past both the Red Sox and the Jays and into first place.

My win, on May 30, was extra sweet: It came against the Indians, in my first trip to Cleveland as a Yankee. This called for a party. We probably would have gone out with a big crew no matter how the game had turned out, but beating the Indians made it even better. Johnny Damon and his wife, Michelle, came along, plus Cliff and Kristen Lee, and a whole bunch of friends from Cleveland. We went out to dinner and then to The

View, in the Flats, one of our old hangouts, a big, loud dance club. I was good and drunk by the time we arrived and don't remember many of the details. Amber was ready to leave, but I kept saying, "One more drink!" At some point I backed up from the bar and bumped into a girl. She spilled her drink on me, so I offered to buy her a new one. Then it got loud. People were pushing and shoving and cursing. Cliff Lee was pulling on me: "Come on! We got to go!" So then I started trying to fight Cliff. He wound up punching me in the face just to get me into the car.

The whole mess ended up on the Cleveland TV news the next day. That was the only unusual thing about it, though. Me getting drunk, me getting into arguments and near-brawls—that was common. That was how a lot of my nights ended. But just like my pre-game bullpens, I had developed a strict routine. The two days before I was scheduled to pitch, I dried out. As soon as I'd done my work and come out of the game, the drinking cranked back up. With the Yankees, we had these tall green plastic Gatorade cups in the clubhouse. They held maybe thirty ounces of liquid. I'd fill one up with Crown Royal and Sprite, or whatever I happened to feel like drinking at the time, and head to the shower. Refill it for my ride home to New Jersey. It was the culture of our clubhouse at the time; I certainly wasn't the only one leaving the ballpark carrying a giant Gatorade cup cocktail. But I was the only one who would keep drinking hard for the next three days, sweating some of the booze out during a workout in the afternoon and then drinking until I passed out at night. The only thing that kept me partly sober was knowing I had to pitch, and right on schedule I would clean it up.

Yeah, I had some bad hangovers. Yeah, there were some close calls in bars where someone could have gotten hurt. But as messy as it might have been at times, my routine was working. I went from 3–3 in mid-May to 19–8 at the end of the regular season. The Red Sox kept pace with us until August, when we pulled away for good, winning the AL East by eight games. We won 103 games, the most the Yankees had won in seven years. And we had a blast doing it.

A.J. introduced a new tradition, something he'd done when he played for the Marlins and the Jays. If we had a walk-off win at home, typically the guy who delivered the winning hit would be interviewed immediately afterward on the field by the YES Network, the station that broadcast our games. A.J. would sneak up behind the player being interviewed, carrying a towel filled with whipped cream, and "pie" him right in the face. The first time was in the middle of May, when we scored three runs in the bottom of the ninth to beat the Twins, and Melky Cabrera was the hero and A.J.'s first victim. A.J.'s young sons helped create another tradition. They gave Johnny Damon a toy plastic championship wrestling belt. Johnny decided that after victories the belt needed to be awarded to our "player of the game"; soon we had a ceremony to go along with it, and the winner had to deliver a speech. Halfway through the season the belt got an upgrade when Jerry "The King" Lawler, the pro wrestler and WWE announcer and a big Cleveland Indians fan, sent me an official one made out of leather and sparkling with rhinestones. This stuff sounds kind of silly when it's written out, but in a long season it's the kind of thing you need to keep things fun and to build a tight unit out of twenty-five very different people.

There was also one epic night that pulled us closer together. A-Rod was living in this incredible mansion in Rye, a town that's a little more than twenty miles north of Yankee Stadium, and on a Saturday night in late July he threw himself a thirty-fourth-birthday party. Everyone was invited—players, coaches, wives. Jay-Z was there. He's loved the Yankees since he was a kid. The food and the music were phenomenal. But A.J. and I quickly spotted the outdoor, Olympic-sized swimming pool. We started talking about jumping in and told Al our plan. We didn't expect him to go for it.

An hour or so later, A-Rod blew out the candles on his cake. Everybody finished singing "Happy Birthday." And Al made a run for the pool—wearing his suit, watch, shoes, everything—and did a cannonball. Instantly it was mayhem. There had to be eighty people splashing around, including Joe Girardi, who's about the straightest guy you'll ever meet.

As a team, we were together on the bus or the plane all year, and groups of guys would hang at dinner or clubs, but that's not really being together. This was the first time where almost everybody on the roster came, and we had a blast. Maybe you don't bond with this guy or like that guy too much, but if you're all splashing around in a pool together, you see him in a different light.

In October, when it was time for the playoffs, I was incredibly nervous. I didn't know if I could be good in New York when it mattered most. We didn't have many team meetings, but we had one right before the first round. Joe Girardi spoke, along with a few players. But it was Gene Monahan, our trainer, who made the biggest impact on me. Geno stood up and said, "Hey, it's eleven more wins." Something about the calmness in the way he said it got through to me and settled me down.

This time I put to use everything I had learned in the past eight years, and especially from my failures in the playoffs the past two years with Cleveland and Milwaukee: **Set the tone from the start, dominate, but don't think you have to win the game all by yourself.**

I dodged trouble in the first inning without any runs scoring, but in the third, with two outs, I gave up three straight hits, then bounced a pitch, and we were down 2–0. **Shit.** When we finally ended the inning, I was sitting on the bench with my heart racing. Jeter sat right next to me. "You all right?" he said.

"I'm good, I'm good," I replied.

Jeet said, totally calm, "All right, I got you." With Melky Cabrera on second, he went up and hit an absolute bomb into the left field seats. Tie game. Stadium rocking. All the weight lifted from my shoulders. I cruised into the seventh not allowing any more runs, and we won 7–2.

We basically crushed the Twins' spirit in the second game, scoring two to tie it in the bottom of the ninth on an A-Rod homer, and then winning it in the bottom of the eleventh on a leadoff walk-off homer by Teixeira. I'd thought I'd heard loud stadiums in Cleveland and Milwaukee, but Yankee Stadium was absolutely shaking when we ran out to mob Tex as he crossed home plate. Game three, in Minneapolis, was close, but never really in doubt.

The Angels swept the Red Sox in the other AL Division Series—which only added to the motivation for me. Now I could remind Anaheim what they'd missed by giving me a half-assed offer as a free agent. I shut them down twice, in games one and four, throwing a total of sixteen innings and allowing only two runs. We closed out the Angels in six games. I was in a groove and finally going to the World Series for the first time.

I had been aiming for this moment my whole life. This was why I'd overcome my hostility to playing for the Yankees—because now I had a real shot at winning a championship. All season long, before every one of my starts, I had listened to Kanye's "Champion": "Tell me what it takes to be number one." So you would think I'd remember every detail of my first World Series start. It's strange, but I don't. That night is mostly a blur. The thing that stays with me the most is that I was on the verge of one of my biggest dreams—and who was I up against as the starting pitcher for the other team? Cliff Lee! The Indians had traded Cliff to the Phillies at the deadline in July, and he was a big reason they had won the National League. Starting pitchers always tell reporters they don't care who is on the mound for the other team— your focus is on the opposing hitters. Which is mostly true. But when it's one of your best friends, and it's the first game of your first World Series, you notice. Cliff and I had always competed, even when we were on the same team, pushing each other, trying to get better. Two years earlier we'd been hanging out together every day in Cleveland, playing Nintendo R.B.I. Baseball. Now here we were pitching against each other in the biggest game of the baseball season—a few months after he'd punched me to protect me in a bar brawl! It made it more fun, and more intense.

I pitched pretty well—but Cliff pitched even better. I went seven innings and made just two real mistakes, each of which Chase Utley hit for a solo home run. Girardi pulled me after seven innings with us down 2–0, though the way Cliff was pitching, it felt like we were down 10–0. He was dealing and wound up throwing a complete game, striking out ten with no walks; we scored just one unearned run. Sure, I was disappointed, but I wasn't down. We were still the better team. I had another start coming in three or four days, and I was going to be even better.

My turn came around in game four, in Philadelphia, and it was an even bigger spot than starting game one. We had won the previous two; take game four and all we needed was one more to be champs. Lose and the series would be tied, with the Phillies at home for one more game. Game four was a battle; I wasn't at my sharpest, but I kept making key pitches when I needed to. We jumped out to a 2–0 lead in the first, but Utley got me again in the bottom of the inning, doubling in Shane Victorino. The Phillies tied it in the fourth on a couple of singles and a stolen base; we went back up in the fifth when Jeter and Damon drove in runs. I was feeling good and got two quick outs in the bottom of the seventh. Then Utley hit his third homer of the series off me. This one wasn't even a bad pitch. But that made it a one-run game. Joe decided I was done, and I spent the rest of the night in the dugout, hanging over the railing, chewing on a towel, praying for our bullpen to come through.

In the eighth Pedro Feliz, the Phillies' third baseman, hit a homer off Joba to tie it. But the toughness we'd built over the past seven months kicked in. With two outs in the top of the ninth, Damon singled, then stole second and third; the man had huge balls. Tex got hit by a pitch. A-Rod doubled in Damon to put us ahead. Then Posada knocked in Tex and A-Rod. It took Mo just eight pitches to get the final three outs. I didn't get credit for the win, but it didn't matter: I gave my team a chance to win, and now we were on the edge of winning the World Series.

The Phillies stayed alive by winning the next night, but that was fine: It meant we would end it in New York, which would be even sweeter. Andy got the start, which I loved because the Yankees had seemed close to letting him leave the previous winter, even after all he'd meant to the team. He took a pay cut to stay and try to win another ring, and when Joba replaced him in the sixth inning we were up 7–3. With the finish line in sight, Joe Girardi was taking no chances: He brought in Mo early, in the eighth, for a five-out save. No one is perfect, but Mo was as close as it will ever get in baseball. I knew we had it locked down. But A.J. and I were so nervous, we stood together in the dugout gripping the rail so tightly we could have squeezed the stuffing out of it, all the way up until the last out, a Shane Victorino grounder to Robbie Canó. Then we flew up and over the railing, sprinting for the mound and that championship dogpile we'd been visualizing ever since we first picked up a ball.

The team took a victory lap around the Yankee Stadium warning track. It was the kind of thing you grew up watching Bob Costas describe on TV, and now I was in it, I was in the dream, running with Andy and Mo, slapping hands with the fans. The stadium sound system played Sinatra's "New York, New York" over and over again, as it does after every Yankees home game. But 2009 was the year that "Empire State of Mind" came out, and it became the anthem for that team. Hova and Alicia Keys performed it live before game two of the World Series, on a stage on the outfield grass just behind second base. The whole team was watching from the dugout, and I got a chill when Alicia hit "In New York / Concrete jungle where dreams are made of / There's nothin' you can't do / Now you're in New York." Still do get a chill whenever I hear it. It reminds me of coming to New York, the new stadium opening, all eyes on me, me wanting so bad to succeed. There's so much history with the Yankees, it's hard to make yourself even a little part of it—but in 2009 we did, we etched ourselves into those history books. We wrote our own Yankee Stadium story. Jay-Z said it: "I'm the new Sinatra, and since I made it here / I can make it anywhere." I was living it, right down to the ticker-tape parade on Broadway.

With Amber, distributing back-to-school supplies
at PS 47, in the Bronx. Our PitCCh In Foundation
has raised and spent more than $6 million
to help kids in New York and Vallejo.

# 13

THE VICTORY CELEBRATION CONTINUED FOR most of the winter. There was the standard stuff—TV interviews, awards dinners. The highlight for me wasn't an official Yankees event, though it felt close to one, considering the guest of honor. In early December, Beyoncé threw a surprise fortieth-birthday party for Jay-Z at a resort on the southeast coast of the Dominican Republic and invited roughly fifty people. We were all flown in by private plane, and the party had a 1920s/1940s **Scarface**-type theme, which was cool: Everyone was dressed as if we were walking into the Cotton Club in its prime, or maybe hanging at Jay Gatsby's estate. I had known Hova since 2007, and I had been around famous people for years. But here were me and Amber, two kids from Vallejo, standing next to a shimmering pool where forty synchronized swimmers were performing, looking up at a private fireworks show, drinking vintage Dom Pérignon, surrounded by Diddy, Kanye West, Alicia Keys, Kate Hudson, and A-Rod.

It was amazing, but for me it was also scary. It

always made me anxious to be out with a group of people who weren't close friends and to try to be fun and interesting, but this was taking things to another level. Yeah, I was a big part of the new World Series–winning team—but did I really belong here, with people who were artists, who were famous all over the world? And couldn't what I was achieving, in life and in baseball, be taken away in a minute?

Before we went down to the D.R. I had promised Amber I wasn't going to drink. That promise didn't hold for long. Drinking helped with my nerves, so I figured drinking more had to help more. Not that I was even being that logical. Once I got started, I didn't know when to stop. People told me later that the party finally ended at 5 A.M. I don't remember. What I remember is Amber waking me up. There had been plenty of times where I got drunk, passed out, got out of bed, and went sleepwalking; on road trips with the Indians and the Yankees I had locked myself out of hotel rooms and gone wandering the hallways in the middle of the night until security or a teammate intercepted me. Maybe that's what happened this time. Amber woke up in our cabana the morning after the party and saw I was gone. Then the housekeeper knocked on the door and quietly told her, "Ma'am, your husband is down there by the pool." Amber came out and found me facedown on a lounge chair, passed out, completely naked. Someone had covered my butt with a beach towel.

Amber woke me up, wrapped me in a bathrobe, and steered me back to our guesthouse. We went on with the weekend as if nothing had happened, though I know she was embarrassed. Fortunately, none of the other guests mentioned it. I don't like to think about who else may have seen me out there. But this was the pattern: Something big and good would happen in my life, and then there would be a big fall.

I knew that my drinking caused trouble, and that it wasn't good that I kept breaking my promises to Amber to dial it down. But recognizing a pattern is one thing; wanting to change it is something else. And I didn't, not really. For all the lows, I was having plenty of fun, and I hadn't done what I considered real damage. Hadn't hurt myself or someone else; hadn't gotten arrested. Sure, I missed some events at the kids' schools. But I never got drunk and was violent with Amber or slept with another woman. As loaded as I got, those were lines I would not cross. Amber never threatened to leave—though I knew that if she made up her mind, she wouldn't threaten; she would be gone. So I told myself that if I just managed the drinking a little better, I wouldn't need to stop. Or need to deal with the emotions that the drinking was covering up.

Besides, the bigger, brighter stage of New York was helping us do good things off the field, not just getting us invited to celebrity parties. I had donated to charities for years, but it had mostly been random: A teammate would be doing a cancer fundraiser, so we'd buy a table at the dinner. The Vallejo high school athletic fields needed to be renovated, so we'd write a check. But we wanted to do something deeper and sustained, something meaningful that could help lift people. The real push came from a robbery. In March 2009, somebody broke into the office of the North Vallejo Little League, trashed the computers and trophies, tore down a poster of me, and stole 150 uniforms and all the food and candy from the concession stand—the same concession stand where my mom would still work during games in the spring. Amber and I knew that life in Vallejo had gotten rougher— a lot of closed businesses, a lot of our friends out of work. In May 2008, Vallejo became the biggest city in California to ever declare bankruptcy. We certainly couldn't fix that. But maybe we could help give inner-city kids some hope, and not just in Vallejo.

The Boys & Girls Club had made a big difference in my life; Amber and I wanted to create something that could have the same kind of impact. We came up with the PitCCh In Foundation, and did our first event in Cleveland in 2008. We got a bowling alley to donate a night, and we sold tickets so fans could bowl alongside Indians players. We took the money we raised, plus a few thousand dollars more that I donated, and bought hundreds of backpacks, stuffed them with school supplies, and handed them out to elementary school students in Vallejo. As a kid, I never had many back-to-school supplies; our idea was to send kids back to school excited. But we could see the need was much larger than Vallejo—and me and Amber, we don't ever do things small. We kept coming up with ideas. In late December 2009, we did our first Christmas Caravan, a weeklong series of events. With the help of Vallejo Youth and Family Services, we took twenty teenagers on a shopping spree at the mall. We partnered with Kaiser Permanente, the health-care company, and went to a children's cancer hospital in Vallejo, where we visited patients and handed out Nintendo DS game systems. We laid new carpet and hung new curtains and built new bookshelves inside Rosewood House, a residence for women recovering from drug and alcohol addiction. By the time we came to New York we had two annual events in place—the backpack giveaway at the start of the school year, and the caravan in December. But it was clear that the foundation was just getting warmed up. That first year we gave away five hundred backpacks; within a couple of years we were giving away five thousand, at schools in both Vallejo and the Bronx. One reason we were able to expand was that being a Yankee opened doors to do a whole lot more good. For instance, we teamed up with the Shawn Carter Foundation to establish a scholarship at Vallejo High that is awarded every year to four outstanding senior student-athletes.

We named it the Nathan Berhel Scholarship, in honor of my late cousin. There is no way to bring Nate back. But he was a determined, courageous man, and my hope is the scholarship passes on some of his spirit to kids from our neighborhood, and maybe helps them chase their dreams. I sure needed all the help I could get, even when it looked as if I was on top of the world.

It felt like I had two faces. The one that laughed belonged to CC the All-Star pitcher and generously charitable guy who the public saw and praised. The one that snarled belonged to drunk CC, and it came out for my friends and family, who had to clean up my messes.

On the mound, I kept chasing another championship. Off it, I was heading for a crash.

# 14

T HE 2009 CHAMPIONSHIP WAS THE TWENTY-seventh for the Yankees. It was my first. But all of us—the franchise, the fans, me—believed that more rings were right around the corner. Which is what made the next three seasons so frustrating and disappointing. The everyday starting lineup stayed essentially the same; the biggest change was that Posada gradually—and grudgingly—gave way to Russell Martin at catcher. The starting rotation was less stable in those years. Javier Vázquez and Freddy Garcia and my old Indians teammate Bartolo Colón cycled through. Joba moved back to the bullpen. A.J. left as a free agent. Andy retired for 2011, then returned for two seasons.

In 2010 I felt stronger than I had since probably my rookie year, and more confident than probably ever. Winning the World Series in my first year with the Yankees relaxed me mentally. It certainly wasn't that I was satisfied with one ring—winning once made me hungry for more. But I knew that if we hadn't gotten it done in 2009, the pressure would have built both outside and in my mind: **We brought Sabathia** here and paid him all that money to win a championship—when is he going to deliver? That burden was gone, and I could just compete for myself and my teammates, free and easy. Even the birth of our fourth child and second son, Carter, fit perfectly into the flow that summer. Amber and I planned it so that she would be induced on the one off-day during a seven-game homestand.

I won 21 games in 2010, the most victories I would ever have in a single season. Personal statistics never meant much to me, but this was an exception: It meant that I had joined the Black Aces, fulfilling the promise Mudcat Grant had seen in me ten years earlier. That's special, being only the fourteenth member of a club that includes Mudcat, Bob Gibson, Ferguson Jenkins, and Dave Stewart. Not that it took the sting off the Texas Rangers knocking us out in the 2010 AL Championship Series.

In 2011 we took a step backward, losing to the Tigers in the Division Series, three games to two. At the end of that season my contract allowed me to opt out and become a free agent again, and all the sportswriters expected me to test the market. But I loved that the Yankees, as a franchise, were all about winning. In New York, more so than in any other city in MLB, the fans and the organization keep the pressure on you to be good no matter what. With the Yankees, there's always a sense of urgency. Even when you're working out in January, you're thinking about pitching good all the time, every game, in June, in October. You fail a lot, but with the Yankees you expect to be great, and New York holds you accountable.

The pinstripes are heavy. We know the players who came before us. Yogi and Whitey and Reggie and Pettitte—you feel that when you put the jersey on. It's a heavy-ass jersey. It's not for everybody. There's been a few guys here I thought could handle it, but they didn't. People talk about being a "true Yankee." I don't know what that is, and it's not for me to judge whether I qualify. I do know I felt the pride and the history every time I buttoned that jersey, and that it's different and better than any-where else in the league.

Besides, we had settled happily into our Alpine house. So when the Yankees offered to basically add two years and $50 million to my deal, it was an easy call. The details didn't get hammered out until a few hours before the deadline, which made things look dramatic. I wanted to be paid what I was worth, but the money was never really an issue. It was adding as many years as possible that mat-tered to me. I never had any real intention of leaving New York. I wanted to end my career as a Yankee.

We knew that 2012 could be our last chance to win a World Series with this core group. Jeter was thirty-eight, A-Rod was thirty-six, Andy was forty, and Mo was forty-two. We took a huge hit in May, when Mo was shagging fly balls during batting practice and tore the ACL in his right knee. He was out for the rest of the year.

Age wasn't my main problem, but my body was breaking down, too. Fans and the sports media are always criticizing athletes for being soft, for not playing hurt. What I've seen is just the opposite. Players and teams are almost always shading the truth in what they say publicly about injuries— they're understating the severity. Players are trying to keep from getting benched, or to protect their contract bargaining position; teams are hiding the degree of damage to maintain the value of a possible trade. Now and then I've seen guys who I thought were being too cautious in coming back from a serious injury. In playing with hundreds of guys over the years, though, I've only ever had one team-mate who actually faked injuries: If we were due to face a pitcher who owned him, this guy suddenly had a sore back or bad cramps in his legs.

Most players have really high pain thresholds and will do anything to stay on the field, whether it's taking painkillers or hours of treatment. Some-times you can't avoid surgery, though. The burgers and the booze pushed my weight over 300 pounds for most of my twenties, and on every pitch I threw my right leg took the full force of that weight. I also landed with the toes of my right foot pointed to the left, across my body, increasing the torque on my knee. The first time I went under the knife was in September 2006, after a season in Cleveland, to repair torn cartilage in my right knee. The same problem flared up again in the middle of 2010, but I was throwing so well that I just kept icing it and taking Toradol on the days I pitched; five days after the Rangers beat us in the playoffs, I had it scoped to repair the meniscus.

In 2012, though, the injuries started to multiply. In June, during a start against the Mets, I felt a pull in the left side of my groin but didn't tell anyone. Two days later, when I was throwing my regular bullpen between starts, the pain got worse, and the Yankees insisted I spend fifteen days on the disabled list, for the first time in my career. I hated it, hated the sitting around, hated not contributing.

I was thirty-one years old at the beginning of the 2012 season, and I must have thrown a million pitches by then, but my arm never bothered me. That changed late in the spring. I started feeling stiffness in my left elbow, but the sensation would come and go. In May, the elbow started swelling up like a water balloon after games. My whole body is normally super limber, but I couldn't touch my left shoulder with my left hand or straighten my arm out completely, there was so much inflammation. In between starts we would crank on it, crank on it—massages, ice, exercises, anything to try to get my left arm as straight as possible. The treatment usually hurt more than when I pitched, even though I was taking Celebrex and Toradol. By July, whenever I snapped off a curveball there would be a sharp pain, like a jolt of electricity. I got an MRI in early August; it didn't show any structural damage, so I made my next start. The results weren't terrible—I went 6⅔ innings, struck out seven, we beat the Tigers. But I couldn't extend my arm all the way; I couldn't finish my pitches. My best fastballs were only 88 miles per hour, when for most of my career I'd been around 95. And my elbow hurt so badly I couldn't sleep. Bad as that pain was, it was nothing compared to the emotional hurt I inflicted at the end of August. I got an early start on a Thursday morning, an off-day for the Yankees. It was warm and our three oldest kids were in our backyard pool, so I joined them. Conveniently, we have a bar about ten feet away from the pool, so I was getting lubricated both inside and out. After an hour or so it was time to go to Lil' C's football practice. My extra-good mood must have made Amber suspicious, because when I said I wanted to drive, she insisted on taking the kids separately, in her car. When we got to practice, I kept my buzz going. I was joking around with people as much as I was watching football. At some point I stood up and began parading Cyia around on my shoulders. My cellphone must have fallen out of my pocket, because Amber spotted it on my chair. Then she saw a bunch of texts I had sent that day to a woman she did not know.

I was loaded, but when I came back I was clear-eyed enough to see that Amber was fuming. We weren't going to have a scene out there in front of the other football parents, so after practice we drove back home, Amber steaming, me knowing I'd fucked up by being drunk at our son's practice. But instead of explaining when we got home—that as bad as it might have looked, there was nothing to those texts but chatter—I walked through our front door and headed straight to the basement to hide. I cracked open a bottle of vodka. By the time Amber was done with the kids, taking baths and getting them to bed, I was passed out on the couch in front of the TV. It was probably about ten o'clock at night by then.

Amber came down to the basement and woke me up. "Get out," she said—quietly, but with knives in her voice.

I sputtered, "What? What?"

"Nah, dude," she said. "You got caught texting another woman. I deal with enough."

I told her it was nothing, that it was just some girl I had met at the stadium. "We were texting about some dope shoes!"

Amber wasn't having it: "Just get out."

I walked out into our driveway. This was bad, and I didn't know what to do. **Maybe I should leave, let things cool off. No, I should go back inside and apologize.** I turned around and tried the doorknob. Amber had locked me out.

Somehow I didn't have my keys to the house, but I did have my car keys. A couple of years before, I had bought a 1972 Olds Cutlass, a drop-top, the car my cousin MeMe had owned when I was a kid, the car I'd always dreamed of owning myself. I'd bought one as soon as I had some money, and I'd had it overhauled Raiders-style: silver paint on the outside, black interior. I got in the Cutlass, lowered the roof, and headed down our hill. It's a twisty road, and there are no streetlights. Just before you reach the stop sign and intersection at the bottom there's one last curve to the left. I turned left, and I guess I kept turning, because I hopped the curb and went smashing through a ten-foot steel fence onto someone's front lawn. The Cutlass didn't stop until we hit a tree.

I sat there for a while in the dark, pissed off, embarrassed, confused. I wasn't hurt, but I'd wrecked my beautiful car, and maybe my marriage. All I could do now was walk back up the hill and finally try to get some real help. It was after midnight, absolutely silent. From the spot where I had crashed to our front door is less than a mile, but it felt like the longest walk I had ever taken.

The door was still locked. When I rang the bell there was no answer. Amber was furious, she had no idea what had happened after I drove away, and I guess she had decided I was going to stay locked out for the night. My Hummer was parked in the driveway. I climbed behind the wheel, but this time, in maybe my first smart move of the whole day, I didn't start the car. I called our driver, Danny, and told him I needed him to come get me. He checked me into a hotel about ten minutes away, in Tenafly.

The calls and texts must have started flying then. Word reached my agent, Amber, and my mom, and their fix-it mode kicked in. Later they told me that a tow truck was called to retrieve the totaled Cutlass before the sun came up and anyone spotted it. The owner of the house where I had crashed was kind enough not to call the police; we paid to repair the fence.

And a few hours after I'd hit the tree I was in the Bronx, at an elementary school, smiling and posing for photos beside Amber, passing out backpacks, because I cared about being there for the foundation. I had a responsibility to those kids to show up. I'd also had a lot of experience in pulling things together quickly. After a few hours of sleep and a shower, I still had a nasty hangover and my eyes were a bit glassy, but I had my public face back on for the kids.

Back home, though, I was exiled to the guest room for the next month. I had known, for a long time, that I was putting an unfair burden on Amber. At some level I understood that my neediness, my anxieties, my fears of failure and of abandonment, came at a heavy cost to her. Out of love she tried everything she could to help me deal. We have been together so long—longer than we haven't been together, in years—that we are each a part of every-thing the other one does. So I understood the stress she was under. I wanted to save our relationship, to straighten things out for her, so we started couples therapy the week after the crash. But I was still in a bad place. I said I'd stop drinking only to get Amber and my mom off my back, but staying sober for somebody else doesn't work. If I could just drink and nobody gave a fuck, I would still drink. It sounds selfish, but I had to want to stop drinking for myself, not for us. I was the one who had to want to change, for me.

My mom had flown in the day after the crash, because she was always part of the cleanup crew when something went wrong with me. Mom was genuinely worried about me—especially that if Amber didn't forgive me this time, I would get myself killed while I was drinking, or drink myself to death. Amber being mad gave me another excuse to drink more, so Mom decided she would keep an eye on me by following the Yankees when we left, two days later, on our next road trip, to Tampa.

The backpacks we gave the Bronx kids included a book called **Today's Superstars: CC Sabathia.** "It's the story of a talented young man," the book says, "whose positive attitude and hard work helped him become one of the most popular baseball players today." All true. It just wasn't anywhere close to the whole story—a story that would need to get worse, even after a car crash, before it could get better.

The time on the DL healed my elbow just enough that I finished strong, going eight innings in each of my final three regular-season starts, giving me 15 wins. I stayed on a roll in the ALDS against the Orioles—on the road in the opener, going 8⅔ innings to get the win, then at Yankee Stadium in game five, closing out the series with a one-run, four-hit, nine-strikeout complete game. Those were probably my two best-ever playoff starts.

Back in September Jeet had bruised his left ankle but kept going; a month later he fouled a ball off his left foot but kept going. Now, in the first game of the ALCS against Detroit, in the top of the twelfth inning, the Tigers had just grabbed a 5–4 lead. Jhonny Peralta hit a roller up the middle and Jeet took about four steps to his left to field the ball, the same way he'd done ten thousand times before. Only this time his left ankle fractured. When Jeet fell, crumpling onto the infield dirt, we instantly knew it was bad, really bad. I have never heard forty-seven thousand people go silent so fast. In the dugout, I was holding back tears.

The price of my two strong starts in the first round, against Baltimore, was that now my elbow was roaring again. My start against Detroit was pushed back until game four, with us down 3–0 in the series and needing a win to stay alive. But I had no command and got rocked for eleven hits and six runs, getting pulled in the fourth inning. With the Tigers sweeping us, Jeter on crutches, and me heading to elbow surgery, it was a miserable ending.

At least I could go to Alabama and have Dr. James Andrews fix my elbow. I didn't know how to repair the relationships that were fraying badly.

Playing pool with MeMe.
He was my hero growing up,
and his sudden death sent me to a dark place.

**15**

ONE OFF-SEASON WE ORGANIZED A TRIP WITH extended family to Costa Rica, probably fifteen of us in one big house. The highlight was going to be a deep-sea fishing trip. I couldn't wait to go fishing, and I wanted to be on my best behavior the whole week. "Babe," I told Amber as we were getting ready to head south, "everyone else is going to be drinking. I don't want to feel weird. So I'm just going to have one beer at dinner." I'm sure she didn't believe me. But I made it through the first dinner with one beer. The next morning, at breakfast, I had a coffee cup, but no food. Amber asked me if I wanted breakfast. "Nah," I told her. "Not hungry. I'm just going to have coffee." It wasn't coffee in the cup.

By the time we got to the beach, I was yelling at her. Amber's brother, Joe, stepped in. Joe is a big dude, six-four, and he was in the Army. I started trying to fight Joe, who probably could have killed me with three moves. "I don't want to do this, CC!" Joe was shouting. "Please get out of my face! I'm not going to let you talk to us like that, and if it's me or you, it's going to be you!"

They wrestled me back into the house—where I started cussing out Amber's mother: "You're ungrateful! We take care of you!" She stormed out, crying.

At that point my mom stepped in. Eventually she calmed me down, got me to sleep it off.

When everybody got back after having a great time fishing, I didn't apologize—I got mad that they'd left me behind. Somehow Amber was able to laugh. "Yeah," she said, "we're not bringing angry CC out on the boat." I had missed the boat, in every way.

We spent some of each winter in California, too, and I made sure to coordinate the trip with a Raiders home game. From when I was five years old my dad would pack us into the car at 2 A.M. for the six-hour drive from Vallejo to the L.A. Coliseum. I wanted to keep the tradition alive, so as soon as I signed my first Indians contract, I bought Raiders season tickets. Even after the Raiders moved back to Oakland we would wake up early, at 4 A.M., so we could be at the parking lot gate when they opened it at six. Our tailgate starts with breakfast burritos. In recent years my little cousin Darnell Jones, who's a chef, has done the cooking. He grills up tons of ribs, chicken, burgers, sausage, and hot dogs, plus he makes beans, greens, and mac and cheese. We invite fifty or sixty people, including baseball friends and former teammates who are Raiders fans, like Matt Garza and Aaron Hicks, and we hook up a TV so we can watch the early NFL games while we eat lunch. I always got jealous when I drove into Yankee Stadium before a big game and saw people tailgating and throwing the baseball around in the parking lot. In Oakland, I can throw the football around and wear my number 52 Raiders jersey, with my name on the back, and some years I'll paint my face silver and black. There is no such thing as a casual Raiders fan.

At the end of 2011, after the Yankees contract extension was done, we were set up to really enjoy our time out west, and things started out good. One December afternoon we were hanging at our house, friends and family coming in and out, watching games on TV, eating and drinking. Plenty of drinking. I don't know how many hours we had been going, or what exactly set it off. But suddenly I was in the backyard, raging at my cousin MeMe. He was a huge, strong guy, too—in addition to playing college ball, MeMe had been drafted by the Raiders and played four years for the Barcelona Dragons of NFL Europe. We had so many good times together over the years; MeMe would come to New York four or five times a season and watch me pitch, and between games we'd spend every minute together. Now here we were face-to-face, inches apart, screaming and cursing, with other people holding us back. The alcohol allowed me to say all the stuff I had been holding back when I was sober, and say it in the meanest possible way. It was me being a drunken asshole, and not knowing how to deal with anger in any kind of productive way. MeMe had been my idol growing up, and we had become even closer as adults. But after that night, I didn't know if we could ever make peace.

We didn't speak for months. A little bit on the phone in February, when I was at spring training. In late May 2012, the Yankees made a West Coast trip, and MeMe and Glo and Nieci came down to Anaheim. That was the first real chance we had to hash things out—the jealousies, the misunderstandings, the hurt feelings. This time we didn't do any drinking, and by the end of a couple of hours we had kind of gotten back to normal. MeMe even came to visit in New York a few months later. We still had a few things to resolve and I was looking forward to seeing him after the season.

Then, in December 2012, ten days before Christmas, we were packing to fly out west when the phone rang. My mom was screaming: "He's gone! He's gone! I can't believe it! We were in the emergency room—" She was in shock, and so was I when it became clear what Mom was talking about. MeMe had played pickup basketball that morning at a court near his house outside of Sacramento, something he'd done a couple of times a week for years. Then he went home, and with no warning, his heart gave out. Forty-six years old. Gone.

I sat down and cried. I was grateful we had mostly patched things up, but losing MeMe added a mountain of sadness on top of all the other grief I kept inside—Dad, Uncle Aaron, Nate. MeMe was my hero when I was a kid; I wanted to grow up to be like him and to have him be proud of me. Now, instead of heading to Vallejo for a Christmas celebration, we were traveling to another funeral.

This one was packed. MeMe had been loved far and wide. The church had to make an announcement that it would be a fire hazard to let anyone else into the service. Aunt Glo, MeMe's mother, asked if I would speak, and I wanted to, for her and for him. I got up and looked out at all those faces, including MeMe's daughter and his three sons. I started to say a few words about my friend, how much he'd meant to all of us, but I couldn't get through it. I was too distraught. Losing my dad, now losing MeMe—it sent me down a dark path. No matter how old you are, you always want a male figure in your life, somebody solid you can lean on. I didn't have that anymore. I felt abandonded.

We had our regular Christmas events in Vallejo, and then Amber, the kids, and I went on to Maui, as we had been planning to do. But it felt like a big part of me had stayed behind, buried with MeMe. It would be years, with a lot more drinking, before I confronted what his death meant to me. When I did, his memory would be part of what saved my life.

Derek Jeter was the first Yankee player to text me when I signed with the team. During the next six seasons we would become close friends.

# 16

FOR A POWER PITCHER, HAVING A LIVE FASTBALL IS as essential as being able to breathe. February 2013 was the first time I had ever arrived at spring training after surgery on my arm, and I was nervous. Was I going to need to become a different kind of pitcher, the type who nibbles around the corners instead of blowing hitters away? I'd been playing catch in a gym in New Jersey for a few weeks. I felt a little stiff, but the pain in my elbow was gone. Still, I was a little fearful when I stepped on the mound for the first time, and I hesitated to really turn it loose. All the tension disappeared as soon as I heard the thwack of the ball in the catcher's glove, though. I had to rebuild some strength. But within a few weeks my fastball velocity was back.

I'd made the All-Star team the past three years, and I was gunning to keep the streak alive while helping the Yankees bounce back into the World Series. I could not have guessed that I was about to head into the roughest three years of my career.

As a big kid, I was always sensitive about how my body looked. I could hoop, but if we were playing shirts and skins at school, I wasn't taking my shirt off—I'd have to be on the shirts or I was out. For years my main motivation for working out wasn't to get into shape to play. It was so I could eat as much as I wanted. When I was drafted, I weighed 255. I went and played in the minors that spring and summer, then came home. I was eighteen and Cleveland had just given me a million dollars—you think I'm gonna work out during the off-season? I weighed 278 when I showed up for spring training, and the Indians were panicking. But I pitched well, and for me mass equaled gas: I had to be heavy to throw hard. Now, though, I was thirty-three years old, and in the past few seasons I had been up to as much as 325 pounds. I knew the weight was bad for my health, especially my knees. So over the winter I went on a no-carb diet, and in two months I dropped thirty pounds and came into camp at 265, the lightest I had been since high school. I felt great; my body was strong. I just couldn't pitch. I was off-balance, falling all over the mound on my follow-through; I couldn't even hold the ball tight enough. A lot of my velocity disappeared with the weight. I couldn't generate the same arm speed. The best thing that happened to me was losing that weight and sucking, because nobody fucked with me about my weight anymore.

I won more games than I lost in 2013, and so did the team. But that was about the most you could say for that season. The lineup went through a lot of turnover, because of age and injury, and on many days it was a patchwork of guys who were unproven or on the downhill side of their careers: Lyle Overbay at first, Eduardo Núñez at short for Jeter, Vernon Wells and Ichiro Suzuki in the outfield, my old buddy Travis Hafner at DH. After a decent start we faded in late June and never recovered, finishing far back in third place, twelve games behind the Red Sox, missing the playoffs for the first time in five years.

There is no patience for losing in the Yankees culture, even if George Steinbrenner is gone, and that's one of the things I love about the organization. So we spent big in the off-season, almost half a billion dollars, bringing in Brian McCann at catcher, Jacoby Ellsbury for center field, and Masahiro Tanaka as a starting pitcher, re-signing Kuroda for the rotation and Carlos Beltrán at DH. It didn't work. For all the great individual players, we never came together as a team, and finished twelve games back again, this time behind the Orioles, and missed the playoffs again, for the second straight year. That hadn't happened in two decades. The starting pitching underperformed, and I was one of the biggest reasons.

I had come back too fast from the elbow surgery the previous year, and my arm never felt right. This spring the pain in my right knee flared up during training camp, but I figured it was manageable, like it had always been. I'd alternate cortisone shots with getting the fluid drained and I'd make it through the season fine, I figured. And I pitched decently for the first few weeks of the 2014 regular season. Then came a home game against Seattle, at the end of April. When I went into my windup, I could barely raise my right leg to my waist. When I landed on it, the pain shot up and I automatically jerked my foot back up off the ground, as if I were barefoot and stepping onto hot charcoal. Two more short starts and my season was over, on May 10. The first losing regular-season record of my career.

I flew down to Alabama to see Dr. Andrews. The good news was that the meniscus tear had not gotten worse. The bad news was the knee joint itself was slowly breaking down. "Degenerative" is the medical term. There was no cure, short of an eventual knee replacement. Oh, the cartilage damage wouldn't be as quick if I stopped playing. But that wasn't going to happen. We tried cortisone and stem cell injections to see if I could get back on the mound, but around July 4, when I tried throwing again, the pain came right back. It killed me to agree to surgery, because it meant missing the rest of the year—and because I had to listen to all the critics saying my contract extension was already a huge mistake by the Yankees. But if I wanted to pitch in 2015, I had no choice.

Sitting and watching as the team struggled felt terrible, worse than the knee injury. On top of that I was missing out on being part of Derek Jeter's final season. Back in February, two days before the start of spring training, he had announced he would be retiring at the end of the 2014 season. Jeet's legs were giving him trouble, too, and at thirty-nine, with five World Series rings, he decided it was time to go. So our season started with the extra goal of sending Jeet out with one more championship. We battled until the last week of the season, when a loss to the Orioles eliminated us from playoff contention. Our final home game of the season, his final day on this infield dirt, was the first time Jeet had ever played a meaningless game at Yankee Stadium. And it still felt like the biggest game ever. A sellout, of course, and a crazy game. We're up three runs going into the ninth inning, but Baltimore scores three to tie it. Jeet had 3,462 hits, five World Series rings, all these highlight reel accomplishments, and now he was coming to the plate in the bottom of the ninth with a shot to win the game? No chance. If you had put that in a movie, I wouldn't have even watched it. But sure enough, Jeet drove in the winning run. I was fresh off knee surgery, I hadn't done any running, and I was the first one out onto the field to congratulate him. Stevie Donohue, our trainer, was looking at me: **What are you doing?**

It wasn't the way we wanted it to end for Jeet, and I felt like I had let him down after all he had done for me and for the Yankees. He and Pettitte were the first ones to reach out to me when I signed as a free agent in 2008. The fact that Jeet was as regular as a guy could be with that level of celebrity was an interesting thing to see up close. You knew Jeet was the biggest thing in New York, but when you were around him, you weren't in awe of him, you didn't admire him, you didn't even really think about it, because of the way he handled it; that's just who he is. Though I did love to go out at night and hang with Jeet, because people would swarm him and leave me the fuck alone. It was awesome.

Jeet saw me drunk more than once, and he'd say, "What the fuck are you doing?" That was about it. It wasn't that he didn't care—I know that he did. It was his style, for better or worse, to treat people as adults and expect them to take responsibility for themselves. He wasn't going to lecture you or hold your hand. My relationship with Andy was very different. Partly because as fellow starting pitchers we naturally spent more time together, but mostly because of his personality. The day after he'd seen me drunk on the plane or in the hotel, Andy would hang back and find some quiet time, maybe when we were in the outfield during batting practice or in the clubhouse grabbing something to eat during the game. "What's up?" he'd say. "What's going on with you?" And he genuinely wanted to know. I'd give him some answer that seemed logical, like I'd had an argument with Amber or I'd pitched bad and was just blowing off steam, but I'm sure he could see my drinking was too regular for that kind of explanation. Eventually I'd talk to him about how I was worried that I didn't really know the reason I was drinking so much, or how I could change. Andy didn't push me to do anything specific—to get therapy or go to church or go cold turkey. Which I appreciated, because I probably would have rejected his suggestion if he had. He knew I'd figure it out on my own schedule.

The car crash got my attention. For years I told myself I wasn't an alcoholic. Alcoholics are people who drink every day, and I could go days without drinking. Hell, I could go weeks if I wanted, and sometimes I did. I could turn the drinking on and off as needed, at least during the season. Or if we had a bad vacation trip one year, I'd make up for it by going dry the next year. An alcoholic? Nah. I had a lot of lines that I used on Amber or Andy and in my own head: **I'm fine. I was only drinking because I was celebrating. It was just a binge.**

After the crash was the first time I was willing to seriously consider that I really was an alcoholic. I remember the first time I said it out loud to Amber. It felt strange, and I still didn't completely believe it. But I was willing to try couples counseling. Amber and I were partners in every way, and she knew me best, so she should be there; plus she had been suggesting we do it for years. Couples therapy, instead of me alone, was also a way I could keep from taking on all the responsibility for my problem.

At least that's how I went into it. The first three sessions were pretty relaxed—us telling the therapist about how we grew up, our family backgrounds, some of the bad scenes that had been caused by my drinking. I was very cooperative, a good patient, I thought. Then the doctor said, "No, this isn't primarily about the two of you. I would like to just see CC by himself. You have some issues that we really need to work out. This goes way deeper than you think. This is addiction. This is alcoholism."

Her words stung me. I knew she was saying it was a disease, but it still felt like I had failed somehow, and it made me defensive. I went to solo appointments for three years, on and off. She prescribed Antabuse, a drug that makes you sick if you drink alcohol. I liked that, because it was medicine—a pill I could swallow and be fixed, rather than fixing myself. The doctor had Amber control the supply of pills, giving them to me on schedule and making sure I took them—but that quickly became weird for both of us, because it sort of put my wife in the role of being my mother. So we switched it to a more neutral person emotionally, a trainer with the Yankees.

Sometimes I took the Antabuse. Sometimes I didn't. Sometimes I flushed the pills down the toilet after making it look like I had taken them. This became part of my larger strategy: I didn't need to stop drinking completely—I just needed to hide it better. So during the season, I would only drink on road trips. I didn't announce this to anyone on the team, of course, and the system worked pretty well for all of 2014, at least in terms of fooling Amber. She thought I had stopped drinking. And I had, mostly—because the knee injury ended my season in the middle of May, I was around home most of the summer, which meant Amber could keep a closer eye on me. So we were getting along great.

That off-season I was working out, rehabbing from the knee surgery, lifting, doing a lunge. My left leg was back, my foot was in a flexed position— and something popped. My left big toe fucking hurt, bad. It wasn't dislocated, but we couldn't figure out what was wrong. A foot doctor put me in a boot, but when I went back after two weeks the pain was even worse. More surgery: This time they removed a sesamoid bone from under the big toe joint. A small thing, you would think, but that turned out to be the worst, most painful surgery to come back from. The incision took forever to heal. Plus I had to wear this big-ass pink thing to try to protect the foot.

In December 2014 our family trip, a dozen people, was to Jamaica. I was still doing rehab after the surgery on my right knee, and my right foot was in a boot from the toe surgery, so I was using one of those scooters to get around Newark Airport. We had gotten everyone up at 4 A.M., and we'd arrived at the airport two hours early, gone through all the hassle with our passports. Somehow we were never notified that it was time to board the plane. When they refused to let us on, claiming we'd arrived too late, Amber and I got mad and started yelling. The airline called the cops, and the whole stupid thing ended up in the papers.

We went back to Newark the next day and finally made it to Jamaica. The bad joke was that this was one mess where I wasn't even drinking. Maybe it was a sign of the trouble ahead. I would soon turn thirty-five, which is getting old for a pitcher, and I was heading into the new season on two sore legs, with a drinking problem I needed to correct—and a growing fear that I didn't know how.

Throwing the cutter, the pitch that extended
my career on the mound after
I saved my life off the field.

**17**

EVERY PITCHER TINKERS. YOU HAVE YOUR BASIC grips and your go-to pitches; for me, for the first fourteen years of my career, it was pretty simple—four-seam fastball, slider, changeup. But you never know exactly what's going to work from day to day, or even from inning to inning. You go out there and the ball feels heavier in your hand. Or it's hot and you're sweating a lot and you can't get the feel of the seam in order to make the slider break sharply enough. You lose the feel for a pitch all the time. My change or cutter would be there for two weeks, and then it'd be gone. When that happens, trying to change your grip doesn't work—you get away from what you're trying to do. You just have to throw the pitch a lot more. You can usually try to correct it playing catch. It's all about a feeling, the way the ball comes out of your hand. So you are always experimenting in the bull-pen, or when you're playing catch in the outfield, fooling around with your fingers in different positions, trying to make the ball move in ways that will be harder to hit.

The way I came up, starters were expected to go seven or more innings, which meant you were going to face individual hitters three or four times in a game. For a long time I could overpower them no matter how many times they'd seen me that day, but it was always good to have an extra wrinkle available. Pitchers are mad scientists that way.

Back in July 2005, when I was with the Indians, I was going through a stretch where I was having a tough time getting out lefties. We were in Oakland and I had gotten destroyed, one of the worst starts of my career until then: eight hits and eight earned runs in just over two innings. Carl Willis, our pitching coach, said, "Man, we've got to teach you a cutter—something that looks like a fastball but that breaks in on righties and away from lefties." He suggested the cutter because that's a pitch you throw hard, like a fastball, and I wouldn't have to think about slowing down my arm and trying to make the ball break, the way you need to do to throw a slider. So two days later we went out to the visitors' bullpen. "I'm gonna give you the grip, and I want you to throw the shit out of it," Carl said. "Throw it as hard as you can." We worked on it for maybe a half hour, and pretty much right away it was working really good. Here's the funny thing, though. Carl was teaching me a cutter; I was throwing it like a cutter. But instead of running in at 95 and breaking tight over the plate, the way a cutter does, the ball was slicing like a slider, a really good 83-mile-an-hour slider. For years, though, I called it and thought of it as a cutter, to keep the same mentality of how I was throwing it. If I had started calling it a slider, my mind would have gotten in the way—I would have tried to throw it differently, like a true slider, and that would have messed up the pitch. People give these pitches names just to be able to communicate. But it's really all about what you can make the ball do.

My next start was in Seattle. Bottom of the fourth inning, we were up 2–0, and Ichiro was leading off. He was a great hitter, so he was always a very tough out, and he was a lefty—a perfect situation to break out my new toy. **I'll fool him with a pitch he's not expecting,** I thought. The count was 2–1. I flipped the cutter, but it didn't really break; it just kind of drifted across the middle of the plate. Ichiro hit it over the right field fence.

Okay, so I hadn't executed the pitch properly. That was no reason to give up on it. And I've always been stubborn, so I was going to show I could do it right. Bottom of the sixth inning, game was tied 2–2, Ichiro leading off again. Cutter. Home run. We ended up losing, 3–2.

Three years later, in Milwaukee, the same thing had happened when I tried a new pitch. My very first bullpen with the Brewers, the pitching coach, Mike Maddux, said, "Hey, what do you think about throwing a two-seamer? You're in the National League now; it could help you get some ground balls." Why not? I threw eight or ten in the bullpen and the ball felt good coming out of my hand right away, and I was getting really good downward break. A few weeks later, against Houston, we were up 6–1 in the top of the sixth. The Astros' left fielder, Ty Wigginton, was hitting, and our catcher, Jason Kendall, called for the two-seamer, the first one I had ever thrown in a big-league game. Wigginton hit it off the center field scoreboard.

Maybe giving up home runs the first time I threw each new pitch was a good sign, because the cutter and the two-seamer became two of my most important weapons. Throwing more cutters was a big reason that everything finally came together for me as a young pitcher at the end of 2005. I won nine of my eleven starts down the stretch after getting beaten by the Mariners on Ichiro's second homer. In 2008, when I was piling up all those innings in the final month's push with the Brewers, the two-seamer was exactly what I needed. Hitters thought they knew what to expect, and the two-seamer kept them guessing and a little more off-balance.

Over the years I learned as much about pitching from talking to hitters as I did from talking to other pitchers. Eddie Murray was a Hall of Fame switch-hitter, mostly with the Orioles, and when he retired he became a hitting coach with the Indians for three-plus seasons. We would sit and talk about hitting for hours during games, or all day if we weren't playing. Eddie had hundreds of pitch sequences in his head—what series of pitches a certain pitcher had thrown in certain situations in games going back years. He understood the psychology of hitters and how it changed with the flow of a game, and he could spot mechanical mistakes I was making. Even when I went to New York he'd come to Yankee Stadium and sit next to the visitors' dugout and give me signals to make corrections.

A-Rod was also brilliant at analyzing hitters. His baseball IQ is off the charts. Where Eddie generalized things, A-Rod could tell you specifically how to get guys out. In 2009, in the ALCS, I was concerned about facing Bobby Abreu. A-Rod walked over to me from third base and said, "Pitch him backward. Throw him sliders early, heaters late." Abreu came up against me six times in that series. I struck him out four times and allowed no hits.

But you also had to be careful not to be too generous with information when you talked with hitters. Raúl Ibañez is a great guy, and hugely knowledgeable about the game. We were teammates for one year in New York, the 2012 season, and Raúl went out of his way to sit with me in the dugout during games and ask me how I would pitch to guys on the opposing team. About halfway through the season I realized that what Raúl was really doing was stockpiling information on how I would try to attack him if we ever faced each other in a game again. Which we did, the next season when he played for the Mariners. The clever son-of-a-bitch went two-for-three and hit a two-run homer off me.

In Milwaukee, when I added the two-seamer it was a bonus. Same with the cutter in Cleveland. I added them during seasons when I was still young and strong and dominant. Those pitches helped, but I never used either of them more than a quarter of the time; I still lived and thrived with my four-seam fastball. In those years the cutter and the two-seamer were options, extras. But between the knee surgery and the foot surgery, I was all fucked up, and I came back too soon in 2015. Especially after missing most of 2014, I just hated the idea of starting the season on the disabled list. But I pitched shitty, losing my first five decisions of 2015 and giving up buckets of hits and runs. Most days my four-seamer was barely averaging 90, which will get you killed by big-league hitters. I was used to starting seasons slowly, so I figured the velocity would come back by the summer. When it didn't, that was alarming, and I didn't have a consistent curve or changeup to keep hitters off the fastball. Nothing worked. I didn't know what the fuck to do.

The Yankees' pitching coach, Larry Rothschild, had been working on me for a while about adding a true cutter, not the slider that I called a cutter. "If you want to stay in the big leagues, you need to learn this pitch," Larry said. "You need to buy into it. But you can do it. Otherwise, the way you're going, you're going to be out." I listened to Larry, I understood what he was saying—I just didn't want to hear it. I'm stubborn.

In late June 2015, we played a series in Houston. Andy lives down there. I hadn't seen him in a long time, but he came to a game and we went out to the bullpen. "I need you to teach me the cutter," I said, and I meant it: I needed his help, and Andy is someone who I have always trusted completely. Both Andy and Mo were the rare athletes who could perform at an extremely high level and also explain how to do it. I always learned better by watching, though, especially by watching right-handed pitchers—I could stand alongside them on the mound and mirror their delivery exactly. Instead of having them say, "The ball needs to come out of your hand this way, at this arm angle," and all that analytics bullshit, I wanted them to just show me, and then I could do it.

Over the years Mo had shown me his cutter grip: middle and index fingers sewn together and fingertips extending just past the seams, across the horseshoe of the ball. Andy taught me the delivery. In my head, the arm action was the same as if I was throwing a football—your hand is closer to your ear, and you keep your arm more cocked, instead of extending it completely. Andy would talk about trying to slice the ball in half as you let it go; for me, that's just like throwing a football.

I'd had a great relationship with Brian McCann, our catcher, ever since he came to the Yankees for the 2014 season. We'd talk and talk between starts, spend extra time working in the bullpen. Poor Mac—he was racking his brain during the 2015 season, trying everything to help me. He moved me from standing on the left side of the rubber to the right, then to the center. He was hunting down videos of similar pitchers; he was showing me videos comparing my good and bad starts. At one point we tried throwing a comeback two-seamer, which is supposed to break left to right across the plate, almost like an old-fashioned screwball. Didn't work. I was out on the mound making up shit during games. I felt bad for Mac.

I felt scared for me. I was in the fourth year of a guaranteed five-year contract extension, but the way I was pitching, the Yankees would have found a way to trade me or cut me loose over the winter, eating the money rather than having me drag the team down. As I pitched badly, I drank more, and even though I knew the drinking was making things worse, both with Amber and on the mound, the only way out seemed to be alcohol rehab. But if I went to rehab after having a terrible season, that would guarantee that I'd be out of a job. Nobody would want an old, losing pitcher who had just come out of the drunk tank. The end was coming up faster and uglier than I could have ever imagined it. I felt trapped.

In July 2015, for my thirty-fifth birthday, we threw a Coachella-themed party at our house, and I managed to get through that without drinking. The next day Amber was unwrapping the gifts people had brought for us, and she opened up a box to find a bottle of Johnnie Walker Blue. Then another. Then another. Dellin Betances was one of my best friends on the team, so Amber called his wife, Janisa, and asked why they'd gotten me the bottle of Johnnie Walker Blue. "Oh, Dellin said that's what CC brings on the plane," Janisa told her.

The therapist had repeatedly suggested I should go to alcohol rehab. Now she was insisting. I wouldn't. **No way. Maybe after I retire. Okay, fine, after I retire, I'll go to rehab.** But I wasn't willing to do it while I was playing, because it would end my career. Guys would look at me as weak. I would feel like I was letting them down. I wouldn't pitch as well with people knowing I was an alcoholic. If I went to rehab, the Yankees would look at me as damaged goods and find a way to cut me loose. No way.

By August both my career as a Yankee and the Yankees' season were increasingly on the line. We were in first place in the AL East, but our lead over the Blue Jays had started to shrink. I pulled out two of my best games of the year, going six innings and giving up one run as we beat the Red Sox. Then we went to Cleveland, which always gave me a jolt of adrenaline. We lost, 2–1, and went from a half-game up to a half-game behind. But I had gone six solid innings again. I left town feeling a strange mix of vulnerability and hope—maybe things might be turning around, at least enough for me to finish the season strong.

The next stop on our road trip was Toronto. I've always loved Toronto—the mix of people from around the world, the food, the nightlife. After our first game against the Jays I headed back to the hotel and tore my way through the minibar. Then Dee and I went to a downtown club, with Dellin Betances and a couple of other guys. A friend of one of my teammates had hooked us up with some spot, and they showed us straight to a table in the VIP section. I ordered bottles of Hennessy, champagne, Grey Goose. Destroyed those and ordered more. Just chilling, hanging out. A pretty normal night for me. Which included getting mad at Dee. The mood I was in, the way I was drinking, he'd seen it plenty of times before and knew where things were going. So he wasn't drinking himself, in order to be our unofficial security.

Dee is four years older than me, and he hadn't been as lucky with his mistakes—when he was twenty he got busted for possessing and selling drugs and spent five years in prison, mostly in Folsom. When he came out Dee was determined to make the most of his second chance, and to find a better way. He was still a lot of fun, but I appreciated—needed— his soulfulness and maturity. So in Toronto, Dee was being responsible, as usual, but I was drunk, and his reserved attitude was pissing me off: "You need to be having a good time! Stop standing over there by yourself!"

After two or three hours, Dee decided we should leave. I ignored him and put away a couple more rounds, but it was about 3 A.M., and I needed to be at the ballpark in roughly seven hours for our game, so I finally agreed to go. We were walking toward the front door of the club and some guy said . . . well, I don't know what he said, but it was something smartass. I wheeled on him and started shouting that he should shut the fuck up. Dee got between us and started pushing me toward the door. But by that point I was amped up, and this dude was still talking. Then one of his friends started pointing at me and yelling, "Let's go Yankees," but sarcastically.

I snapped. I charged the second guy, taunting him, daring him to hit me. The guy was a lot smaller than me, but he wasn't backing down—maybe because what looked like twenty of his friends, big guys in hockey jerseys, suddenly surrounded us. The situation had gone from zero to 100 in a second. Dee was yelling, "We got to get you out of here!" but I was fighting him so I could get to the other guys and fight them. "Dude, we're not going to win this fight!" he shouted. "These guys don't care!"

I didn't care, either. I was cursing and shoving. We were out in the street at that point, outside the club, and it was mayhem. One of my shoes, a big red Jordan high-top, was gone. Dee's cousin, who was with us, was challenging some of the Canadian guys, trying to deflect them away from me, while Dee somehow stopped a taxi and started forcing me into the backseat. Dee got the door closed and was still standing on the street, telling the driver to go to the hotel, when the Canadian dudes surrounded the cab. One of them jumped on the hood and started pounding. They were trying to pull the doors open. Dee was yelling at the driver, "Drive! Drive! Drive!"

The cabbie was panicked. He pointed at the guy on the hood and screamed, "I can't!"

"Drive or you'll get us killed out here!"

I don't know whether the Canadian guy climbed off or fell off, but we started moving forward. At the end of the block, for some reason, we stopped—and I got back out and started barreling back toward the Canadian guys, wearing one shoe, drunk out of my mind, and raging.

Dee intercepted me: "No, man, it's not worth it, C, it's not worth it." I hauled off and punched Dee in the nose. He was bleeding, but somehow he kept cool, even as I was cussing him out worse than I ever had before. "C, come on, man, this is getting ridiculous," Dee said, still trying to talk me down, trying to push me back toward the cab. "You want to fight me? We can fight anywhere, just not here! You got to get back in this cab."

This time Dee got in with me, to make sure I didn't escape again. I was ripping him a new asshole, calling him every bad name I've heard in my life. Dee just said, "Dude, you tripping! You almost got us killed back there, dog!"

I yelled back, "I don't care! I don't care! Fuck that!"

"You got to care!" Dee said. "We got families at home! I got a newborn! You have to care!"

"I don't give a fuck about your newborn!"

And I didn't, not then or any other night I was drunk. I didn't care about Dee, his kids, my kids, Amber, or myself. All that mattered was the anger and letting it flow.

I had somehow gotten my sneaker back, but we were still a mess when we got back to the hotel, with Dee's nose bleeding and me still furious. Dee wanted to keep an eye on me, but I kicked him out of the room. The hotel, being efficient, had refilled the minibar, so I got to work again.

A few hours later Dee, who had held on to the extra key to my room because he was worried, found me on the bathroom floor as the sun was coming up. "This is really bad," he said.

Fuck, I knew that. So what? I'd had plenty of bad nights before, and by the next morning I'd slept it off and forgotten most of what happened, gone to the ballpark, and dried out in time for my next start. I didn't have to pitch for a few more days, so this didn't matter. I bent over and puked. Again, nothing new. I cussed at Dee some more and told him to get me some fucking wine out of the mini-bar. It was around 5 A.M.

"No, man, this is really bad," Dee said. "This is serious. This time we got caught acting the fool. They got us on camera."

At that moment I didn't comprehend what he was saying. I was still drunk and combative: "Fuck that shit. I don't care!" It wasn't until I got to the stadium and my head had cleared some that I understood why this night had been different.

When I'd gotten to the big leagues, back in 2001, almost nobody had a cellphone. And somehow I had regularly been drunk and belligerent, often in public places, for the next fourteen years without someone getting it on video. But my luck ran out that night in Toronto. Someone had sent TMZ, the celebrity news site, cellphone footage of the street brawl.

At the stadium I went in and told Girardi about it, hoping he'd hear about it from me first. Then I had to answer questions from the Yankees beat writers. I didn't hide. I stood in front of my locker and told the reporters the truth: I shouldn't have lost my temper, and it was going to be hard to explain to Lil' C. At home I had done a pretty good job of hiding my drinking from our kids, but Lil' C was twelve now, and there was no way to keep him from going online and seeing his dad acting stupid. What I didn't tell them was that I had no idea how

I was going to stop drinking, and no real intention of stopping.

The thing I did still care about deeply was pitching well, but that was quickly slipping away. My first start after the Toronto brawl was okay—six and two-thirds inconsistent innings in a game we won against Minnesota. My next time on the mound was a disaster. I wanted so much to pitch well that day, not just because we were battling for a playoff spot but because before the game the Yankees held a ceremony to retire Andy Pettitte's number, 46. My friend and mentor, a guy I looked up to. In the clubhouse before the game Andy hugged me, said he knew I was going through a rough stretch but that he also knew I'd get out of it. Instead I had nothing on the ball, walked four guys in 2⅔ innings, and gave up a two-run homer. Probably the best pitch I threw was a 91-mile-an-hour fastball to strike out Yan Gomes, but that was my last pitch that day. When I landed, my right knee, the one that surgery was supposed to have fixed a year earlier, felt like it had been soaked in gasoline and set on fire. An MRI showed pretty much what we already knew: The surgery had cleaned up some of the cartilage, but the knee was continuing to deteriorate.

This time the Yankees didn't just skip one of my turns in the rotation; they put me on the fifteen-day disabled list. I couldn't even get mad. We were sinking in the standings, trying to hold off the

Rangers for a wild-card spot. Maybe rest and treatment would allow my knee to calm down enough for me to make a few big starts down the stretch. As soon as my knee felt a little better, I went to the bullpen and started tinkering, trying to find a pitch that could get me through September, help get us to the playoffs, and maybe prop up my chances of pitching in 2016.

Every summer Amber and I picked a couple of road trips where we could bring the whole family along. One of those rolled around now. Even though I wouldn't be pitching, Amber and the kids came along for the weekend in Atlanta. The team hotel didn't have a pool, so we got a nice big suite at the St. Regis; our kids can't live without a pool in the summer. The suite also came with a balcony, and on Friday I went out there to smoke a blunt, wearing a Cavs LeBron jersey, Cavs shorts, and Minion slippers, from **Despicable Me**. It made for a pretty funny photo—except for the fact that we weren't the ones who took it.

On Saturday morning, the kids were splashing around in the pool and Amber and I were lounging in beach chairs when she got an email from our publicist: Someone was shopping a photo, saying it showed me standing out on the balcony the night before, doing something I wasn't supposed to be doing. They were going to sell the photo to one of the New York papers—unless we bought it first.

Amber immediately went into fix-it mode.

She's always been a strategic thinker, and living in New York, she had quickly learned how to play the media game. "If we buy it, they think we're gonna bury it," she said, "and one of the papers is still going to get it somehow." She stopped and thought for a moment. Finally she said, "So why don't we just post it ourselves? That way we get ahead of the story, and if the papers run it, they'll have to credit C's Instagram account and our caption saying it's just a cigar." Which was really clever, and so that's what we did. I argued that I shouldn't lie—that I should admit I'd been smoking a blunt. And if you read between the lines of the caption we posted, I basically did admit it. But coming out and saying it to reporters directly probably would have gotten me suspended by MLB, so everyone talked me out of it.

I had seen Jeter, A-Rod, and lots of my other famous friends deal with the paparazzi for years. But until now I hadn't been on the receiving end of it. Between what had happened in Toronto and now in Atlanta, I was making myself a target—that person everyone wants to catch on video doing something wrong. Sure, I had been a public figure, an easily recognizable one, for years. And I had brought the negative attention on myself: Nobody had told me to fight in the street in Toronto. Nobody had made me go out onto that balcony in Atlanta. But it was still super creepy to realize that when I was away from the stadium people were out there watching me and taking pictures, waiting for me to mess up.

In late September we made another trip to Toronto. I stayed away from the clubs this time, but trouble still found me. I got a text from my agent: Thanks to the photo on the Atlanta balcony, Major League Baseball wanted to schedule me for a drug test, for marijuana.

Now, I had been smoking weed on and off since I was a teenager, first at parties. Where we grew up—not just Vallejo but the whole state of California—it was no big deal. Smoking took the edge off and helped me be more social. Later, it seemed hypocritical that baseball would happily shoot you full of cortisone to keep you on the field, but I couldn't smoke a joint when my knee hurt? And it had become part of my strategy to cut down on booze: If I smoked weed, I didn't need to drink. I never smoked and drank at the same time—that would have gotten me too fucked up. But now it looked as if baseball was going to take the weed away from me. I was mad.

Things were spiraling down, both on and off the field. I felt like the walls were closing in. If Andy Pettitte hadn't told me how close I was to figuring out a new way to pitch, I probably would have quit. I am terrible about returning texts and phone calls—everyone gives me shit about it, and it's become a good running joke with people like Jeet. But in June, when Andy texted saying, "Hey, pick up the phone," I got back to him pretty quick. Andy was the Yankees teammate I had always trusted when I had trouble, someone I could talk to about baseball or drinking or family or anything else. He was also the one who had first started teaching me the cutter. When I was frustrated in 2015, it was Andy I talked to the most, and he kept saying that it was just a matter of getting used to the pitch, that he kept seeing flashes of me throwing great cutters, and that he was confident that I was going to put it all together.

"The tired old lefty"—that's what Andy called himself. His confidence was crucial, because mine was eroding. I couldn't throw the cutter consistently because my knee hurt so badly that I couldn't land properly. In 2014 I had tried wearing a brace, because Carlos Beltrán encouraged me to do it. His knee was probably even worse than mine, and wearing a brace enabled him to play nearly every day. A guy like Beltrán, a veteran who seemed to be on his way to the Hall of Fame, tells you to do something, you should listen. So I had one made, the same style as 'Los's, but it felt awkward. Plus, I stubbornly thought, **I don't need a stupid piece of equipment! I'm gonna tough this out.** So I was in pain every time I landed, and I never fully committed to the cutter.

The lack of commitment was as much mental as physical, though, and probably even more so. I knew, objectively, that it was getting late in my career and that I was struggling, and that my body was breaking down. But changing the way I pitched meant surrendering a part of myself, saying good-bye to what had gotten me here: the power, the domination, the big fastball. It meant acknowledging I was getting old. That I was mortal. That I was never going to be twenty-two years old again and throw 95, blowing the ball past everybody.

Everything in my life felt uncertain, in limbo. I was going back and forth between drinking and not drinking. I was throwing the cutter for a couple of innings, then giving up on it for whole games. In late June I started against the Phillies, and I came out throwing the cutter and I was cutting their ass up for the first three innings. The fourth inning I said, **Fuck it, I'm going back to my old shit.** And bang—I gave up five runs in one inning.

I spent the next four days thinking, **What the fuck am I doing?** I needed something to stabilize me. I needed to commit to something again, to ride or die with it. After a terrible start against the Indians in late August, when I couldn't make it out of the third inning, the Yankees put me on the fifteen-day disabled list again. I tried not to read the papers or listen to sports radio during the season, but you'd hear things—your friends would tell you what was being said, or you'd see something on your phone and couldn't avoid taking it in. And the way Girardi told reporters I was going on the DL, it sounded as if he thought I was never coming back. That I was done for the year. Maybe for good.

That hurt, and it pissed me off. I gave in, out of desperation: **Fuck it. I'm wearing the knee brace. I'm throwing the cutter. This is who I am now. I'm a sinker-cutter kind of guy now. If I can't do this, then I'm out of the game.** What I was also realizing was that it wasn't really about grips or pitch selection—it was as much about attitude and confidence. Transitioning to not throwing as hard, I still needed to have the same mentality. I wasn't throwing 97 and 98 anymore, but I was still me on the fucking mound. I'd still fight you.

The results weren't great right away—that first game back from the DL, against the Orioles, I didn't make it past the fifth inning, but I threw the cutter for twelve out of my eighty-five pitches, more than I ever had in a game, and I got five strikeouts. Eleven days later, against the Mets, came a breakthrough: I racked up seven strikeouts and my first win in two months. On October 1, with just three days left in the season, we could clinch a wild-card spot and mathematically eliminate the Twins and the Angels. I got the start, against the Red Sox, and the chance at redeeming my season.

I pitched. I didn't just throw, as I had on many nights for fourteen years. I moved the ball in and out, up and down, in the strike zone. The Red Sox had runners on in every inning, but it was a walk here, a single there—I was keeping them from making really solid contact. I used my new toy, the cutter, more than I ever had. In the second, Beltrán hit a homer and Brendan Ryan singled in a run, so I had a 2–0 lead. My only serious trouble came in the fifth, when Boston strung together three singles and scored one run. But I got Jackie Bradley Jr. on a weak grounder for the second out and then intentionally walked Xander Bogaerts to load the bases and face Travis Shaw, a lefty hitter. Adam Warren was warming up in the bullpen; Girardi was on the top step of the dugout, ready to pull me. This was the game for me. With two balls and one strike, I threw a slider that stayed a little too much out over the plate, and Shaw drove it high and deep to center. I sucked in all my breath and turned to watch Brett Gardner. He was cruising back easily, to about ten feet in front of the warning track, where he made the catch. I exhaled and exploded as I charged off the mound: "Fuck, yeah!" Compared to where I'd been all season, I was lights out in September. Pitching was fun again.

I watched the rest of the game from the dugout as we added two runs and my little brother Dellin Betances came on in the ninth to close it out. We were going to the playoffs again. I had shown the Yankees I could still get big outs, and salvaged my spot on the team for the next season. I'd gone to the cutter out of desperation and had started to reinvent myself—on the mound, anyway. In the clubhouse celebration, I sprayed a ton of champagne on other guys, but I drank nothing. Once we got on the bus to the airport, though, somebody handed me a bottle of white Hennessy, and I finished it before we got to the plane. I drank on the plane to Baltimore; I drank on the bus from the airport to the hotel. That was all just a warm-up for the damage I would do inside my room, where no one could see me and I could really let loose.

Maybe what fueled my drinking marathon this time was relief that I had made it to the end of the season and ended it on a high note. Maybe it was me trying to wash away all the tension that had built up over the past six months. But two days into my Baltimore blowout someone sent Amber a new photo. This time the sender was trying to help me. It was a picture of me passed out on the couch in the locker room, with a note saying I had come to the ballpark all messed up, that I was slurring my words and talking crazy to people, and they were worried that it was going to be obvious to reporters. They asked Amber how to stop my binge. It wasn't that Amber didn't care—she always cared, so much that it hurt. It wasn't that she'd given up, not exactly. But she had tried everything, and nothing had gotten through to me. Amber had run out of ideas. I would need to bottom out, and hope no one got hurt on my way down, if I was ever going to change my life off the field.

Drunk inside of the Camden Yards storage

room—that was when I hit bottom, finally. As fucked up as I was, the realization that I was too drunk to throw my normal bullpen—that I couldn't do my job, that the drinking was keeping me from picking up the ball and throwing it, the thing that had changed my life and given my family every-thing good—hit me, and somehow this time the mix of sadness and fear and exhaustion got me off the concrete. Chad Bohling, our mental skills coach, spotted me and said, "Bro, what are you doing?" I think I started crying, and I told him, "Man, the drinking has gotten to be too much."

Chad went and grabbed outfielder Chris Young, a player I was close to. I staggered into the locker room, and the two of us sat down. "Man, I think I need to go to rehab," I told him.

C.Y. knew I drank too much, but he was like, "What do you mean?"

I said, "Man, because I've just been drinking the whole weekend. I think I need to go get help."

C.Y. told me, "This is a decision that you need to make for your life. We'll be fine. We're your boys, we're going to be here, but if you feel like you need to go, then go."

My whole life I had only made baseball decisions, not life decisions. Everything had always been about baseball and what was best for the team. When I was seventeen and my grandmother died and my family needed the money? **Forget college, I'm signing with the Indians.** My knee is fucked up but the team needs me? **I'm pitching.** This time I made a life decision.

This time was different because I was older, and I knew that my physical gifts couldn't cover for my recklessness anymore. It was different because Amber had run out of patience, and was running out of hope that I would ever really change. Something precious was slipping away, and not simply the career I had worked so hard to build for twenty years, but maybe the last chance to deal with the emotional pain and make myself whole. To save my life.

I walked into Joe's office.

I didn't want to hear about waiting until after the playoffs, checking myself in quietly during the off-season when no one would notice. I was going to rehab now. I didn't give a shit who knew. I didn't want to live this way anymore. If I didn't change, I was going to die.

My dad, the A's, and a Big Wheel.
What else could a kid want?

# 18

ROLLED INTO REHAB HAMMERED. THAT WAS probably a good thing: It cut down on any last-minute resistance. If I had arrived sober, I probably would have freaked at the reality of being confined for a month and forced to dive deep into my emotions. It was by no means a conscious strategy, though. It was only a continuation of my Baltimore binge.

Just because I had walked into Joe Girardi's office in Baltimore and said I realized I needed to go to alcohol rehab didn't mean I slowed down. As soon as I left Joe's office I went and got another bottle. If these were going to be my last hours of drinking, I was going to make the most of it. I bought a bottle of Hennessy for the ride. Amber had called Mike, our driver, and insisted that he drive me straight from the hotel to our house—no stopping! She knew me too well. I went to work on Mike right away: "Man, I'm going to rehab, this is my last time, I'm never drinking again. You got to stop!" We had barely made it out of Delaware before I threatened to fire Mike if he didn't exit right away and find us a liquor store so I could refuel. We stopped. I slumped in the backseat, draining more cognac. You know that scene in **A Star Is Born** where Bradley Cooper leaves the concert and makes his driver find a bar? That was basically me, but I didn't run into Lady Gaga off the New Jersey Turnpike.

By the time we got back to Alpine my spot in rehab had already been booked. Amber knew that if I was ever going to go, we needed to take advantage of the momentum and do it now, or I'd start backing away from the decision and keep drinking. The only debate that was going on, with Amber and our publicist and the Yankees, was how to get me checked into a rehab facility without the media finding out where it was. Which seemed kind of pointless, because there was already a circus outside our house: TV trucks with satellite antennas lined the street by the gate to our driveway, trying to catch a shot of me or Amber. Reporters even followed our kids to school Monday morning, which pissed me off.

But as fucked up as I was after a solid three days of drinking, I was clear enough on one thing: I knew I didn't want to hide anymore. If this was going to work, I **couldn't** hide anymore. I was tired of hiding and tired of pretending that I wasn't an alcoholic and that I wasn't drinking all the time. If I had started rehab by sneaking in, it would have been starting off trying to get better by lying again. Lying was the addiction, as much as drinking. I knew that going into rehab: I was more tired of lying than I was of drinking. To me, lying was **the** problem; it was more exhausting than being drunk. So covering up going to rehab would have solved nothing, and it would have given me an out in my head: **Nobody knows I went to rehab, so if I start drinking again, it doesn't really count as me failing.** Besides, if we tried to hide and the media found out where I was, there would be cameras up at the rehab facility, and everything would have gone crazy. I wasn't ashamed of people knowing I was an alcoholic or of admitting I needed help. I was scared of continuing to be an alcoholic and not knowing how to get help.

My therapist recommended a place called Silver Hill, in Connecticut. She thought they did good work, and they had plenty of experience dealing with famous people. Mariah Carey, Nick Nolte, and Jon Hamm had all gone through the Silver Hill program, though I didn't know any of that at the time. As we climbed the winding, hilly driveway in the woods, the stone buildings that came into view looked like the campus of a small college. I didn't know what I was getting into, and I was nervous walking through the front door. As I sat and answered what seemed like hours of medical history questions and filled out endless paperwork, my head started to pound with the beginnings of a hangover—the perfect condition for entering the detox unit. I don't know how long it took me to sober up. But there was one moment of clarity in those first few hours, a procedure that snapped me to attention: when they took away my shoelaces and my belt. Did they think I would try to kill myself? Did other patients try to kill themselves?

The booze was mostly out of my system by the second day, but they had given me some kind of meds and I was drowsy and relaxed. Then things got super strange. When I was admitted, they asked if I wanted to use an alias, to protect my privacy, and so the staff was calling me by a fake name. But as I walked from the dorm building to the cafeteria, the other patients turned and looked: **We know who that is.** If anyone was still fooled, they weren't that night, when a group of us gathered in the lounge. On the TV was the American League Wild Card Game, the Yankees versus the Astros. And here I was sitting in rehab, watching my teammates, the guys I had been in uniform with just two days before. It was super weird. But I could see even more clearly than if I had been in the dugout that the home plate umpire was squeezing Tanaka. We ended up losing, 3–0, ending our season. I didn't feel helpless, exactly. But I wished I was still there, in the clubhouse, with my boys, saying goodbye for the off-season, instead of sitting with a bunch of strangers in the middle of nowhere, fidgeting and wondering if rehab would really work or not.

Giving me an alias was kind of silly, but the purpose behind it was worthwhile: to protect my privacy, but even more to encourage the idea that in rehab we were all the same. We were all there to work on a problem we couldn't control. Whatever our roles in the outside world, we all had some kind of hurt we didn't understand that was messing up our lives.

Everyone's rock bottom was different, but no one's hurt was better or worse than anyone else's. Everybody's got shit in their lives. You could be the richest person on the planet and still be fucked up and still need to come to rehab. Everybody's on the same level in there. I liked that concept, and I thought it would help me open up and talk about my drinking. We were equals in our addiction. So for the first time since I had been in the low minor leagues, I had a roommate who was not a friend or relative. He was a dude in his late fifties; I'll call him Frank. He was basically a nice guy, though at night he snored really loud. That wasn't the real problem, though. The first night we told each other a little bit about ourselves. Frank was addicted to both alcohol and pain pills. He'd been arrested and a court had ordered him into rehab. Something about that unnerved me. Not that I was afraid of Frank. I knew I was messed up, and I knew I needed to be here, but I was telling myself that I was doing rehab for the right reasons, for positive reasons. Talking to Frank didn't make me feel guilty about my addiction. But hearing how he'd come to rehab made it feel like I had done something bad and we were in jail. My anxieties started kicking back in big-time. After two nights I told my counselor I needed a private room.

The timing was good, in a way, because after the first couple of days in the detox unit, they said the alcohol was finally completely out of my system and I was ready to move to one of the group residential units, called Scavetta House. Many of the other patients in the house seemed to have troubles beyond drinking—depression, bipolar conditions. In some ways I felt relieved to think my problem was simpler— but it also made me worried that maybe my drinking was caused by another illness I didn't know about yet.

The days at Silver Hill were highly scheduled. There were group sessions in the mornings, and individual meetings with your doctor and your therapist in the afternoons. During one of my first conversations with Tom, my therapist, I told him I was already feeling much better. Tom said he was glad to hear that, but then he said something that I would hear again and again, in different versions from different people, for the next month. "You may feel like you could go out and pitch a game tomorrow," he said. "But in fact, if you do that, you're at extremely high likelihood of relapsing. Getting serious about your sobriety means accepting that you have a lifelong vulnerability. Fans look at you and they see a hero, but you're an alcoholic, and you're as vulnerable as everybody else here to drinking again. In some ways, more so. So you're going to have to change fundamental things about your life, and we're going to give you that structure over the next twenty-eight days. By the way, twenty-eight days is a drop in the bucket. If you really want it, this is a lifelong change. Don't think that we're going to do this to you. You're going to do the change. We're just going to provide you the tools to do it. You may think being in the World Series was hard. This change is going to be harder."

I did really want to change. I didn't know if I really believed that I could change, or if changing would actually be good for me. As much damage as I had done to other people and to myself when I was drunk, for fourteen years I had been an elite major league pitcher while regularly getting loaded between starts. I hated changing even small things about my routine, like the roads I took to get to Yankee Stadium. Drinking had become a much bigger part of my life than that. The times I had stopped drinking on my own, I had pitched worse. What if I needed to drink to pitch well? Maybe that doesn't sound completely logical, but in my first few days at rehab, that's how I was thinking.

One night I picked up a book. I am much more of a movie and TV guy than a reader, but Amber had put a couple of books into the bags I'd be taking to rehab, knowing I would need ways to keep my mind occupied. This one was called **Five O'Clock Comes Early,** and it was written by Bob Welch with George Vecsey, a sportswriter for the **New York Times.** I remembered that Welch had pitched for the Dodgers and the A's when I was a kid, and that he had been pretty good. I didn't know anything about his life story, though—including that Welch had been an alcoholic. Some of his biography was very different from mine: Welch had grown up in a Detroit suburb, he had gone to college, and he went to rehab after just his second season in the majors, when he was twenty-three years old. But larger, more important parts of what he went through were really similar and hit very close to home for me: the history of family addiction, the drinking to overcome social awkwardness, the binges and the blackouts and the fights with friends. There were also a few direct connections that made the book feel more personal. One of Welch's Dodgers teammates and best friends in the eighties was Rick Sutcliffe, and twenty years later Sut had become like a big brother to me when we went on a Nike off-season baseball trip together with our wives. Reading Welch's book while I was in rehab was hugely inspiring and reassuring. No matter how many people had encouraged me to get help, I was still fearful that they would look at me as weak if I went to rehab, and treat me differently when I got out. Welch's book talked about how Sutcliffe and other teammates had been supportive of him, which made me more hopeful that my teammates and the baseball community would support me for going to rehab. And Welch had gone on to have great years as a pitcher after he stopped drinking. It could be done. It felt like Bob Welch's book was talking to me: **It's okay. You needed to do this. You made the right decision.** That started to put my mind more at ease.

Some other parts of rehab were also a relief, in smaller ways that helped me focus on myself. They took away my cellphone, for instance. I loved that. No one could get hold of me, no one was asking me for anything. I hated being away from my family, but the peacefulness of being in rehab was unmatched. I haven't been that much at peace before or since. That atmosphere is necessary, because every day in rehab is intense, and you are being asked to go deep into dark places inside yourself that you don't want to visit—that you became an addict to avoid visiting. There are boxes of tissues everywhere inside Silver Hill, and they get a workout.

Once a week I would meet with a psychiatrist, Dr. Eric Collins, whose specialty was alcoholism. He and Tom worked with me on developing techniques to avoid drinking, and to avoid the situations that led me to drink. I had always known that problems with drugs and alcohol ran wide and deep in my family, but at Silver Hill I finally understood how much of it was hereditary; they broke down the brain chemistry and the genetic links, not to give you an excuse, but to give you an understanding of how the vulnerability to addiction is wired into your system.

There were rugged family sessions. In one of them, parents and brothers and sisters and kids read a letter, out loud, that they had written about how addiction had hurt their family. Amber surprised me, and probably everyone in the room: She thanked alcohol. Amber said that understanding I was an addict allowed me to see that my destructive actions were because of drinking, not because there was something inherently wrong with me. She wasn't shifting the blame or making an excuse, and neither was I. I was responsible for all the shit I'd done when I was drunk. The point Amber's letter made was that even though I was flawed, alcohol wasn't who I am. At least that's how I heard it, through all the tears we were crying.

What helped me the most, though, was hearing the other patients talk about their lives, whether it was in meetings or when we were just sitting around. Seeing people at different points in their lives and their addictions made a big impression. There were younger guys who were defiant: **I'm just here because my family made me come. Fuck this, I'm drinking when I get out because I still need to party.** When I heard things like that I'd think, **That's not going to be me—I've done all that and I don't need it anymore.** One guy who lived in Scavetta House with us made the most powerful impression on me. He had been drinking his whole life, and his relationship with his wife—well, now his ex-wife—was totally severed. His motivation, the only thing that really kept him moving forward, was trying to rescue his relationships with his kids. Patients can make a small number of calls to the outside world each week on the Silver Hill phone line, and this guy would always call his kids—but they wouldn't answer. I had a lot of sympathy for his situation. But his life was a mess. **I can't let myself become him.**

The toughest class focused on trauma. Every day, ten of us would sit in a circle as the counselor prompted us to talk about the most devastating days or events in our lives. This was intense. As good as the counselor was, people were slow to open up, and that was understandable, because eventually they were describing suicides and physically abusive husbands and sexual abuse. Talking about all the deaths of people close to me sure wasn't easy, but compared to the shit other people had experienced, my stuff did not seem heavy at all. I cried constantly in those group conversations. But it was nothing compared to an exercise we did after about two weeks.

The assignment was to write a letter to someone you loved, someone who you thought was involved in a major trauma in your life. Which would have been a tough assignment all by itself. But after you wrote your letter, you would need to read it out loud to another patient, who was playing the role of the person receiving the letter.

One person wrote to a child who had died. Another wrote to her parents about all the ways they had fucked her up. It took two days for all the patients to read our letters, and after the first day of listening and crying and watching people relive the hell they had gone through, I went back to my room and said, "Fuck that. I'm not doing this stupid fucking letter. I am not doing this assignment." I have always found writing hard, but that wasn't the main problem. The counselor had suggested that I write the letter as if I was Lil' C talking to me after I had died from drinking. He was twelve at the time, and as I sat there, a picture of his beautiful young face in my mind, the idea of imagining and acting out the pain my dying would cause Lil' C was just too much. I wasn't going to play that game.

But as I was trying to push away confronting that awful possibility, one of my neuroses took over. I absolutely hate not being prepared. I couldn't start a game and not be ready; I couldn't go to a class and not have my homework done. So I took out the little notebook they had given us, started writing, and didn't stop for an hour.

The next day my partner, a guy named Chris, went first. I sat directly across from him, about two feet away, playing the role of his best friend. The rehab code is that once you're out, you don't talk about the specifics of what you've heard during the program. It's part of the trust that allows patients to open up and share their pain. So I'll just say this about Chris's letter: Everyone in the room tried to clap when a letter was finished, but when Chris was done, all you could hear were sobs, including mine. Chris could barely finish reading what he had written.

We took a break, and then it was my turn. To my surprise, my hands didn't shake, my voice didn't crack. Looking at Chris, my partner, who was pretending to be me, I started reading as if I was Lil' C. I'm not sure when exactly it happened, but somewhere in the middle, as I read what I had written about Lil' C missing his father so badly, I realized that what the counselor had suggested was a brilliant trick.

It wasn't Lil' C, my son, speaking to me about his pain; it was me, CC, the son, the young boy, speaking to my father about how deeply it had hurt to lose him, and not understanding why. It was so real that it felt like my dad was right there in front of me.

When I finished, I could barely stand up. I was drained—and at the same time, I felt a new lightness come over me. In that letter was all the stuff I never got a chance to say to my dad, and never gave myself a chance to feel. Saying out loud how much losing him hurt, then and now, allowed me to stop running from the pain. My dad's death and MeMe's death, which I'd never grieved, were the two biggest things that had sent me to rehab. Reading that letter out loud lifted that fucking darkness off me as plainly as if someone had pulled a thousand-pound anvil off my chest. Not that I was never going to get sad again thinking about my dad and MeMe. But the grief would never again propel me to drink.

That night, when I got back to my room, I sat on the bed where I had written the letter and thought, **Lil' C is never going to read a letter like this to anybody, because I'm going to be here for him and for all our kids. Whatever I need to do to stay healthy, to stay sober, I'm going to do. I am not going to have my sons and daughters suffering like I've been suffering all these years for my dad.** I knew there would be hard days ahead. But after all these years, it was over.

The beast comes out. After rehab my mind felt freer
than it had in years, and the game felt fun again.

## 19

SECRECY HELPED KILL MY DAD. FIRST HE TRIED to hide his drug addiction, and the friends and family who could have helped him before things got worse were in the dark. Then when he got sick from HIV, he kept quiet about it and suffered alone for too long, until he couldn't hide it anymore. I understand why Dad was secretive: He was embarrassed and scared and didn't know how to reach out. But after rehab I was determined not to make the same mistake. In fact, I wanted to go in the opposite direction: I wanted everyone to know that I was an alcoholic and that I had gotten treatment. In some ways I didn't have a choice, of course. My leaving the Yankees and entering Silver Hill had been big news at the end of October 2015. But a month later, when I was finished with the program, I could have turned down all the interview requests and said I was spending time with my family, at least until spring training, when I would be forced to deal with reporters. People probably would have understood it as a request for privacy during a difficult time. Instead, two days after I got out of Silver Hill, I put on a gray cardigan and a gray tie with black stripes, and Amber and I sat down to talk with Robin Roberts of **Good Morning America.**

My reasons were selfish, in some ways. Going on national television and talking about my alcoholism was a way of eliminating any possibility of secrecy, and asking for everyone's help in staying sober: If anyone saw me drinking again, they would call me out. And just in case a month in rehab hadn't completely gotten through to me, talking about my troubles out loud, in public, was another way for me to buy into the reality of being an alcoholic.

But it was also 1,000 percent freeing. All the years of trying to hide my drinking from my team-mates and all the people I loved—it had been damaging, and it had been work. With everyone knowing that I had been to rehab, I could be myself. The love that came back was a revelation, and a relief: I didn't have to drink to relax or to have people want to be around me. I was free.

I also hoped that by talking, without shame, I might be able to help someone else. Guilt had fatally damaged my dad; fear of being seen as weak had kept me from getting help for way too long. Maybe if we had seen other people, particularly other Black men, acknowledge an addiction or a mental illness without hesitation, we would have acted sooner to save ourselves. Whatever platform baseball had given me, I was going to use it to try to tell people I understood what they were going through and to show them it was possible to get better.

I was amazed by and grateful for the response. I got dozens of texts from people in baseball saying that they supported me. Even better, many said they were going to finally tackle their own drug or drinking problem or reach out to a relative who they knew was struggling with addiction. Probably the highest-profile example was Steve Sarkisian. In 2015 he was in his second season as the head football coach at USC, one of the most prestigious jobs in college sports. Under Sarkisian the Trojans were winning, but one morning in October he reportedly showed up drunk for a team meeting. The next day USC fired him.

On the Monday night of what turned out to be his final week at USC, though, Sarkisian was watching ESPN and saw Scott Van Pelt do a **SportsCenter** commentary segment. I had just announced that I was going into rehab, and SVP praised my decision, which was a nice gesture of support. Scott also talked about how alcoholism had killed his own father. Sarkisian later said that hearing SVP talk about me propelled him to finally go into rehab himself.

Sark called to thank me when he had finished his program and he said pretty much what he later told reporters about what me going public had meant to him: "I thought to myself, 'Whoa, here's some-body who is like me, who is in a very high-profile position in sports—ace pitcher of the New York Yankees—and was being relatively commended or almost celebrated for going to do what he did.' I knew I needed to [go]. I didn't know how to go about it. But that thing gave me a feeling of, 'There's a like person that is going to do this. I know I need to do it. Now how, what, when.' So I made the decision to go do it. It's been the best decision of my life." Knowing that speaking up had helped even one person is phenomenal. And being public has allowed me to help a bunch of people in base-ball: Once I returned to the game, at least once a month a player from another team would come up to me on the field asking about rehab: "What's it like? How did you do it? How did you know you needed to go?" They weren't asking just because they were curious; they were struggling, too. That's why I have included all the messy, ugly details of my drinking in this book, in hopes that it might help someone else turn things around before it's too late.

As the 2016 season approached, my mind felt freer than it had in years. Physically, though, I was still trying to figure out a new way to pitch. My right knee felt like Rice Krispies—but it wouldn't just snap, crackle, and pop every time I moved it, it would grind and crunch, too. It hurt all the time, even when I was sitting still. When I was lying down, it was so sore I couldn't let my knee touch the mattress. My pre-game routine before a start now took up to two hours: a hot tub, having my leg and shoulder muscles rolled out, a massage, light weights, a series of stretches, all before I even got on the field and picked up a ball. My fastball only averaged 92.3 mph now, so I couldn't beat most hitters with that anymore. In my prime I had thrown the four-seam fastball more than 60 percent of the time; in 2016, it sank to 34 percent, the lowest ever for me. My new best friend was the cutter. I mixed it with a slider, the idea being to get soft contact on breaking balls that hitters couldn't barrel up—producing ground balls and weak fly balls instead of line drives and home runs. But I was bullheaded and kept throwing too many pitches in the center of the strike zone, instead of to the corners. I still didn't totally believe in finessing hitters. So the results were uneven—I'd get knocked around for nine hits and seven runs one start, and then give up just three hits and one run the next. Our season was a disappointing muddle, too: We hovered around .500 for most of the summer before making a little bit of a run in September, but it was too late, and we finished fourth, way behind the Red Sox.

Probably the best part of the season was that I never felt any real desire to drink. We took a few precautions. Amber got rid of all the booze in our house. The Yankees told all the hotels where we stayed on road trips to empty the minibar in my room before the team arrived. I found ways to fill the hours I used to spend drinking. In rehab I had learned to play chess. I'd had a TV in my room since I was three years old; now, instead of binge-drinking, I'd binge-watch shows, like **Game of Thrones, Peaky Blinders, The Get Down, The Americans, Black Mirror, Power, Homeland,** and **Patriot Act with Hasan Minhaj.**

I had a lot of help from my friends, too. At first it was kind of awkward. We would go out to dinner after a game, and guys who would automatically have a beer were ordering soda. I told them I appreciated the effort, but they needed to do what they wanted, and it wasn't going to change anything I did. The first year after rehab I had sessions with my therapist in New Jersey twice a week, but I didn't go to follow-up anti-addiction meetings or have a formal "sponsor," the way it's done in programs like Alcoholics Anonymous. A couple of friends filled a similar role, though, especially Scott Elarton. We had become good friends during the two years he pitched in Cleveland. Like me, Scott had been a first-round draft pick and signed when he was eighteen. He was six-seven and threw hard, and he had some great years early in his career, but injuries and drinking dragged him down. We were similar in that way, too: Scott wouldn't drink every day, but when he did, he went all out, and things could get ugly in a hurry. After leaving the Indians in 2008 Scott went to a thirty-day program. He had always been a thoughtful, caring dude, but getting sober also made him a happy guy again. I talked to him every couple of days during 2016. The changes and the support helped. But the biggest thing was that I had something new to prove. I never came close to slipping up and relapsing.

In other ways it was a strange and difficult year off the field. Police abuse of Black Americans has a long and bloody history, and the past few years had added terrible new killings. Michael Brown in Ferguson, Missouri. Tamir Rice, twelve years old, shot down while playing with a toy gun in a Cleveland park. Freddie Gray, battered to death in the back of a Baltimore police van. Sandra Bland, pulled over for supposedly failing to signal a lane change and found dead in a Texas jail cell three days later. In July 2016, on back-to-back days, came the police shootings of Alton Sterling in Baton Rouge and Philando Castile in Minnesota.

The Yankees happened to be on a road trip that week, to Chicago and Cleveland. During one of the flights someone was watching the news about the latest killings, and one of my White teammates said, "Why don't they just obey?" Over the years, as I had become a veteran and taken more of a leadership role, one of my main rules for team peace and unity was "No talking politics." If it came up in the clubhouse, I'd just say, "Shut the fuck up." Because you didn't want to hate guys. Our views might be different, we grew up different, but in there we needed to be pulling in the same direction every day to win games. And if the country wasn't having that conversation, we couldn't be having it on the team. Most of the White boys couldn't see our perspective, so there was no point in talking about it.

But when I heard that about "Why don't they just obey?" the heat rose in my chest. I couldn't let that go. I didn't get mad. I tried to explain. I told this group of guys about growing up young and Black in a poor neighborhood and having the cops pull us over for no reason, point their guns, and order us to get facedown on the pavement. We had no idea whether we would be arrested or shot right there on the ground. Fortunately, neither one happened that time, but the exact same situation had ended badly for hundreds of Black kids just like me. My teammates—all of them young, White, and having grown up in the suburbs—didn't believe me. Their response was that one of us must have done something wrong—cops didn't act that way without a good reason.

Now I was the one in disbelief. They were trying to tell me what my life was like and how the world worked. They hadn't really even been listening. If they didn't want to hear anything outside their experience or to admit that racism existed, then fuck it. I gave up trying to educate them.

Soon, NFL players started a peaceful protest against police violence, and in September would begin taking a knee during the national anthem. It brought overdue attention to an important issue, but taking a knee didn't feel like the best way for me to contribute to the larger cause. Through the PitCCh In Foundation, we've tried to slowly and steadily lift thousands of kids, most of them Black, giving them the tools to build a better life in a world stacked against them.

Inside the game, I had all seventy-two of the active Black players and a lot more retired guys on a group text. We exchanged information on everything from where to find a good barber on the road to who to be cautious around. Not as dramatic as protesting on TV, maybe, but I hope and believe that these grassroots things make a difference. Besides, the media expectation that Black athletes are also supposed to be social leaders is a double standard: Of course we should speak up when we see something wrong. But most of us are having a tough enough time just being Black and trying to succeed in our jobs and in society. And it isn't Black folks who have the real power and the responsibility to change the racial dynamic in this country.

The baseball-related issues with the Yankees weren't nearly as serious as what was happening in the outside world, but 2016 was an unsettling year inside the clubhouse, too. Any realistic hope of making the playoffs was gone by the end of June, and the Yankees front office started overhauling the roster, trying to get younger and more athletic. In early August 2016, Beltrán was traded; one week later A-Rod retired; Teixeira and McCann would soon be gone. At thirty-six, with a bad knee, I didn't know how much time I had left to play, and I sure didn't want to spend it on a losing team going through a rebuilding process. Amber and I would have conversations at night: **Is it time for me to go somewhere else, too?**

Then, later in August, Gary Sánchez arrived. We'd seen him in spring training, and he looked good, but a lot of guys look good in Florida in March. Now Gary came up from the minors and absolutely raked—twenty homers in two months. Right behind him were this monster outfielder, Aaron Judge, and a twenty-two-year-old pitcher with a lightning arm, Luis Severino. It seemed like rebuilding took all of about ten days. By the end of September, I knew I wanted to stick around. Not only would these young guys give us a better chance to win, but I saw a chance to help them adjust to life in the big leagues and in New York, in contrast to how I had been treated when I was a rookie in Cleveland, where instead of being mentored you were hazed.

Didi Gregorius had been the first of the new wave of key players on the roster, and he was under a lot of pressure as the guy replacing Jeter at shortstop. But Didi is an outgoing, confident guy, and he handled the attention gracefully and played well right away, which made things a whole lot easier. He is also a guy with a lot of interests outside baseball—he's a talented photographer and animator. Didi grew up in Curaçao and, like me, he loves to travel around the world, so we got along easily and quickly. In 2017, Judge took over in right field and Sánchez was behind the plate, and both of them immediately made big impacts. Judgie drew a lot of attention his rookie year because he's huge and he hit 52 home runs. Because Sanchie was the new starting catcher, he and I talked mostly about how we were going to attack hitters. Both of them aren't just terrific players—they are eager to learn and to work their asses off to get better. That's always how you evaluate guys, more than whether they're having success on the field every day. The media and the fans would give Gary a lot of shit during his first few seasons for not being better at blocking balls in the dirt; I wasn't worried, because I saw how many hours Sanchie was putting in during practice before games, determined to improve. And he did.

I certainly don't expect everyone to act the same, and having a range of personalities makes a clubhouse stronger and more interesting. But I believe everybody needs to communicate and to buy into the group. A baseball season is a long grind, and even the best teams go through bad stretches, so to be an effective leader you must know how to get through to each guy, how to boost them when they're down or kick their ass when they deserve it. Sometimes being a good leader is as simple as being a good friend. Actually, you've got to be a guy's friend before you can lead him anywhere.

For instance, in spring training 2011, Dellin Betances was one of the Yankees' top prospects. I saw a lot of myself in him: a big guy, a confident kid, but quiet and kind of in awe at being around guys he had grown up watching play. A big part of succeeding in the big leagues is feeling comfortable, feeling like you belong. In Cleveland when I was young, I was more worried about what was gonna happen with my older teammates off the field than I was about pitching: **Am I sitting in the right seat on the plane or are they gonna give me shit?** Why would you want to suppress someone's personality and pick on him for shit all the time? We were trying to fucking win, and that wasn't going to help. So I introduced myself to Dellin right away, found out he loves fantasy sports, too, and made sure to include him when we went out to eat. That September, Dellin was called up from the minors and made his major league debut. He was nervous, and he walked the house! Four walks in two-thirds of an inning of relief. That night I sent him a text: "Hey, don't worry about it. It was your first time. Congratulations! Keep your head up. Keep working."

Other guys, it takes more time to get to know them. Luis Severino is reserved and fairly quiet, and it didn't seem like we had much in common: me a lefty, him a righty; me from Cali, him from the Dominican. But you are going to talk to me, especially in the clubhouse, my clubhouse. So whenever Sevy was sitting on a chair alone in front of his locker, I kept pulling up a chair right next to him, looking him in the eye, talking about music or food—anything except baseball.

The thing that finally broke through? Turns out Sevy and I share a love of **ThunderCats**. I'd watched the original episodes in the eighties when I was a kid, and I guess they play old reruns of the show in the D.R., so he got into it at the same age as me, only more than a decade later. Once we figured out we had Lion-O and Tygra and Cheetara in common, we were set. He was like, **Oh, I like this motherfucker now!** It was the weirdest thing. But he opened up, and we began to talk with no problem, practically like he was my little brother.

As the roster got younger, the atmosphere in the clubhouse changed. We always had fun—the perception of people on the outside that the Yankees were always all business was never completely true. We just never showed much personality when the clubhouse was open to the media. Now, though, with all the young players, things loosened up in ways that everybody heard about, especially with social media. Judgie is a fantastic DJ, and he took over the clubhouse sound system, putting together an amazing pre-game mix every day to get guys pumped up. Somebody brought in strobe lights and a fog machine so that after big wins the club-house turned into a nightclub. I love the pure emotion of the World Baseball Classic, when guys represent their home countries every four years, and I wish MLB could be more like it. I don't want to hear about "unwritten rules," "the Yankee way." You've got to change with the times. So I loved all the new celebratory stuff we were doing—but it came from the young guys, and it was true to them.

All this new blood on the roster reenergized me, and it made the team better, maybe even sooner than anyone expected. To win you need to have talent, but you also need to learn to pull in the same direction. That's a hard thing for a young team especially, and a turning point came in late August. We had been playing pretty well, but we couldn't seem to make up any ground on the Red Sox and we were in danger of missing the playoffs. We dropped two out of three games in Boston and then went to Detroit, where we won the first two games of the series. We were up 3–2 in the fifth inning of the third game, looking for a sweep we badly needed, when Michael Fulmer hit Sanchie in the left thigh—probably because Gary had already hit four homers in the series. The next inning Tommy Kahnle sailed a fastball behind Miguel Cabrera. Kahnle got tossed; Girardi got tossed for arguing. Then Miggy said something to Austin Romine, who was catching that day; Miggy dropped his bat, shoved Ro in the chest, and threw a punch.

Most baseball fights are lame: Guys stand around and yell and hold one another back. Some are vicious, though. Probably the most serious beating I ever saw delivered was in 2009, when Jorge Posada whipped on a left-handed Blue Jays reliever so hard that I was screaming for Sado to stop. This fight in Detroit was plenty real. Ro tackled Miggy, the benches and bullpens cleared, and there were bodies all over the field. Eight players and coaches ended up getting ejected.

Fights can unite a team or they can break you up. The Tigers were already having a bad season, but the brawl destroyed them as a group—Victor Martinez and Nicholas Castellanos and Justin Verlander ended up yelling at one another in the dugout. We lost the game that day, but that fight brought our team so close together that we went on a tear, winning twenty-three of thirty-six down the stretch and taking the wild-card slot.

For the first time in five years I felt mostly healthy all season. My cutter had become a real weapon. Mixing it with the two-seamer and the backdoor slider, I'd found a new formula. But it wasn't really about pitch selection. It was that in my head I had turned into this new pitcher. I had embraced being a guy who loved the chess match of getting hitters out, the art of moving the ball around the strike zone and getting soft contact instead of double-digit strikeouts. When I was younger, I always felt like I was my team's best option, even when I'd thrown a hundred pitches in a game; I was pissed every time a manager took me out. Now, I still wanted to throw complete-game shutouts, and I was mad every time when I didn't. But in 2017 I completely bought into the idea of going five or six solid innings, keeping my team in the game, and then turning it over to our great bullpen.

As much as I had learned about how to pitch, I never wanted to think too much on the mound. All the data and technology in modern stadiums made keeping your mind clear harder and harder, though. What each guy hits with runners in scoring position, the velocity of each of your pitches—they have so much shit up on the scoreboards, and so many scoreboards, that you have to work to avoid it. At Yankee Stadium, there's a screen directly above and behind home plate, so as soon as you look up, it's in your face. I hated it. I wanted as little information as possible in my head when I was on the mound so that I could feel the game situation, what was working, and my energy level; I wanted to clear my mind and focus only on the next pitch. So I developed tunnel vision. In every stadium I found a place where I could look between pitches and not see any scoreboards—a visual dead spot. At Yankee Stadium, when I was standing behind the mound I would look into our dugout.

When I was on the mound, I would look at Amber and Mom and the kids in their seats a little to the right of the plate.

All those little tricks helped, but the biggest thing in 2017 was that I was being honest with myself about where I was in my life and in my career, and it paid off: I went 14–5 in the regular season, tying Sevy for the team lead. It was my best year in a long time. By September I was certain I would be playing another season, somewhere, even if we ended this year by winning it all.

We took care of the Twins in the Wild Card Game, then the Division Series matched us up with the Indians. Every time I pitched against them, even in the regular season, was weird. Every time. This was the organization that had raised me as a baseball player; pitching against them felt disloyal, as if I was pitching against Vallejo High. But 2017 was even more intense. I was supposed to have taken Cleveland to the World Series—and I'd failed, letting myself down and letting the city of Cleveland down. I hated being part of that fucked-up Cleveland sports history: Earnest Byner fumbling, LeBron leaving, MJ shooting daggers in '89 and '93, José Mesa blowing the save. Now, ten years after failing with Cleveland in the playoffs against the Red Sox, here I was with the Yankees, trying to keep the Indians from reaching the World Series one more time. And on top of all that, both my Division Series starts that year came in

Cleveland: in game two of the series, which we lost, and then in game five, the elimination game. I'd grown up there, I'd learned everything there, I still had friends there. I felt guilty. But once I got on the mound? Oh, yeah, I was trying to fucking bury them, 1,000 percent. And we did. I went a little over four innings, struck out nine, and we beat the Indians 5–2. On to Houston.

It turned out to be an incredible series. We dropped the first two games, both by 2–1, both in Houston. Losing game three wouldn't end the series, mathematically, but it would put us in an almost impossible hole. Back in New York, though, with me starting, we changed the momentum— I went six shutout innings, we won 8–1, then we took the next two, putting us one game away from getting back to the World Series.

Game six was in Houston, though. That gave them home field advantage—we just didn't find out how much of an advantage it was until two years later, when **The Athletic** broke the news about the fucking sign-stealing scandal. Justin Verlander shut us down. So once again the season was on my shoulders. It had been only two years since I had bottomed out in Baltimore, but as I took the mound for game seven that felt like a lifetime ago. No matter how this game turned out, earning this start was a validation of all the changes I had made in my life. But I wanted to win, very badly.

It was 0–0 going into the bottom of the fourth,

and I was feeling sharp—until I hung a slider to Evan Gattis, the leadoff hitter, who hit it for a solo homer. I walked my old friend Brian McCann on a 3–2 pitch and got Marwin González to ground into a force play. When Josh Reddick hit a grounder to the left side, I thought it was a double play and I was out of trouble—but the ball went past Todd Frazier, who was playing third base. Joe pulled me for Tommy Kahnle, who got us out of that jam, but Charlie Morton and Lance McCullers Jr. shut us down, and we ended up losing 4–0.

We had come so close to playing for a championship again. This loss stung, bad. I know we would have beaten the Dodgers in the World Series. Joe made a little speech, telling us he was proud of our effort. Mike Harkey, the bullpen coach, gave me a hug, and I immediately broke down. I hadn't cried after a baseball game in a long time. But I was devastated, because I was so attached to this group of guys. The chemistry we had was incredibly rare, and I knew how hard it would be to get back to this point next year. I also knew I was pitching on borrowed time. Sitting in the bare-bones visitors' locker room, listening to the Astros fans roar and celebrate in the seats above us, I cried like a baby.

The infusion of raw young talent had gotten us here, and the experience of competing in the playoffs set us up to be even better in 2018, plus we could use the bitterness of losing to the Astros as fuel. But the youth movement had one large casualty. Five days after we were eliminated by Houston, the Yankees fired Joe Girardi. It wasn't any one thing—no controversial strategic decision by Joe that cost us a game, no confrontation with Cashman or a player. And Joe had supported me in a pivotal moment, that morning in Baltimore when I told him I needed to go to rehab right away. I will always be grateful to him for understanding what I needed to do to get my life together. But at times it could be hard to communicate with Joe, and that became more of an issue as the team got younger and fewer of the players who had started with him were still around. So when Joe was fired I was not surprised.

Baseball is a cold, hard business at this level— and at the end of 2017, my job was in jeopardy, too. Sure, I had just thrown my best season in five years. But by the middle of the next season I would be thirty-eight years old—ancient. I'd already thrown 3,433 innings, and the Yankees had every scan and X-ray that showed the damage all those pitches had done to my body. I hadn't had a drink in two years, but there was no guarantee I would stay sober. And after nine years and more than $205 million, my big contract was finally done and off the Yankees' books. I was sure to get offers from other teams, but I wanted to stay in the Bronx. I'd come here nearly a decade before and had been scared to death, not knowing what was going to happen, not know- ing if our family was going to adapt to the East

Coast. And now this was our home—the kids loved living in Jersey, I loved playing in the Bronx. I wanted to retire the next year after having been in another parade up Broadway. But would the Yankees want me, or a younger, cheaper, healthier pitcher?

I was pretty confident they would want me back; I wasn't freaking out, because I had pitched pretty well. And the initial conversations between Cash and my agent were encouraging. Then things seemed to stall. In early December the Yankees made a huge move, trading for Giancarlo Stanton, who had just won the National League MVP with the Miami Marlins—and who had a contract for $325 million. Even with the Yankees' budget, that's a lot of money. Getting Stanton made me really nervous—maybe the Yankees would let me walk to save a few dollars. By mid-December I was getting more worried every day. We had a three-week family trip to South Africa coming up shortly, and I didn't want to leave the country with the contract unfinished, not knowing where I was going to be playing when we got back.

Two days before we left for Johannesburg, my phone rang, pretty late at night. I was lying in bed with Amber, but I picked up when I saw who was on the other end. It was Cash. He was offering me a one-year, $10 million deal. I told him I'd need to talk it over with everyone before making a decision.

Toronto was interested in signing me, but if I

went somewhere else, I didn't want the team to be in the AL East, where I'd have to play against the Yankees all the time. Minnesota had made an offer for more years and more money than the Yankees: two years, $22 million. Kyle Thousand, my agent— yeah, that's his real name—talked about how not many guys get to finish what they started, especially in New York, especially after signing as a free agent and spending nine years with the Yankees.

I told Amber what Cash had said, and asked her, "What do you think?" She read the mix of relief and uncertainty on my face—the Yankees had made an offer, which was what I wanted, but was I only worth a one-year deal? She laughed a little bit. "Do you know how many players have huge contracts and don't even finish them out on the field?" she said. "You saw it with A-Rod. You're seeing it with Ellsbury. You finished it. You delivered. You lived up to your end of the bargain. You gave the Yankees a World Series win. They want you back, they want you to finish your career in New York, and they're going to pay you $10 million at your age? That is phenomenal! It's storybook."

Everything I had accomplished in the game over the years hadn't erased the fundamental insecurity I carried inside. It didn't click until Amber said it. The Yankees still wanted me. Maybe I really was worthy. I was about to get the rare chance to write my own ending.

Our vow renewal, in a Napa Valley castle,
was spectacular—but I was smiling through some of
the worst pain I had ever felt.

# 20

HAD OUTLASTED TEN OF THE MAJOR LEAGUE stadiums that existed when I was a rookie. Only Ichiro and Albert Pujols, among active players, had been around as many seasons as me. In a spring training game I faced Daz Cameron—the son of Mike, my former Brewers teammate! I didn't need any other reminders that I was really old in baseball terms, and that I had been in the big leagues a long time. I got one anyway that winter when the Yankees stunned everybody by hiring Aaron Boone as our new manager. Boonie had never managed or coached anywhere before—not officially, anyway. We had been teammates for two seasons in Cleveland, and days that Boonie wasn't in the lineup, he'd be sitting in the dugout pretending to manage the game. His father and brother and grandfather had played in the majors, so he had been prepping for his whole life, and he had a light touch with people. The Yankees didn't ask me, but I thought Boonie was a great choice.

We came into 2018 confident, especially after adding Stanton. And we did go on to set a new major league record for team home runs that year. But the regular season was a mess of injuries, and it was amazing that we won 100 games. I contributed 9 wins, but it was a battle just to keep going out to the mound every five or six days. Three times I needed shots of lubricant so my right knee would be flexible enough for me to pitch. Those shots did nothing for the pain, though, and in August it got so bad I had to go on the DL for ten days.

I pitched okay afterward, even though my knee didn't feel a whole lot better. The main highlight came in my final regular-season start, in Tampa. It was the last week of September, game 159 out of 162. A meaningless game, in terms of the standings. We'd clinched a playoff spot and the Rays had been eliminated from contention weeks earlier. We were pounding them, up 7–0 in the bottom of the fifth, when I threw a two-seamer inside to Jake Bauers. He didn't even move to get out of the way, and it clipped him on the right hand. No big deal. But in the top of the sixth inning their pitcher, Andrew Kittredge, threw a 93-mile-per-hour fastball behind the head of Austin Romine. That's crazy dangerous, but I knew what it was about— and I was pretty damn sure where it was coming from. Kevin Cash, the Rays' manager, had been on the Yankees as a backup catcher in 2009. I liked him fine at the time. But now he was on the other side, and I don't like anybody on the other side. And Cash was trying to show us up. He was managing a young team, and he wanted his players to learn a lesson about never being scared and always punching back. But throwing at a guy's head is the wrong fucking way to do it. Not only that, Ro was a catcher, so he was my guy—I had to protect him. Even worse, Ro had recently taken a foul tip square in the mask and gone through concussion protocol. Ro came back to the dugout after his at-bat, after nearly being beaned, and he was spooked. Me, I was pissed. I would show the Rays the right way to send a message.

With my first pitch in the bottom of the sixth I aimed straight at the front leg of their first hitter, Jesús Sucre. Nailed him good, just above the left knee. I've got nothing against Sucre personally. It was Cash I was pointing to and yelling at when the home plate umpire threw me out of the game: "That's for you, bitch!" They were trying to punk us. When the Rays came out on the field, pushing and shoving and acting tough, I yelled, "You got something to say about me hitting Bauers when he could have got out of the way, come out here and talk about it!" None of them said a fucking word.

Did I know at the time that getting tossed could cost me $500,000 because I would end the season two innings short of a bonus in my contract? Sure. I didn't care. Did I think about the fact that this might be the way I left the field for the final time— because there was no guarantee I'd get a start in the playoffs, and my contract was coming to an end?

Nope. It wouldn't have been the way I'd choose to go out, but if that was my exit, it would have been fine with me. Because you always protect your boys.

You need to keep protecting them until your opponents get the message—and until your own guys understand what's up. The way the Rays tried to tell it—"Oh, we got young pitchers, they're just trying to throw inside, sometimes it gets away from them"—well, our guys are young, too. They're talented, but they're young. They don't know what it looks like when a pitcher is deliberately throwing at a batter. They wonder, "Oh, did he do it on purpose, blah, blah, blah?" After the game, after Kittredge almost killed Romine, Didi talked to guys he knows on the Rays, asking if they threw at Romine on purpose. Get the fuck out of here! I know what that shit looks like. People thought I'd lost my mind when I hit Sucre, got ejected, and started screaming at the Tampa Bay dugout. Nope. Oh, I was mad, but I knew exactly what I was doing.

People call that kind of thing old-school baseball; they mean it as a compliment, and I appreciate it. Those same people complain about guys doing bat flips after hitting a big home run. Bat flips don't bother me. You beat me? Fine. Celebrate. You're worried about the guy flipping his bat? Worry about throwing a better fucking pitch! If you don't want to see someone pimp a home run, don't give it up. And when I beat you, when I strike you out with the bases loaded, I get to dance and yell. If you don't want to see me yelling and cussing as I walk off the mound, don't strike out. Simple rules. We're not showing each other up. We're enjoying the moment. Baseball is boring too much of the time. The game needs to change, and I don't mean using more data to shift guys on the infield. I'm talking about the way people say "He played the game the right way" when what they mean is "He played it the White way." What they mean is they don't like the flair that Black and Hispanic guys bring to the field.

When I first came up, there were so many Black players in the league you had the luxury of not liking some of them. The Latino guys all hung out together, because they were the real minority in the game at the time. By this point, though, that was us. We all knew one another. We all talked to one another. We had to talk to one another. I had a million White friends in the game, guys who couldn't be more on the opposite end of the spectrum from me in how they grew up or in their political views. But if you saw another Black dude on the other team, it's automatic: **Oh, we're going to dinner tonight.** It didn't matter that for three hours on the field I did everything I could to beat them; after games I'd hang with Mookie Betts, David Price, Adam Jones, Marcus Stroman. All the Black players were in a text group. It was self-defense, self-preservation. The bond was tight, because we had a lot in common and there weren't many of us. In 2007 I did an interview where I said the shrinking number of Black players wasn't a problem, it was a crisis, and afterward everybody jumped down my throat: "Oh my God, what are you talking about?" But I could see what was happening in the organizations. The A's, the Indians, the Reds, the Pirates—there used to be organizations with a bunch of Black players. Nope. Not anymore. When I said it was a crisis I was the only Black guy on the Indians opening day roster that year.

You can play baseball a long time, have a lot of fun, and make a lot of money. But right now this sport is not for us, and we know that. If the game doesn't change, it's going to be in trouble, and not just with Black people. I know there's been a lot of debate about the "Indians" nickname, but Cleveland is taking a positive step by replacing it. Could I have said that when I was playing in Cleveland? Yes, but taking on racial issues when you're a Black baseball player is incredibly complicated. For one thing, you are almost always in a serious minority. That's why you've seen more Black NFL and NBA players speak out than MLB players—there's strength in numbers. There were plenty of years in Cleveland when I was the only Black player on the roster; New York was better, but even with the Yankees, most seasons I was one of a maximum of four or five Black players on the 25-man roster. That's a lonely place to be at any point in your career, but especially if you're a younger guy trying to prove yourself in the game. You want to hold on to your job and you want to feel like you're part of the team, not an outcast, not the "angry Black guy." And you want the fans to love you. LeBron is probably the only athlete who is so good that as soon as he's back on the court everyone forgets what he tweeted about social injustice. The rest of us, we'd hear about it from the fans and the media.

Even when I was an established veteran I always put being a good teammate over my personal feelings. So if we were sitting around the food table after a game and someone said some racist shit that made me livid, I would just walk out. A few years ago in the Yankee clubhouse, some shit came up— it may have been Trump, it may have been a police brutality case. I was super close to losing my shit, so I just got the fuck up and walked out. When I came back, I said, "We ain't talking politics in here no more. Fuck that. Whatever y'all believe, leave that shit at the door. I'm gonna leave my shit at the door, we're just gonna come out here and talk about baseball or whatever else, but never politics." I guess I had enough seniority or had earned enough respect that it was never a problem again.

It ain't fair or healthy, tamping that stuff down, and over time it eats at your insides—it's part of the dance all Black Americans have done for a long time, learning how to be non-confrontational and non-threatening, just so that we can go about our lives and not be in danger. When Lil' C turned sixteen, I started teaching him how to drive— but the first lesson was what to do when he gets pulled over by the cops, because it will happen. **Put your hands up. Don't move fast. Do not raise your voice. Be super respectful.** That's a stupid and fucking humiliating conversation to have with your son, when I should be teaching him how to actually make turns!

It makes my heart ache. I've worked hard for my success. I've won awards and been cheered by thousands of people. Been called a hero. Amber is an upstanding citizen who has raised and donated millions to charity. And our son will still be looked at first as a big Black kid with locs. Black folks are still marching and rallying for the same civil rights that our grandparents marched for fifty years ago. It's crazy.

I've known players who became obsessed with how they were treated because they were Black. They weren't wrong, but the bitterness became a distraction. Ellis Burks told me early on, "Play their game"—which means being a good teammate, being a leader, all that shit—"and you can play as long as you want." When you're Black in baseball, if you don't play their game, then they can run you out whenever you're not producing. I would've been done in 2014 or 2015, but I got an extra five years by playing the game, by being thought of as a good guy in the clubhouse. And all most of us really want to do is play baseball. You're thinking, **I'm trying to get fucking Evan Longoria out tonight. That's hard enough.**

So I kept my public battles between the white lines. In 2018, after the fun little regular-season finish in Tampa, we knocked out the A's in the Wild Card Game. That bought us a trip to Boston, where we split the first two games of the Division Series. We felt like we were in a good position, coming back to New York with Sevy, our new ace, on the mound. He'd won 19 games during the regular season and made the All-Star Game twice. But the Red Sox jumped all over him in the third and fourth innings, and we ended up getting routed 16–1. If we lost the next game, our season would be over. It would be my first start of the series—and maybe the last one of my career.

It had stung losing to the Astros to end our 2017 season. The feeling after our final game in 2018 was anger. The previous night, Angel Hernandez had blown three calls at first base. For game four, with our season on the line, he was the home plate umpire. I wasn't my sharpest, but Angel was worse, from the very first inning. He kept missing pitches on the corners, forcing me to throw the ball down the middle. After two singles and a walk, the Red Sox had the bases loaded, but I got a cutter down and in on Ian Kinsler, and he flew out to Brett Gardner in the left field corner to end the inning with no runs. After the out I walked straight toward the plate, covered my mouth with my glove, and told Hernandez to get his shit together.

The Red Sox scored three off me in the third inning, and my night was done. I had showered and changed by the time the game was over and we had lost 4–3, but I was still hot two hours after coming off the mound, and I vented to the reporters about Hernandez. "He's absolutely terrible," I said without even being asked. "I don't think Angel Hernandez should be umping playoff games." Was he the reason we lost? Absolutely not. Maybe I shouldn't have said that stuff because it made me look like I was whining and making excuses. When you win, you can say whatever you want. When you lose, you gotta just shut the fuck up. But I had to be honest about how I felt.

Yeah, maybe something about authority figures making arbitrary decisions strikes a nerve with me. One of the things I loved most about pitching is that I had the ball and nothing could happen in the game until I was ready; I loved being in control. The umpires are always trying to take that control away from the players. Or maybe it's just that I hate people who don't care enough to do the hard work to be good.

Part of my anger that night was also about not wanting this to be the way my career ended, letting my teammates down with our season on the line. So I was honest again when the reporters asked me if I wanted to play in 2019. This was a young-ass team—in 2018 Miguel Andújar was a rookie, Gleyber Torres was a rookie, Judgie and Aaron Hicks were in their third season, Sanchie in his fourth—and I think it showed, and it was part of the reason we came up short in the playoffs. We never came to the park with the attitude "We're gonna dominate this series." But I knew this core group was going to win a championship at some point, and I wanted to be part of it. I knew I was near the end, but I was having so much fun I didn't want it to be the end. That's why I was in a rush to have surgery on my right knee, getting scoped for the third straight off-season just three days after we were eliminated by the Red Sox. It gave me plenty of time to heal before spring training.

The bigger fix, though, was that I owed Amber a wedding. A good one this time, with me sober and happy. A vow renewal. A redo, fifteen years later. We planned it for months, with Amber doing most of the work, including picking an amazing location, an actual castle in a Napa Valley vineyard. We invited 250 people, including baseball friends and teammates like Chris Young, Adam Jones, Johnny Damon, Prince Fielder, and Cameron Maybin. We had incredible entertainment thanks to En Vogue and Juvenile. All four kids had parts in the ceremony: Carter was the best man. Jada and Cyia were

Amber's bridesmaids. Lil' C walked his mother down the aisle. I think I looked pretty good in my white tuxedo, but nowhere near as spectacular as Amber in her custom gown and veil. She seemed to glide down the aisle on a white cloud as Anthony Hamilton sang "Her Heart." Lil Duval officiated, and this time I was able to look Amber straight in the eye as we read the vows we had written. My wife, my grandmother, and my mom: Anyone who had one of those women in their life would be lucky. And I've had all three. But Amber is my compass.

Everything at the wedding was beautiful and perfect. One of the best nights of my life. Except that the whole time I was sweating like crazy, and I felt as if I was going to vomit. This wasn't nerves. It wasn't booze. I was drinking grape juice all night, and not the fermented kind. Maybe there was a trace of alcohol in the wedding cake, and it reacted with the Antabuse I was taking? Maybe food poisoning? Whatever the cause, halfway through the reception dinner, I got up from our table, ran out the back of the building, and threw up in the grass. I pulled myself together, then came back in and didn't tell anyone. I was feeling a little better, and there was no way I was going to ruin a second wedding. Fuck that. I'm partying.

At the end of the night, we piled into Sprinter vans to head back to the hotel to drop off guests before returning to the house we'd rented for the weekend. Amber and I were sitting next to Cliff and Kristen Lee, laughing about old times, when the wave of nausea hit me again. "Pull over, now!" I yelled at the driver. I bolted out the door and puked on the side of the road.

Back at the house, in the middle of the night, as I was throwing up a third time, suddenly there was something new—a stabbing pain in my chest. "Babe," I yelled to Amber, "something's wrong with my heart. I think I'm having a heart attack." I was getting scared. Amber stayed calm, though. She's been through so much drama with me that she figured it was just anxiety kicking in again, or that all the puking had strained a muscle in my chest. She talked me down, and I got some sleep. The next morning I was still sweaty, but I made it through our all-white brunch (white clothes, white decorations, that is). For the next two days, I drank Pedialyte and ate crackers, figuring I must have some kind of stomach flu.

The next three weeks were a roller coaster. I'd feel good for a few days. On Thanksgiving we went to my mom's house, and she and my aunts had made a huge feast, as usual, so I couldn't turn that down. But soon I was running to the bathroom with what seemed like the most horrible heartburn I'd ever experienced. Or maybe I had developed acid reflux from all the vomiting. The next day my buddy Jomar was having a party at his house. Another of my best friends, Rickie, made oysters, and I love oysters. Darnell, my cousin the chef, made gumbo, and it was the best I'd ever had. But every half hour or so it felt as if someone was reaching straight through my rib cage and squeezing my heart. This must have happened seven times. I'd go into Jomar's room and sit on the bed. The excruciating pain would last for two or three minutes; it would take another two minutes for me to stop sweating. I thought, **Maybe it's the gumbo. But I'm not gonna not eat the gumbo, because I don't get Darnell's cooking all the time! Fuck it—I'll eat it and then I'll be fine in a couple of days.** I also didn't want anyone to ever think I wasn't still down with the guys. I'll never be the first one to leave and risk anyone saying, "Oh, CC's changed, CC's better than us now." So that day I was eating oysters and gumbo and smoking cigars, even though my stomach was bubbling and my chest was pounding. When I finally did leave, I took a pot of gumbo and put it in the back of the car to bring to my mom. As I was driving, though, the pain kept ripping through my chest, so bad that I'd slam on the brakes. By the time I got to Mom's the gumbo was all over the car.

When it came time to fly back to New Jersey I felt so weak I could barely make it through the airport, and I slept for the whole trip back east. But the next weekend one of my guys was having a bachelor party in Vegas. While I was there I went to Javier's and to the Cabo Wabo Cantina, two of my favorite restaurants, along with Carbone, in New York; one day I ate a big bag of peppered chips. I was constantly drinking Nexium and Pepto-Bismol, chewing fistfuls of Tums. The pain would go away for a while, but it kept coming back, and eventually it started keeping me up at night. But here's how much I love to eat: I'm thinking, **I hope it's a heart attack and not my stomach, because if I have to stop eating some of this food, that's going to be worse.**

When I got home I went to see my physician, who dropped a scope down my throat and saw some inflammation—possibly from throwing up, possibly from an infection, he said. Told me to eat blander foods and take some antibiotics. Thinking I was basically fine, I headed to a meeting with my Jordan rep, to talk about what I wanted to do with my cleats next season. Could I have cancelled the meeting? Maybe. Could I have asked to move it from Sofia, the cigar bar? Sure. But even after all these years, it's a battle for me to tell people no, or to think I'm disappointing them. It's hard to explain, but too often I'll follow through with things I don't really want to do and then just be mad about it afterward.

For three weeks I had felt too shitty to work out, but I thought maybe if I just did my regular routine on Monday morning—go to the gym, ride the bike, play catch with Dellin—it would all go away. I started pedaling. This time the problem wasn't pain. It was that I couldn't breathe. After less than three minutes I hopped off and said, "D, let's go play catch." I was still thinking, **I'm just going to gut through it, the pain will go away, my breathing will come back, I'll be fine, just like always.** Three, four throws in, though, I felt like I was about to fall down on the floor. But I couldn't let anybody know. Somehow I faked it for ten minutes. Now, finally, the alarms started going off in my head. No matter what had been wrong in my life, physically or mentally, I'd always been able to throw. I've weighed 350, I've been hung over, my leg's been fucked up—and I could throw the ball. I could always throw a fucking baseball all day. But when I couldn't make five good throws, even I knew something serious was up.

The next morning I went back to my doctor for a stress test. They take a scan of your heart, and then you're supposed to walk on the treadmill for sixteen minutes at varying speeds, followed by another heart scan. Three minutes into baby walking on the treadmill, I had to stop and lie down. After that, even though they had only gotten partial readings on the EKG, I had to leave, because I was due at Yankee Stadium to shoot a short guest appearance for a TV show. I don't know exactly how I said my lines; I hadn't eaten all day, my chest was pounding, and I felt like total garbage. The show? **God Friended Me.**

Which sounds like a bad joke, and nearly turned

into a really awful joke. The doctor called while I was at the stadium, ordering me to go straight to the hospital. Whatever he had seen on the partial tests that morning was not good. This time they said they were going to pump dye into my heart to see how it was pumping. Amber cut off the doctor: "After you rule out that it isn't his heart, what's the next test? We can't keep coming back to the hospital." I understand her thinking, which was partly a result of years of experience with me and partly denial (it couldn't be something as bad as a heart problem). The doctor looked at her and said, "I'm ninety-nine percent sure he has a blocked artery and we will need to put a stent in immediately." Amber held her tears until she walked out of the room and called my mom.

It didn't freak me out, though, not at that point. I had felt so bad for three weeks that I didn't care: **Slice me open right now, because I need some relief.** The next day, after three hours of surgery, I woke up in the recovery room. Amber was standing next to the bed as the nurses were cleaning me up, and then the cardiologist came in. He told us the procedure had gone well. Then he got really blunt about what a close call this had been. "It was ninety percent blocked," he said. I understood that was severe, but it was the next phrase he used that chilled me: "It was the artery we call 'the widow-maker.'" I had been scheduled to fly to London two days later, with Jackie Bradley Jr., to promote a series the Yankees and Red Sox would be playing there the next summer—and, even more important, I would get to see Liverpool play Manchester. Obviously I wasn't going to be making the trip. The doctor said that if I had tried to ignore my pain and gotten on the plane, the way I was planning to do it, the combination of the blocked artery and the altitude meant I would have likely come home in a box.

In early November I had signed another one-year deal with the Yankees; while I was in surgery Amber, always the organizer and planner, had had the presence of mind to call my agent and make sure the team couldn't cancel it now. But we weren't thinking about baseball right then. Heart failure: What had killed my grandmother. What had killed my uncle Aaron. What had killed MeMe. Now it had nearly killed me.

Except it hadn't. Maybe God really had friended me. Maybe this was another little tap on the shoulder to get me to clean up my life. Or maybe I was starting to wise up and truly understand what they had been talking about in rehab—that I couldn't bury or push through any and all pain, and that I didn't need to do it alone anymore. Whatever the reason, when I finished crying, I was so giddy with relief that I started dialing the phone, lying there in the hospital bed in that funny little gown, calling my closest friends and teammates: "Hey, Gardy, guess what just happened to me!" They were a little surprised.

I felt as if I had been grazed by a bullet. A near miss. Instead of dropping dead of a massive heart attack at forty-six, I'd gotten the warning in time to get treated and make changes. I don't want to be old. But I want to get old. It's a luxury too many of my friends and family, especially the men, never got the chance to enjoy.

When I checked into the hospital I hadn't slept in three weeks and I was exhausted. Now I was rested. I was fixed. I was better. I was back. Now I was going home to the wife and kids who I love more than anything in the world, instead of them coming to my funeral. And I was getting one more chance to win a ring.

In 2019, I came back for one more season,
to try to win another championship. I threw my
final pitches on October 17, with my left shoulder
wrecked and my eyes closed.

# 21

OST PEOPLE WOULD THINK THIS WAS A nothing game. Middle of July, we had the second-best record in all of baseball and a six-game lead in our division, it was a muggy Tuesday night, the fans seemed sleepy. It would be easy to see it as just one game out of 162, one game that wasn't going to make any difference. Which is why it was so important.

I'd pitched pretty well coming into the top of the sixth inning. I had four strikeouts and I'd given up only three hits, but two of them were solo home runs. Both were on cutters that hadn't really broken, and both were crushed. But Edwin Encarnación had hit one out for us, so we were only down 2–1. If I could keep it close here, there was no way the Rays were going to hold down our offense the rest of the game. I got two quick outs to start the sixth—a grounder to third by Travis d'Arnaud, and a strikeout of Tommy Pham, who was a good hitter. Then I beat Mike Brosseau with a cutter in on his hands, but he dribbled it down the third-base line about thirty-five feet. In my younger days, I would have pounced on it and fired him out at first, inning over. Now, though, on my flimsy right knee, I could barely get to the ball, and Brosseau was on first with a cheap hit. Up next was Yandy Díaz; he'd hit one of the homers earlier in the game, and so I was too careful, falling behind two balls and no strikes. I tried to bend a slider over the outside corner and missed again, but Díaz didn't—he roped it into deep left center for a double, scoring Brosseau. Now we were down 3–1, and I was pissed. I ran a full count on Avisaíl García. If I walked him here, the game would start to get away from us, and I'd definitely be out of the game. **Focus. Relax.** Slider, this time clipping the outside corner perfectly, and the home plate umpire, Phil Cuzzi, gave me the call.

As I walked off the field I glanced toward home plate. García was still standing there, staring at me, and his lips were moving. He looked like he thought I'd said something to him. Which I hadn't. But then I did. I shouted: "I could be talking to you if you want me to be!" And then García said, "Man, you crazy!"

"Yeah, I'm fucking crazy! I am! I'm fucking crazy! Just know that!"

We started walking toward each other, and I could see my teammates jumping out of the dugout and heading our way. At first I was simply mad that we were losing, and pissed that I had just given up a double. Especially because being in first place wasn't what mattered to me. Coming into the game, I'd been thinking that we had lost four of our last six, including the previous night to the Rays, who were in second place. I knew how fragile a division lead can be. Not only did we need to start putting together a new winning streak, but we needed to start putting together an attitude. Our team was good, don't get me wrong. Judge, Sánchez, Didi, Hicks, Gleyber, Stanton, Severino—these were some of the most talented young players in baseball, and we had them all. But they were young players. Yeah, we'd made the playoffs the year before, with mostly the same group—but we'd gotten bounced pretty fast by Boston in the Division Series. This group hadn't ever really fought for something together, all the way to the end. And to do that, you need to fight every damn day. You've got to learn how to win the division and learn how to beat these teams that are trying to come after you. You need to go nuts, to get angry, to roar once in a while, not just to convince the other teams that you're confident but to convince yourself that you're confident. You need a primal, killer instinct if you're going to win a championship.

I knew this because I'd been on the other side of it—on the Rays' side of the equation—during my years in Cleveland when the Indians had been the young, underdog team chasing Minnesota and Chicago and trying to show them we couldn't be intimidated. So I understood what the Rays had been trying to do. They were trying to bully us, to knock us off our game, just like they had at the end of 2018, when I hit Jesús Sucre.

I hadn't been surprised when 2019 started with more of the same between us and the Rays. In May, we went to Tampa, and both teams had been playing well. It was still very early, but the Rays were a half game ahead of us, and it looked like we were going to be tangling all year. In the sixth inning of the second game in that series, DJ LeMahieu hit a homer to tie the score. Sure enough, Luke Voit was up next and their pitcher, Yonny Chirinos, damn near drilled him in the neck, instead hitting Voit in the shoulder. I understood what they were trying to do, and I wasn't going to let it go. I'm leaning out over the dugout railing screaming, "Fuck that. This is our year!" But words don't get you anywhere in this game. Two batters later Chirinos hits Sanchez with a pitch. So the next time I was on the mound against them, I'd match what they were doing.

I got my chance six days later, in the Bronx. You need to be strategic about when you're sending a message, so I waited until the fifth inning, with two out and nobody on. It was a 1–1 game, and I was probably going to pitch only one more inning. So I fed Austin Meadows a fastball in on his knees. Then another at his waist. Yeah, I walked him, but I struck out the next guy to end the inning. And I was still pissed.

It all went back to why Buddy Bell had been screaming at me in 2004 in the Indians' dugout. A lot of what I am, and a lot of what you saw on the mound from me, is from people like Buddy Bell and Dick Pole telling me what I needed to be when I was a young player. Teammates like Matt Lawton and Ellis Burks in Cleveland, veterans who would talk to me before we started a series in Minnesota: "You pitch the first game. You've got to set the tone." That's why I did what I did against Tampa— why I went out there barking and shit, going crazy, throwing the ball as hard as I could. **I'm going to beat your ass.**

So two months later, when I started jawing with Avisaíl García, I wasn't thinking about any of that stuff. After nineteen years in the big leagues, I didn't need to think about it. It was just part of me. It was why I had succeeded as long and as much as I did, even more than being six foot six, or throwing 95, or learning how to get outs when I couldn't throw 95 anymore. It's why in my final season, my 552nd start, when I was just about to turn thirty-nine years old, I came out of the game that night against the Rays and busted up a refrigerator on my way back to the clubhouse. Hit it with a bat. I was so fucking mad that we were losing, that I had just given up a double that made it 3–1. Did the Yankees send me a bill for destroying a refrigerator? They didn't care. It was the second refrigerator I'd totaled that year. What the Yankees cared about—what I cared about—was winning. A short time later I was in the training room, in the hot tub, and watching the rest of the game on TV, no sound, as I soaked. In the bottom of the eighth inning, when Judge and Didi hit home runs and we scored six runs to win it, I was screaming. I was going crazy. Part of it was that we won the game, sure. But another part was that these guys had the pride and the hunger to keep fighting to the end.

I have never tried to hurt anybody with a pitch, and I never would. But there's power in aggression, in the creative use of the fear that maybe you **would** hurt somebody, and in challenging someone's character. We took twelve out of nineteen games from the Rays in 2019. Mission accomplished, and not just against Tampa Bay. How many times were we down three or five or six runs in the late innings in the 2019 season, games where we could have rolled over, and instead we came back and won? How many injuries did we go through that knocked out front-line players for long stretches—Stanton, Andújar, Sánchez, Encarnación, Hicks, Betances, Severino, Domingo Germán—where we could have felt sorry for ourselves, and instead the next guy stepped up and played great? Look, I'm not taking credit for all of that, or even much of it. But yeah, I think there's a connection.

That's why I answered the way I did when a

friend sent me a text one day during the summer. In the bottom of the sixth inning of a 1–1 game—against the goddamn Rays again—I gave up a single and a walk to start the inning. But I got García to fly out to right, then jammed Brosseau with a cutter—double play, inning over. I hadn't pitched into the seventh inning all year, and my friend, watching the game at home on TV, figured I was done and sent a text congratulating me for pitching out of a jam, for finishing on a high note. But Boonie did send me out to pitch the seventh, and with two outs I gave up a two-run homer to Nate Lowe. An hour later, when I had calmed down some, I checked my phone in the locker room, and answered the text with a face-palm emoji and three words: "Till the end."

Nothing matters unless you finish it off or empty yourself out trying. That's how I have always thought. In 2019 every game meant a little extra, of course. Back in November 2018, when I signed the new one-year contract, I decided that this would be my final season. Then, after the heart surgery, I wasn't sure that I really wanted to play. They had me taking blood thinners, which meant that if I got hit with a line drive, it could be fatal. But playing one more year meant one more run at a championship; this Yankees team had a real shot, and that doesn't come around often. And playing one more season meant going out on my own terms, something very few athletes, no matter how good, ever get to do.

Those terms included using my final season to multiply the good work of the PitCCh In Foundation. The Yankees played road games in eighteen different stadiums, and in every one we organized a PitCCh In event with the local Boys & Girls Club, including tickets to one of the games we were playing in that city. The home teams all wanted to have a little ceremony honoring me before one of the games; that was great, but we suggested that making a donation to the foundation would be even better, and they were happy to contribute. We ended up raising nearly $1 million, and all the money will go to programming for kids whose families were looking at a steep road ahead of them, just like mine was when I was growing up in Vallejo. We've handed out more than fifty thousand backpacks, and we're just getting started.

People in baseball are obsessed with numbers. If you're a fan, stats are fun to compare and argue about; if you're a player, they're a big part of determining how much you get paid. But I never played for numbers, in terms of setting goals for a season or for my career. If you make all your starts, the numbers will be there at the end. Strikeouts always meant more to me than wins, at least as a stat, because strikeouts are more of a measure of you personally as a pitcher. A starting pitcher's win totals are so dependent on other people. You can pitch great, but if your team can't hit, you don't get wins (think Jacob deGrom). Same if your team has a weak bullpen. I've seen guys win ten or fifteen games in a season and not deserve half of them; I've seen guys win five in a season who should have won twenty.

I had finished the 2018 season close to a couple of big individual career milestones: 3,000 strikeouts and 250 wins. So all winter there had been lots written and said about how reaching those totals was a big motivation for me to play in 2019. It wasn't. I could have finished right where I was in the record books and been totally satisfied with my numbers and with the work I'd done to achieve them. The whole reason to play one more year—the only thing I cared about in any year— was trying to win another championship. Once I decided to play, did I care about 3,000 and 250? Hell, yeah. But mostly because of the players I would be joining on the lists.

Fourteen strikeouts, four wins. That's what I needed as 2019 began. I picked up three K's and a no-decision in my first start, against the White Sox; five more K's and a win the next time out, against the Royals. It would have been perfect to get the 3,000th strikeout at Yankee Stadium in front of the home fans, but my next two starts would be out west, so Amber and the kids hit the road with us. The fact that the club was aiming to win a champi-onship and wanted to win every game helped me stay focused, but at this point I just wanted to get the milestone over with—every question and interview was about reaching 3,000 strikeouts. In Anaheim, with probably fifty of my friends and relatives in the stands, I went five innings but got hit pretty hard and only struck out three Angels. On to Arizona, still needing three more.

First batter for the D-backs? Adam Jones, one of my best friends. We'd had dinner together the night before. Got him to ground out to short. It wasn't until the second inning that I got my first K of the night—David Peralta going down looking. My 2–2 pitch to the next hitter, Christian Walker, was a nasty slider on the corner, a strike—but the fucking umpire said no. **You know what I'm trying to do here! Just call the fucking strike!** Kind of perfect, though—there I was on the verge of something historic and instead I was cursing at the plate umpire. Two pitches later, this time a swing and miss, and Walker was gone. One more left.

Maybe my focus drifted just a little at that point, because the next batter, Wilmer Flores, connected for a homer to deep left, and we were down 1–0. I got ahead of Nick Ahmed 0–2 . . . and he singled to right. Then the Arizona catcher, John Ryan Murphy, was the hitter. Murph had been a Yankee; he'd caught my 2,500th strikeout, in 2015, and I like Murph a lot. Too bad: With the count one ball and two strikes, Sanchie called a changeup, Murph swung over it, and that was 3,000. At first I didn't realize it—I was still so pissed about the missed call to Walker, still so focused on ripping the umpire's head off, that it wasn't until I turned and saw Luke Voit jumping up and down that I understood what had happened. **Oh, shit! That was 3,000 strikeouts!**

In the dugout, my teammates were clapping and slapping me on the back—but they were also laughing, because I was scrambling to get to the bat rack. Arizona is in the National League, so I got to hit, and I was leading off the next inning! On the way to the plate I made a detour, though, to hug my kids, my mom, and Amber. I also saw a few old teammates and close friends who live in Arizona—Ben Francisco, Damon Hollins, Josh Barfield, Chris Young. And Milton Bradley, who was so determined to support me that he'd come to my previous start, in Anaheim, and when I didn't reach 3,000 there, followed us to Phoenix.

Next to them were the two sons of my childhood friend Nate Berhel, whose initials were stitched into my glove in memory of his life and his too-early death. When I got to the plate I was thinking **Go yard!**, but it was tough to hit with tears in my eyes.

My fourth win of the season, the 250th of my career, didn't come until June 19, against Tampa at Yankee Stadium, but it was equally as emotional and satisfying. I was only the seventeenth pitcher in the history of the game to reach 3,000 strikeouts, and just the third left-hander—but more important to me, I was joining Ferguson Jenkins and Bob Gibson as the only Black pitchers to do it. I was the forty-eighth pitcher to win 250 games—and I might be the last one, because starters don't go deep enough into games anymore. More meaningful to me was that with that win I once again became the newest member of a very small club, with Jenkins and Gibson. It didn't really hit me until the next day, when one of the guys on my group text sent me the list of the pitchers with 250 wins and 3,000 strikeouts, with my name there at the bottom. Then something else flashed into my head. Less than four years earlier I had been sitting in rehab, reading Bob Welch's book, wondering if I could come back and play at all. Now there I was sitting on 250 wins and 3,000 K's. It wasn't always pretty. But that made it a cool journey.

With the numbers out of the way, though, reporters asked constantly if I was getting nostalgic as the end of my career got closer. I wasn't. We were trying to win every day and trying to win a championship, so that made staying focused easier. There were some moments, though, when I couldn't avoid thinking about all the time that had passed. When we came to New York, in 2009, Lil' C had been little—just six years old. Now he was six foot three, and at sixteen he was closer in age to some of my Yankees teammates than I was! Or when we brought up this young pitcher, Ben Heller—who's from Wisconsin, and he told me he was at a game I pitched for the Brewers in 2008. He was in high school at the time! Freaked me out. And there were moments in the dugout that would stop me. For instance, Didi and Hicks are the kind of friends who argue about anything and everything, and it's hilarious to listen to them. Hicks missed most of 2019 with injuries, then came back for the playoffs. One night during a game against Houston, Didi said to Hicksie, "Smile, the camera's on you." Hicks replied, "The camera's always on me." The face Didi made had me in tears of laughter, and then he retorted, "First of all, bitch, you only played, like, fifteen games!" And then they were off and running, going at it.

That's the stuff I knew I was going to miss, not actually playing the game. And I wasn't looking for a farewell tour, but some of the tributes and gifts were a lot of fun. In San Francisco the Giants played a video on the big center field board. In Cleveland, the clips showed me when I was young and skinny; even better, the Indians included video of me hitting two home runs.

In June, we flew to London for two games against the Red Sox, to promote MLB overseas. I love London, and the coincidence of the timing added to the specialness of this being my last time around. I was barely healthy enough to make the trip, though. Since early May I'd been having stabbing pains in my upper left torso. We thought the problem was in my neck, so we were taping the shit out of my neck whenever I pitched. But between what we thought was wrong with my neck and what we knew was wrong with my right knee, I was in a huge amount of pain. If I'd been playing on a trash team, with no shot at the playoffs, after I got the 3,000 strikeouts I might have gone on the injured list and stayed there. But I was still pitching decent, and we had a real chance to win a championship.

In July, MLB brought me back to Cleveland for a special ceremony at the All-Star Game, which was really cool. In August we had a West Coast trip, and my right knee was on fire, but there was no way I was going to miss the chance to pitch in Dodger Stadium one last time. Also, I wanted to hit! I came up in the top of the third, and I swung at the first pitch and when my right foot landed, man, I almost fucking fell down. Ended up lining out to deep right, and I struck out seven in four innings. But after the game I could barely walk.

At Fenway, my buddy David Price presented me with a metal plate from the Green Monster scoreboard, painted with the number 52. That was fun. But my final trip to Boston was memorable for another reason. One afternoon I stopped by the Louis Vuitton store with friends, wanting to get a gift for Amber. I stood there for fifteen minutes looking around for help, the clerks ignoring me the whole time. I'm pretty sure it wasn't because they were big Red Sox fans. I didn't get any attention until the security guard—also a Black guy— went over and whispered to one of the salespeople, "You need to help these dudes before they walk out." Now, every Black person has dozens of stories like that. Is that kind of thing anywhere near as offensive as the fact that Willie Mays, when he was playing for the Giants in the fifties and sixties, the greatest player maybe ever, wasn't allowed to buy a house in the wealthy neighborhoods of San Francisco? Of course not. And I remember Mudcat Grant telling me about how, when he was playing for the Twins in the sixties and a White teammate made racist cracks, Mudcat left the ballpark because he knew that answering the guy would have caused him serious trouble—and he wanted to leave before he slugged the guy. At least I could speak up without hesitation when one of my Yankees teammates started praising Donald Trump in 2016—though I also had to hold myself back from slugging the guy. So yes, there's been progress. But this country finds ways to remind you that even if you're rich and famous, many people still see you as just a big Black guy. I'm still the Black kid sitting in an Escalade in the car dealership being lectured by an old White dude.

How far I've traveled in life, and how far I haven't,

was on my mind a lot during the 2019 season, never more so than on an incredible night in the middle of September at the LegaCCy Gala, hosted by our foundation. Jenny Steinbrenner was there, representing her family, who have been so good to us over the years. All of my 2019 teammates were there, plus Boonie and the coaching staff and Brian Cashman. Our friend Angie Martinez was the MC; Desus and Mero were there, too, with Desus getting off a funny line about how he thought I always looked like one of his old uncles when I was on the mound.

We raised $1.6 million for the foundation, which was the real motivation for the event, and truly gratifying. But what I think I'll remember most is standing by this huge floor-to-ceiling window on the twentieth floor of the venue, called The Shed at Hudson Yards, with the lights of the city spread out below us and so many of the people who had been on this journey from the beginning surrounding me: Coach Hobbs, Jomar, Dee, Devin Rogers, Uncle Edwin and Aunt Genia, my mom and her husband, Al Lanier, and Amber. They understood the real distance between Vallejo and this celebration high above New York.

My life was chaotic from the very beginning. But then I got Hobbs, and then I got Mark Shapiro, people who cared about me and took care of me. It was as if God was saying, **Your shit's going to be all fucked up, but I'm going to give you these people,** and if you can use them right, you can figure this shit out. That didn't stop everything from getting as bad as it possibly could at times. But I still had the love around me to get out of it. It's strange. Some people believe in God's will, and that we have no control over our fate. But that's not it. At the same time, it's not pure luck, either, because people as good as Carl Willis don't come into your life by accident. So I don't know how or why it happened. I do know that I feel way more blessed than a lot of people just like me in the hood.

Something else about feelings: I had them all now. For years, I had been able to release many of them in a productive way on the field while numbing them most of the rest of the time. My greatest strength had been my ability to express love, grief, and desire through baseball, but my inability to do that off the field was killing me. In 2015, my pitching career looked like it could quickly be coming to an end, and I broke down. For years I had kept my baseball emotions separate from the rest of my life. I couldn't do it any longer. The fears intersected. Fortunately an impulse to save myself propelled me to rehab. When I came out, my feelings were all mine, all the time—and the strongest one was joy.

I couldn't stay sentimental for too long, though. The 560th and final start of my career was scheduled for two days later, a Wednesday night at Yankee Stadium, against the Angels. I tried to keep everything the same as I had always done it: In the morning at home, I cranked my six songs in the shower—that year they included "West Coast" by G-Eazy and Blueface, a reminder of where I started, and "Ready to Die," by Biggie, a reminder that some things aren't so different on the East Coast. Driving into the park, I made sure I was in a good mood. Being pissed off makes me horrible. I can't function anywhere in life when I'm angry, and that was especially true on the mound. I had to be under control. I tried to put myself in a space where nothing would affect me—not a bad call, not a swinging bunt. It had taken me eighteen years to get to that point. And just as my mind was finally right, my body had started breaking down, so I wouldn't be making this trip much longer.

South on the Palisades Parkway to the George Washington Bridge, looking at the construction workers, thinking about how if it weren't for baseball I might have been out there in a hard hat, too, instead of behind the wheel of a Rolls-Royce Cullinan. Up ahead there's a big sign that reads Exit 1 Yankee Stadium, but that takes you south onto the Major Deegan and usually smack into a traffic jam. So I found a shortcut. I took Exit 2, in Manhattan, forked right then forked left, followed the sign for University Avenue and crossed into the Bronx on the underappreciated Washington Bridge—not only because it was faster, but also because driving on the local streets, stopping at lights and seeing people wearing Yankee hats as they were walking around, it felt like I was going to work instead of just being a visitor passing through the Bronx.

A quick right on Ogden Avenue, then a left on University, then a right on Grant Highway. Just past Shakespeare Avenue, over there on the left, is a place called Jordan Sport Barber Shop. The owner, Jose Moisés Lopéz, cuts hair for us at Yankee Stadium, and a lot of the Latin guys on visiting teams—Pujols, Félix Hernández, Vladdy Guerrero—stop in his shop when they are in the city. I think I'm secretly Latin on the low. I'm going to do my 23andMe and it's going to come back that I'm really from the Dominican.

At the intersection of Grant Highway and Jerome Avenue you can see the 4 train rolling down the elevated tracks. It's the subway line that flashes into view above Yankee Stadium's right field seats. My pulse picks up a notch. I take a right on Jerome and head to a shortcut, just past 164th Street. A big iron roll-up gate seals off a freight entrance running between the left field seats and a parking garage. Blow the horn: **Hurry up, raise the gate!** Out the other side, turn right just past deep center field, onto River Avenue. Underneath a big Bernie Williams poster is the entrance to the players' underground parking garage, my space marked on the wall with a big 52. Half an hour door to door. I came up with that route in 2009, the year we won the World Series, so I have been taking it ever since.

My final start, I only went 2⅔ innings. We wanted to save some bullets for the playoffs, when I would be pitching out of the bullpen. It was also a nice gesture by Boonie, to take me out in the middle of an inning, and I appreciated the standing ovation from the fans. But it was strange knowing that something I'd done every five days for nineteen years was now over, forever.

We felt all season that the true World Series would be us against the Astros in the LCS, and that was the way it played out—just not with the ending I'd been dreaming about. We needed to win game six, in Houston, to stay alive, and we rallied for two in the top of the ninth to tie it, only to be stunned when José Altuve crushed a homer off Aroldis Chapman to end it.

I was so proud of the way we had fought all season, to the last fucking out. So many guys went down with injuries, yet we never hung our heads. That 40-man roster, those guys were savages for real—the nickname we'd adopted from a rant by Boonie during one game in the middle of the season.

After the final loss to the Astros, before the media came into the clubhouse, Boonie said a few words to the team. Judge got up and talked, too. I looked across the room at Gardy, my teammate and friend for the entire eleven seasons I'd spent as a Yankee, and I couldn't say a word.

I sat in front of my locker a long time that night. Took the last bus back from the stadium to the hotel, with Gardy and J.A. Happ, the next two oldest guys on the team; then I got my stuff and flew to New York with the team. Amber and the kids came back a day later, so I walked into an empty house just before dawn, and it all hit me so hard: the loss, knowing how close we'd been to a championship, knowing how fucking hard it is to win, knowing I'd never get the chance again. I was crying like crazy, trying to post on Instagram, texting people, calling people. Crying. It was rough. I needed to get it all out, pour out my emotions, the wins and losses of time and of people, one last time, one big last baseball catharsis, unaltered by alcohol. By the time I collapsed into bed at 5 A.M., I was spent.

My own season had ended two nights earlier, at Yankee Stadium. With two on and nobody out in the seventh inning of game four in the series, Boonie had brought me in to face a lefty hitter— that was my new and strange role in the bullpen. I got Yordan Álvarez to hit a weak grounder to second base, but unfortunately Gleyber Torres couldn't make the play. Two batters later Aledmys Díaz was at the plate, and on the fifth pitch he hit a routine fly to right field. But as soon as the ball left my hand, I knew something was wrong.

My left shoulder had been sore for the past month, bad enough for me to get an MRI in late August. What we'd originally thought was a neck injury turned out to be a cartilage strain in my throwing shoulder. I went on the injured list, though the official, public explanation was that it was to rest my right knee. A cortisone injection helped. I was crawling to the finish line. But when I released the cutter to Díaz, the shoulder popped. It felt as if my shoulder went with the ball toward home plate, leaving my body. As Aaron Judge caught the fly ball I walked in a small circle behind the mound, trying to shake the shoulder back into place, my arm tingling, and climbed back onto the rubber. I have a pretty high pain tolerance, and when you're a pitcher, things grab in your arm all the time, but you work through it. So my first thought was, **Throw another pitch, it'll go away.** But this pain was nasty, like nothing I'd felt before. I could feel my left hand swelling in the ten seconds between pitches. Then the hand went numb. I couldn't grip the ball. As I came set, I just kind of balanced the ball, cupped it, between my palm and my fingers.

George Springer was the next hitter. I was praying he'd swing at the first pitch. As I lifted my arm behind my head, getting in position to throw, I squeezed and gripped the ball, and the pain exploded. It hurt so much I had to close my eyes to keep from screaming. Somehow a 91-mile-an-hour cutter came out of my hand for a called strike. After that I missed with two more pitches, both thrown with my eyes closed. I knew I was hurt, but I didn't want to just walk off like that.

Stevie Donohue, our trainer, and Boonie came

racing out, realizing something was wrong. I told them my shoulder had subluxed—partially popped out of the socket—and then popped back in. We talked for a few seconds, and I told them I wanted to throw a practice pitch and see if I could keep going. Sánchez had joined us and was cleaning his cleats; I was pissed and in pain, so I yelled, "Get back there!" as I waved at Gary to go back behind the plate for a test pitch. I threw the ball one more time, and it reached his glove, but I was done. The baseball gods had broken my shit, just in case I was tempted to come back next year. My time had passed.

As I walked to the dugout I tried to take off my hat, the way I always did after an inning, but I couldn't lift my left arm. When I got down the first few steps, heading for the locker room, it was all so overwhelming, I couldn't walk any farther. I could hear the ovation from the Yankees fans, and that hit me even harder than the pain. I sat down on the first step to the clubhouse tunnel and cried.

A few minutes later the team doctor tried to examine me, but there wasn't any position where I wasn't in extreme pain. I got a shot of Toradol in the ass and they strapped a big bag of ice to my shoulder, but the pain burned through everything. Somehow I got undressed and showered and they fitted me into a sling. When the game ended Larry Rothschild came in; trying to hold back tears, he couldn't look me in the face. Boonie gave me a big hug. And then I got the hell out of there. I didn't want people to see me like that. Everybody was way more emotional than me, and I didn't want to be around that sadness. I also didn't want my team-mates to be around that sadness, sadness that I'd caused. I was a small-ass part of this team; if I got hurt, who the fuck cared? But if I stuck around after the game and became the center of attention and it dragged everybody down, that'd be bad. I wasn't about to let that happen. **We got to face Verlander tomorrow! We got a fucking game to win! We ain't got time to be sad, cuz.**

So I bounced. Didn't let Amber drive, though—hell no, and not because she cried all the way home to Jersey. I drove with my left arm in a fucking sling, holding a tennis ball in my left hand to try to fight off the pain. Didn't help much. Nothing did. I heard from everybody that night: Jeet, Sado, Andy, Drese, David Price. Riske called me, crying. But you know who's the first person that's calling me anytime something happens? Big Papi. David Ortiz and I are really good friends, but that's just the kind of person he is, always wanting to make sure you're good. I was up until 5:30 A.M., catching up on my shows, like **The Blacklist**. I wasn't watch-ing no **SportsCenter**. I already knew what the news was going to be.

Having my shit break wasn't how I wanted to go out. But it was fitting. I had given my body to build a life. People often said I had a lot of heart, which was a huge compliment in terms of character, but ten months earlier my real heart had nearly stopped. Now I had thrown until I couldn't anymore. Now I needed shoulder surgery immediately to go along with the knee replacement eventually. The left arm that had helped the Yankees win a championship, the arm that had lifted me and my family from poverty to wealth, the arm that was tattooed from shoulder to wrist with the names of friends and family who had died—that arm had given everything it possibly could. Till the end.

# ACKNOWLEDGMENTS

The authors would like to thank:

Carsten III, Jaden, Cyia, and Carter. Margie Sabathia-Lanier and Al Lanier. Edwin and Genia Sabathia, Gloria Rufus, and Darnell Jones. Jomar Connors, Dee Johnson, Abe Hobbs, Jennifer Austin and Marcel Longmire, Bobby Brooks, Dave Bernstine, Devin Rogers, Michael Palmer, Jerome Maxwell, and Candy Crary. And especially Amber Sabathia.

JAY-Z, Juan Perez and Desiree Perez, Shawn "Pecas" Costner, Kyle Thousand, Deborah Embaie, Samir Hernandez, Stuart Bryan, and Ron Berkowitz.

Chris Jackson, an extraordinary editor. At Penguin Random House, Carla Bruce-Eddings, Greg Kubie, Carole Lowenstein, and Sue Warga.

David Black, the tenacious and generous literary agent who had the idea for this book in 2016.

Matt Giles: officially the fact-checker, in reality the guy who saved us on most every page. CarolLee Kidd and her team at CLK Transcription.

Andy Pettitte, Mark Shapiro, Gary Sheffield, Ben Sheets, Ryan Drese, and David Riske.

Ryan Ruocco, Jim Trdinich, Bart Swain, Mike Vassallo, Jared Boshnack, Alexandra DeGregorio, and Dr. Andrew Gerber, for providing invaluable research help.

Jason Zillo, the unflappable New York Yankees vice president of communications and media relations, and Michael Margolis, Yankees director of baseball information. Sadye Zillo, Eric Newman, and everyone at HBO Sports and at MLB who helped make **Under the Grapefruit Tree.**

The sportswriters and broadcasters who covered me, the Yankees, and baseball over the years. Extra appreciation to Roger Angell, Mike Lupica, Wally Matthews, Peter Botte, Christian Red, Anthony McCarron, Kristie Ackert, Buster Olney, Lindsey Adler, Kevin Davidoff, Jack Curry, Joel Sherman, Tim Brown, George A. King III, Tyler Kepner, Dale Grummert, Mark Feinsand, Paul Hoynes, Tom Haudricourt, David Lennon, James Wagner, Pete Caldera, Thomas Boswell, Bryan Hoch, Suzyn Waldman, John Sterling, David Waldstein, S.L. Price, Howard Bryant, Will Leitch, Jon Scher, and Jon Schwartz, plus Bill James, Sean Forman, and Baseball Reference. Special mentions to George Vecsey, author of **Five O'Clock Comes Early,** with Bob Welch, and to Jeff Tweedy, author of **Let's Go (So We Can Get Back).**

Steve Etter, Walter Paller, Jon Stewart, Brendan Sullivan, and the late great John Homans.

Joan Serra, Jason Smith, a
Smith. Liane Marooney, Caryn
Brunicardi, and James Brunicardi.
Lisa, Lila, and Jack Marooney (wh
favorite left-hander).

Carsten Charles "Corky" Sabathia
William "Bob" Smith, who first taught u
the game. We miss you every day.

See you all at the ballpark.

Joan Serra, Jason Smith, and Barbara Jordan-Smith. Liane Marooney, Caryn Marooney, David Brunicardi, and James Brunicardi. Eliza Abendroth. Lisa, Lila, and Jack Marooney (who is still Chris's favorite left-hander).

Carsten Charles "Corky" Sabathia and Robert William "Bob" Smith, who first taught us a love for the game. We miss you every day.

See you all at the ballpark.